THE BEST OF **Woodworker's Journal**

BOXES, CLOCKS, LAMPS

& Small Projects

THE BEST OF

BOXES, CLOCKS, LAMPS

& Small Projects

from the editors of *Woodworker's Journal*

**Fox
Chapel Publishing**

1970 Broad Street • East Petersburg, PA 17520
www.FoxChapelPublishing.com

Our friends at Rockler Woodworking and Hardware supplied us with most of the hardware used in this book. Visit rockler.com.

Fox Chapel Publishing Company, Inc.

Publisher: Alan Giagnocavo
Acquisition Editor: Peg Couch
Editor: Gretchen Bacon
Series Editor: John Kelsey
Creative Direction: Troy Thorne
Cover Design: Lindsay Hess

Woodworker's Journal

Publisher: Ann Rockler Jackson
Editor-in-Chief: Larry N. Stoiaken
Editor: Rob Johnstone
Art Director: Jeff Jacobson
Senior Editor: Joanna Werch Takes
Field Editor: Chris Marshall
Illustrators: Jeff Jacobson, John Kelliher
Contributing Writers: Jim Jacobson, John English, John Kelliher, Simon Watts, J. Petrovich, Rick White, John Nelson, Mike McGlynn, David Larson, Nina Childs Johnson, Jim Carroll, Marty Lubbers, Craig Lossing, Brad Becker and Stephen Sheperd

ISBN 978-1-56523-328-7

Publisher's Cataloging-in-Publication Data

> Boxes, clocks, lamps & small projects. -- East Petersburg, PA :
> Fox Chapel Publishing, c2007.
>
> p. ; cm.
>
> (The best of Woodworker's journal)
> ISBN 978-1-56523-328-7
>
> 1. Woodwork--Amateurs' manuals. 2. Woodwork--Patterns.
> 3. Wooden boxes--Patterns.
> I. Boxes, clocks, lamps and small projects. II. Series.
> III. Woodworker's journal.

TT185 .B69 2007
684/.08--dc22

0704

To learn more about the other great books from Fox Chapel Publishing, or to find a retailer near you, call toll-free 1-800-457-9112 or visit us at www.FoxChapelPublishing.com. For subscription information to *Woodworker's Journal* magazine, call toll-free 1-800-765-4119 or visit them at www.woodworkersjournal.com.

Printed in China
10 9 8 7 6 5 4 3 2 1

Note to Authors: We are always looking for talented authors to write new books in our area of woodworking, design, and related crafts. Please send a brief letter describing your idea to Peg Couch, Acquisition Editor, 1970 Broad Street, East Petersburg, PA 17520.

INTRODUCTION

Making a major piece of furniture can eat up months of weekends. That's why a lot of woodworking hobbyists look for small and manageable projects to build. Something a little more finite, in terms of time and expense, than a highboy chest. A small project like a lamp or a cigar humidor might have a great many pieces and require a considerable amount of exacting work—it just doesn't consume vast amounts of material or time—you can get it done in and around your already busy life.

That's the appeal of small projects from the woodworker's point of view. The other side of the coin is their appeal to the lucky recipient, the person who receives a beautiful hand-crafted object like the ones shown in this book. It's an instant heirloom, something to be treasured forever.

And who would not want to own the gorgeous chessboard on page 122, the bird's-eye maple lamp on page 52, or the Irish parlor clock on page 76? These are first-rate projects, requiring skilled craftsmanship and beautiful materials. And if it's a real challenge you're after, have a look at Nina Childs Johnson's lovely letter box on page 96. Featuring handcut dovetails and exacting craftsmanship, her project will certainly test your skills and keep you busy in your shop for a few weekends! On the other end of the spectrum, you'll be in and out of the shop on a Sunday morning, in plenty of time to watch the big game, if you decide to tackle John English's simple "Picture Frame for Two" on page 16. Whatever your mood, this book has some great projects with which to hone your skills.

Larry N. Stoiaken, Editor-in-Chief

ACKNOWLEDGMENTS

Woodworker's Journal recently celebrated its 30th anniversary— a benchmark few magazines ever reach. I would like to acknowledge both the 300,000 woodworkers who make up our readership and Rockler Woodworking & Hardware (rockler.com), which provided most of the hardware, wood and other products used to build the projects in this book. Our publishing partner, Fox Chapel, did a terrific job re-presenting our material, and I am especially grateful to Alan Giagnocavo, Gretchen Bacon, John Kelsey, and Troy Thorne for their commitment to our content.

Larry N. Stoiaken, Editor-in-Chief

CONTENTS

By Jim Jacobson

ARTS & CRAFTS PICTURE FRAME

Build a stylish picture frame over the weekend. We've included details for a traditional Arts & Crafts look or a more contemporary style with inlays. Either way, a handmade picture frame is a nice opportunity to do a small-scale project that still offers full-size satisfaction when you're finished—and they make great gifts.

Several years ago we nominated Gustav Stickley as the preeminent woodworker of the 20th Century. In honor of that recognition, I designed a picture frame that would feature Stickley in an appropriate way for my article. The picture frame got such rave reviews from readers that it became a project in it's own right. I also expanded on the theme and created a more contemporary version—one that would perhaps be more suitable for a modern woodworker—like Norm Abram.

The Arts & Crafts version of this frame includes square corner plugs, chamfers and quartersawn stock. For the contemporary version, I selected some beautiful quartersawn sycamore and accented it with ebonized plugs and strips of inlay (see page 13).

Setting Up: Tools and Materials

The essence of Arts & Crafts furniture was simplicity. The idea was to incorporate pre-industrial age values (such as hand-built quality) into the machine age. An Arts & Crafts piece was sturdy, functional and attractive but never gaudy or over-dressed in the way that Victorian pieces had been. This Arts & Crafts picture frame

follows those guidelines: it is sturdy and durable, attractive in its own right, but not so ornate that it overpowers the image in the frame.

Construction is vintage Stickley. The material is quartersawn white oak, and the frame is assembled with open mortise and tenon joints. The uprights are mortised into the feet and pyramidal plugs are prominently used to evoke that pre-industrial age feeling.

While the frame's construction is relatively simple, it does require a fair bit of tooling. For example, you'll need access to a tenoning jig for the table saw, a mortising machine or attachment for your drill press, and a power miter saw. You'll also need a sander and a bearing-guided rabbeting bit for your portable router. Once you've assembled your tools, keep in mind this is the perfect project for setting up a production run.

Starting with the Frame

There are two distinct subassemblies in this project: the frame and the base. The frame is made up of two sides, a top and a bottom (pieces 1 and 2). After cutting these parts to the dimensions shown in the *Material List*, page 12, lay out the open mortise and tenon joints that hold

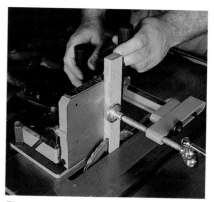

Figure 1: *Use a tenoning jig to form the tenons on the ends of the frame top and bottom and then reset it to plow the open mortises in the sides.*

them together. All the dimensions are provided on the *Technical Drawings* on pages 14 and 15. Use your table saw's tenoning jig to create the tenons on the ends of the frame top and bottom, then reset the jig to plow the open mortises in the frame sides *(see Figure 1)*. Test all these cuts on scrap before milling the actual workpieces, paying special attention to how the parts fit together. You need a tight fit, but not one where you have to force the pieces together, which could risk splitting the walls of the open mortise.

Glue up the frame, applying glue to each mortise and tenon. Clamp the

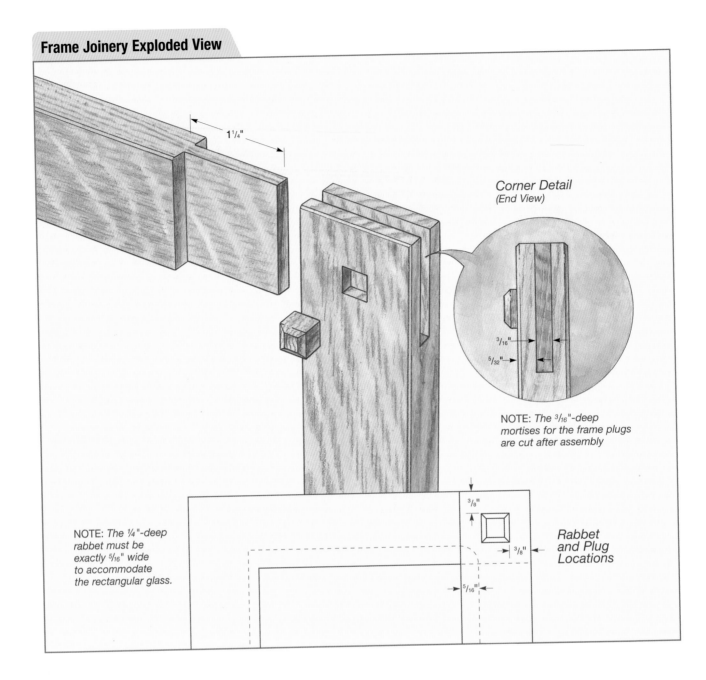

1¼"

Corner Detail
(End View)

3/16"

5/32"

NOTE: *The 3/16"-deep mortises for the frame plugs are cut after assembly*

NOTE: *The ¼"-deep rabbet must be exactly 5/16" wide to accommodate the rectangular glass.*

3/8"

3/8"

5/16"

Rabbet and Plug Locations

assembly so it is square and the joints are tight, then use four more clamps on the corners to ensure good contact between the tenon cheeks and the mortise walls.

When the glue is dry, sand the entire frame before creating the rabbet for the back and glass (pieces 3 and 4). Refer to the *Technical Drawings* and the *Elevation Drawings* for the dimensions and location of this rabbet, then mill it, as shown in *Figure 2*. Use a piloted bearing bit to create a rabbet exactly

¼" deep by 5/16" wide. You want to be precise here to ensure the rounded corners of this cut will accept the rectangular piece of glass you'll install later in the assembly process.

Making the Feet Next

After cutting the feet and base rail (pieces 5 and 6) to their overall dimensions, lay out the chamfers on each foot, following the dimensions on the *Technical Drawings*. Use your miter gauge with the stock clamped

tightly in place to form these chamfers on the table saw. Since there will be some overlapping joinery, I recommend you complete the dado and tenon joint between the feet and the base rail now. Set up your table saw with a dado head and form the dado at the center of each foot. Use the same basic setup to mill the cheeks on the base rail. Once you've got a tight fit, set up your mortising machine with a ½" bit and chisel and form the shallow mortises that will accept the plugs on the outsides of the feet. Now go ahead and glue the feet to the rail, taking care to keep everything square.

When the glue is dry, create another mortise on the top of each foot for the uprights (pieces 7). While you're at it, form the mortises toward the top of these uprights (for the plugs) and drill a small through hole for the nail that will hold the frame in place later. Check the *Technical Drawings* for all the dimensions and locations. As the mortising machine bit is a set size, while tenoning jigs are adjustable, it makes sense to chop your mortises first, then mill the tenons to fit. Once you've cut the mortises for the uprights into the feet, move to the uprights and form the tenons at their ends. These tenons can be milled on the table saw using the same jig you used earlier to build the frame. Check their fit in the mortises you just formed, then use the power miter saw to trim the chamfers at the tops of the uprights and on the plugs. (Use the same method described in the *tint box* at right.)

Assembling the Frame

Before starting your assembly, move back to the mortising machine to form the four mortises for the pyramidal plugs (pieces 8) on the face of the frame. Test the fit of these plugs, as well as the four on the base subassembly. Now sand all parts through the grits to 220 grit, slightly chamfering the edges, then apply the stain of your choice. Traditionally, this would be a dark reddish brown: Stickley used to treat his oak pieces with ammonia to achieve this, but now we can use much safer and simpler stains to gain essentially the same results.

The influence that medieval architecture and design had on the Arts & Crafts period is evident in the widespread use of pyramidal plugs found on turn-of-the-century Mission, Roycroft and other furniture lines. These plugs resemble the beaten heads of iron nails, used extensively in the carpentry and leatherwork of medieval European households.

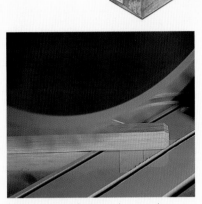

Begin making the plugs by setting your miter saw to 45° and attaching a piece of masking tape to the bed of your miter saw. Rip a piece of stock to ½" square, then set it on the saw and make the first chamfered cut, as shown at right. Before moving the workpiece, mark the stock's location with a pencil line on the tape, then simply line up the end of the stock with this mark as you rotate the piece 90° to make the other three cuts. Trim the plugs to length on the band saw: your miter saw is far too aggressive for this cut and the plugs will just go airborne.

Your power miter saw *is a good choice for forming the chamfered tops on the plugs. Just be sure to switch to the band saw when you're ready to cut them to length.*

Install the frame plugs and the two on the feet, but hang onto the two at the top of the uprights for now. Dry-fit the uprights in the feet and, using small brass washers (pieces 9) as spacers, nail (piece 10) the uprights to the frame. (Note: Drill pilot holes in the uprights just large enough to provide a snug fit for the nails. Also, be sure to extend the pilot holes into the frame to prevent splitting.) When everything fits well, glue the uprights to the feet, keeping the frame in position so the uprights dry at 90°. Plug the last two mortises, apply a satin finish to all the stained parts, and set the photo and glass in the frame to test their fit.

Cut the frame back to size and band saw, then sand the corners to perfectly fit the rabbet in the back of the frame. Apply your stain, and finish both faces of this piece. When the finish has dried,

Figure 2: *The size of the rabbeting bit and bearing is critical. The goal here is to fit a square cornered piece of glass into an opening with rounded corners.*

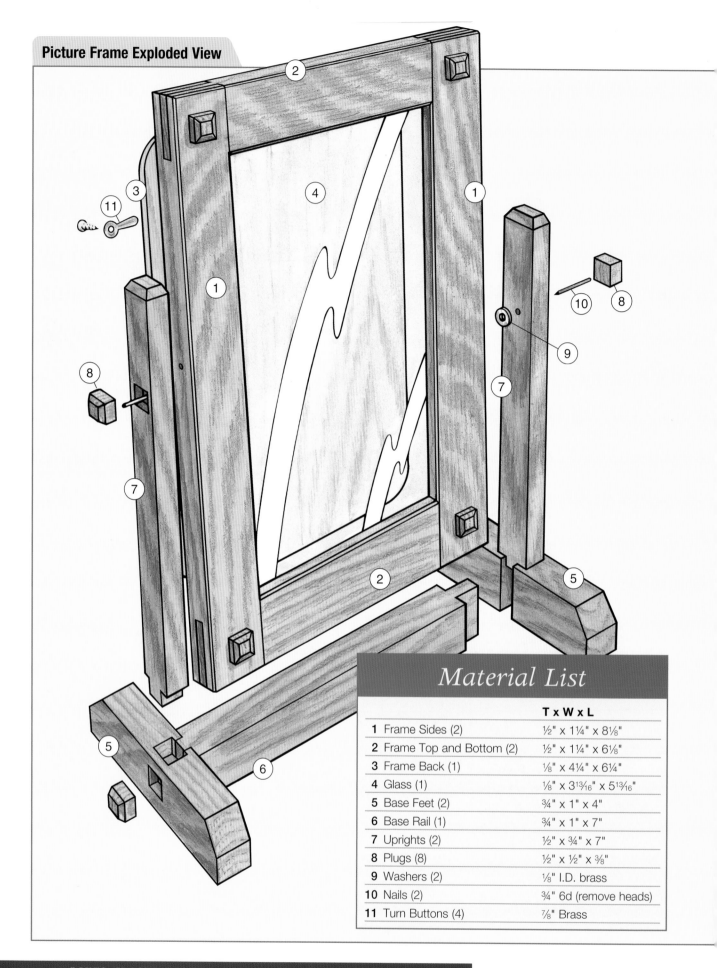

Material List

		T x W x L
1	Frame Sides (2)	½" x 1¼" x 8⅛"
2	Frame Top and Bottom (2)	½" x 1¼" x 6⅛"
3	Frame Back (1)	⅛" x 4¼" x 6¼"
4	Glass (1)	⅛" x 3¹³⁄₁₆" x 5¹³⁄₁₆"
5	Base Feet (2)	¾" x 1" x 4"
6	Base Rail (1)	¾" x 1" x 7"
7	Uprights (2)	½" x ¾" x 7"
8	Plugs (8)	½" x ½" x ⅜"
9	Washers (2)	⅛" I.D. brass
10	Nails (2)	¾" 6d (remove heads)
11	Turn Buttons (4)	⅞" Brass

Base Rail Tenon (Top View)

1/4"

1/2"

(Side View)

Base Joinery
(Side View)

1/2"

1/2"

4⁵/₈"

1/2"

1/2"

1/4"

1³/₄"

In the world of fashion, if you can't find the right color, it's standard practice to "go with black." In woodworking, black also gets the nod, but it's more typically employed as the perfect accent color, complementing without competing. For years, ebony was the species of choice for this role, but today it is in short supply. It's also something of a waste, since you can achieve the same look, often with desirable grain highlights, by using a simple chemical reaction to transform oak's natural color to pure black—ebonizing it.

Of course, you could choose to paint the accents, but paint fills the pores and blends the grain configurations, masking the natural beauty. Staining will add color to oak while retaining its character, but stains can be messy to use and difficult to apply evenly. The following ebonizing process is easier than staining and creates a deeper black than can be attained with stains or dyes.

Try ebonizing something small at first, like the plugs on the frame at right. You can move on to small jewelry boxes, or even the top of an end table, once you get the hang of it. If you are working with previously treated wood, be sure to strip the finish and sand to 280 grit or finer.

The process couldn't be simpler. First, completely immerse a handful of steel nails in a cup of white vinegar (use a wide-mouth container, such as a peanut butter jar). Let this steep for about a week, or until the liquid becomes murky. Try some of your brew on an oak scrap to see how it responds. It may be ready in as few as four days. No pressure, though: it will still be ready after a month. When you're happy with the appearance of your mixture on the scraps, liberally brush the solution onto your accent pieces. As it reacts with the tannin in the oak, the darkening begins. Apply several coats, allowing the wood surface to dry between coats. This takes about half an hour. When the oak is as black as you like, brush on household ammonia. It neutralizes the vinegar acid, stopping the reaction in its tracks. Once the piece is dry, it's ready. You'll find that your ebonized stock finishes nicely and accepts glue with no problem.

This contemporary frame *struck us as more suitable for a turn-of-this-century woodworker, like Norm Abram. Check out the Technical Drawings for the inlay locations.*

install the back, photo and glass with four turn buttons (pieces 11) at the locations shown in the *Technical Drawings*.

Now that you've completed your first frame, it may be time to clean up the shop and set it up for a production run. After all, framed photographs do make for wonderfully personal gifts.

The back should fit perfectly, *since this frame may be viewed from either side. Use brass turn buttons, and finish both sides of this piece to prevent cupping.*

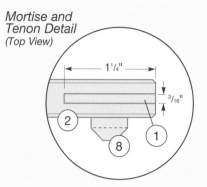

Mortise and Tenon Detail (Top View)

NOTE: *the inlays are optional and more appropriate for a contemporary version. From a design perspective, it is important to stop them short of the pyramid plugs.*

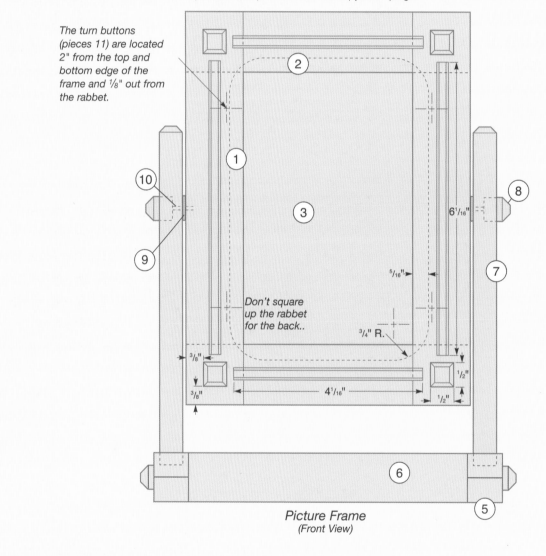

The turn buttons (pieces 11) are located 2" from the top and bottom edge of the frame and ⅛" out from the rabbet.

Don't square up the rabbet for the back..

Picture Frame (Front View)

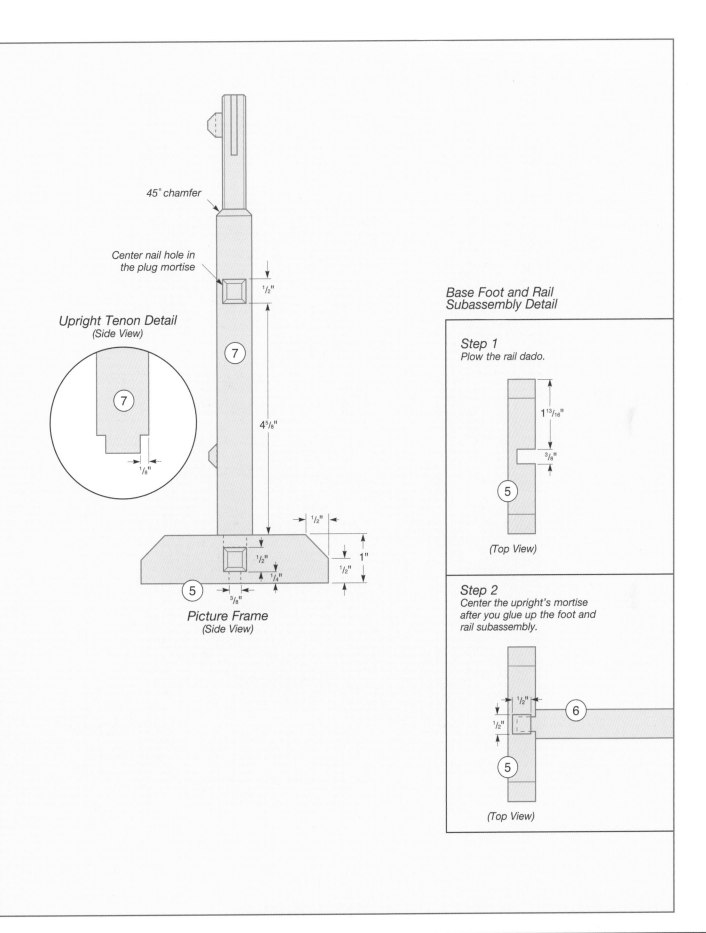

45° chamfer

Center nail hole in
the plug mortise

Upright Tenon Detail
(Side View)

7

7

1/8"

1/2"

4⅝"

⑦

1/2"

1"

1/2"

1/4"

5

3/8"

Picture Frame
(Side View)

Base Foot and Rail
Subassembly Detail

Step 1
Plow the rail dado.

1¹³⁄₁₆"

3/8"

5

(Top View)

Step 2
Center the upright's mortise
after you glue up the foot and
rail subassembly.

1/2"

1/2"

6

5

(Top View)

PICTURE FRAME FOR TWO

Build a simple router jig from scrap and you can create enough picture frames to satisfy everyone on a holiday gift list. While you're at it, you'll also get a little practice with Corian®, a nice alternative to wood for this accent project.

by John English

High-end countertop *material meets weekend woodworking in this easy-to-build picture frame project.*

This elegant picture frame may be the perfect answer to gift giving. It's easy to build and, with the help of a simple routing jig described on the next page, you can turn out a dozen frames in a weekend. The double-sided frame uses Corian® solid-surface material (sidebar, page 19) and bird's-eye maple.

Get started on this project by selecting some of your nicest maple scraps and cutting your bases (pieces 1) to overall size. Now rout a ¼" radius cove around the top of each base. I used Corian® turning blanks (available through lathe-turning supply catalogs) for the tops and sides (pieces 2 and 3). These are fairly small pieces to machine, but with the help of a sled, you'll have no problems.

Building and Using the Sled

The sled is designed to hold each Corian® blank safely on your router table as you cut the dado for the glass (see Figure 1). Using a stop block to limit your length of cut to 5", plow a ½"-wide by ⁷⁄₁₆"-deep dado in the center of the sled. Now insert a Corian® blank in the dado. (Note: your turning blanks probably have two dull surfaces and two shiny surfaces. Make sure you cut your dadoes on one of the dull surfaces.) Without moving the fence, switch to a ¼" straight bit and plow a ⅛"-deep dado in your workpiece. Continue this process, creating three dadoed pieces (a top and two sides) for each frame.

Assembling the Frame

Using a sharp carbide-tipped blade (with at least 40 teeth) in your table saw, form the miters on the tops of the sides and then trim these pieces to length. Move on to cut the two miters on the ends of the top, making sure to back up all these cuts with scrap wood to avoid tearout.

End-boring the frame sides for the two studs (pieces 4) requires an accurate fence setup on your drill press. Set the fence ³⁄₁₆" from the center of the bit and clamp a square 1x4 stop exactly ¼" to

the left of the bit center, as shown in the Figure 1 inset. Now rip a piece of scrap wood to the exact size of your frame sides and hold a 5"-long piece tight to the fence and stop block to test

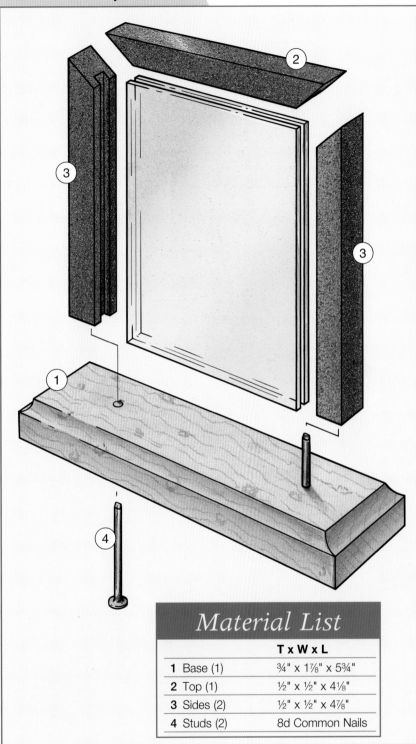

Material List		
	T x W x L	
1 Base (1)	¾" x 1⅞" x 5¾"	
2 Top (1)	½" x ½" x 4⅛"	
3 Sides (2)	½" x ½" x 4⅞"	
4 Studs (2)	8d Common Nails	

Figure 1: *A scrap sled keeps the routing operation safe and creates perfectly centered cuts on each frame piece. Once the sides are dadoed, a fence and stop block on the drill press (right) ensure accurate holes for the studs.*

your setup. An 8d common nail has a diameter of about ⅛" so use a %₄" bit to drill these holes. When you're satisfied with your setup, move on to the Corian® sides and, with the dado

facing out, drill a 1¾"-deep hole in the base of each one.

While you're at the drill press, drill the holes in the base for the nails using a countersink bit to recess the heads.

Bend each nail slightly toward the center to provide the necessary tension for a good friction fit.

Now you're ready to glue up your miters. Corian® requires Special "T" glue, a thick adhesive that fills gaps and sets almost immediately. If your miters are clean, you'll get a virtually invisible joint in about 20 seconds.

Finishing Up

Use non-reflective glass, and a piece of cardboard between the two glass pieces keeps everything tight. As noted in the *sidebar* (page 19), you have to sand Corian® in four stages. Start with 180 and wrap up with 400-grit silicon carbide open coat paper. Follow up with a buffing, using a green Scotchbrite pad. Then finish the maple base with a few coats of oil.

*Quick*Tip

Production Turning Aid

To gauge the accuracy of cylinder turnings, here's a homemade jig that's easier to use than calipers. The jig amounts to a ¼"-thick plywood panel with lines spaced 1" apart and parallel to the lathe bed. While turning, simply sight over the top edge of your workpiece to compare its shape with the lines, which reveals any high or low spots immediately.

Carbide bits *are essential when routing Corian®, which is a synthetic material three times more dense than most hardwoods.*

Corian® is the most popular brand name of a family of products called solid-surface materials—plastics with color patterns that permeate the material. They usually come in ¼", ½" and ¾"-thicknesses. Originally, it was used just for countertops, but innovative fabricators have found many new uses for Corian®: from showers and plaques to cutting boards and wall panels.

What once was a specialized product for countertop installers is now becoming increasingly available to the general public. This picture frame project, for instance, uses Corian® blanks you can buy from pen turning suppliers in various colors and patterns.

Corian® is relatively easy to work. Standard woodshop equipment is quite adequate, but to achieve quality results, you must equip your machines with carbide blades or bits. Sharp cutters are essential to prevent chatter and surface irregularities, because Corian® is three times as dense as most hardwoods.

Cutting straight lines in Corian® is best done with a router. If you use a table saw, the cut will have kerf marks that will have to be removed with a router anyway, so you may as well use the right tool to begin with. Also, when using a router and a straightedge, the tool moves across the surface of the material.

A table saw, on the other hand, requires that you push the entire surface of the workpiece across the tabletop, so scratches are far more likely to occur.

Wearing protective gear is a must with Corian® and similar products. Although the dust is chemically non-toxic, it can be pervasive and constitutes a respiratory nuisance. Eye protection is also recommended by the DuPont Corporation, which manufactures Corian®. The product, though extremely durable, is somewhat brittle, so particles can fly under certain circumstances. It's also heavy. And that density prompts one more piece of advice: When routing a decorative edge, or using a router to cut Corian®, make several passes rather than removing all the waste in a single pass. This is easier on your tools and improves the cut.

Achieving a matte finish on Corian® is also easy. Start sanding with 180-grit paper and work your way through 400. Use a silicon carbide open coat paper, and change papers often as the fine dust tends to clog even open coats rather quickly. Wash off the excess dust with cold water, and buff with a green Scotchbrite® pad to achieve a smooth, polished luster.

by John Kelliher

FRAME SHADOWBOX

Every family has its stories to tell, and some deserve to be shared in a visible way. This frame shadowbox is the fruit of John Kelliher, one of our art directors, to showcase his father's memorabilia received during World War II. It's custom-sized to fit specific things, but the box is certainly adaptable to other collections of treasures your family has to display. Here is John's story and his method for building the project.

"What medals? ..." I e-mailed back to my sister Mary. Soon, I was on the phone with my folks: Mom on one line, Dad on the other. I knew Dad was in World War II and that he was a radioman (he's still liable to use Morse code on the arm of his chair during a close football game). But he hardly ever talked about the war... "I just wanted to get on with my life," he explained recently. After all these years, he decided it was time to find a more suitable place for a number of medals, photos and other memorabilia from his war days. I immediately volunteered to create this "more suitable place."

The design process started with my parents. First, they decided that a wall-hung cabinet with a glass door would be the perfect container for the items under consideration. My mom had just the spot for such a cabinet (which helped dictate the final size) and an idea of which species she'd like: "Cherry...that's kind of reddish, right? That would be nice."

Sorting through all of the stuff my dad sent took the designing process to the next level—deciding how to lay out the inside of the box. The commendations seemed like such humble documents—no foil stampings, no script, just a blue ribbon in an old manual typewriter, probably banged out somewhere on a beach. I was happy to see that some photos were included. While the medals were the reason for the case, Dad's face in all of those situations made the medals and commendations seem more personal.

Considering "Detail" Design

Ian Kirby, one of our regular contributors, outlines four types of design: functional design, spatial design, structural design and detail design. The first three aspects were pretty well covered already, but the "details" still eluded me. Kirby recommends creating full-size mock-ups at this stage, and I realized that, with a little help from

True to form, *art director John Kelliher used a computer to assist in his case design. After employing a flatbed scanner to capture each medal and photo, he turned to familiar publishing software (Quark XPress®) to position the scans and dividers until he was happy with the layout. He then created a full-size pattern with our plotter (check with your local print shop) and had a few extra copies made— future gifts for his siblings.*

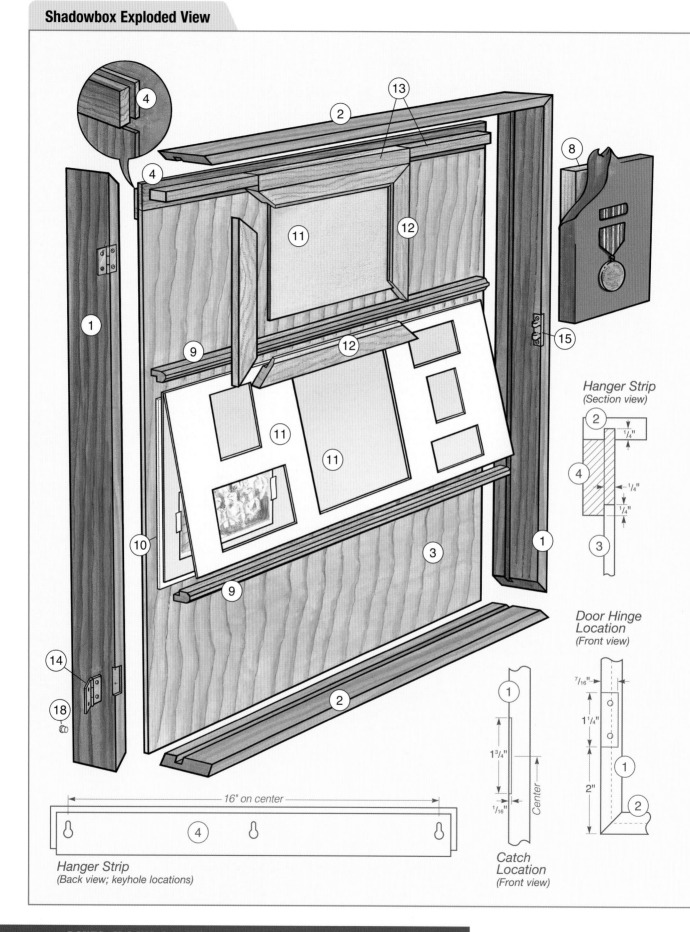

Hanger Strip
(Section view)

Door Hinge
Location
(Front view)

Catch
Location
(Front view)

Hanger Strip
(Back view; keyhole locations)

16" on center

1³/₄"

1/16"

Center

7/16"

1¹/₄"

2"

¹/₄"

¹/₄"

¹/₄"

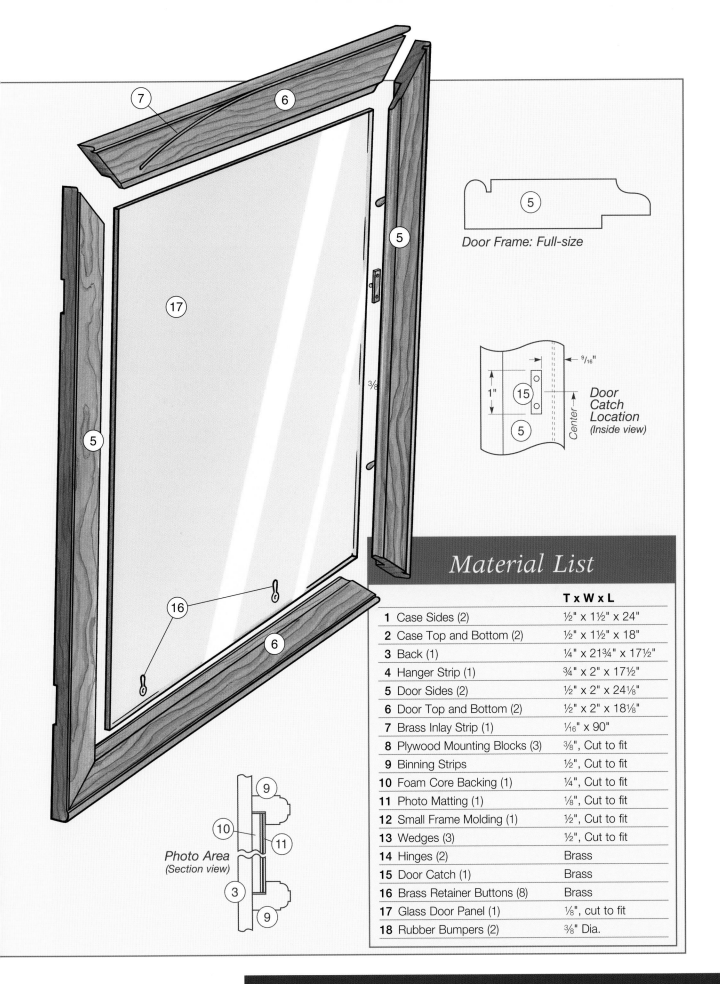

Door Frame: Full-size

Door Catch Location
(Inside view)

⁹/₁₆"

1"

Center

Photo Area
(Section view)

Material List

	T x W x L
1 Case Sides (2)	½" x 1½" x 24"
2 Case Top and Bottom (2)	½" x 1½" x 18"
3 Back (1)	¼" x 21¾" x 17½"
4 Hanger Strip (1)	¾" x 2" x 17½"
5 Door Sides (2)	½" x 2" x 24⅛"
6 Door Top and Bottom (2)	½" x 2" x 18⅛"
7 Brass Inlay Strip (1)	¹/₁₆" x 90"
8 Plywood Mounting Blocks (3)	⅜", Cut to fit
9 Binning Strips	½", Cut to fit
10 Foam Core Backing (1)	¼", Cut to fit
11 Photo Matting (1)	⅛", Cut to fit
12 Small Frame Molding (1)	½", Cut to fit
13 Wedges (3)	½", Cut to fit
14 Hinges (2)	Brass
15 Door Catch (1)	Brass
16 Brass Retainer Buttons (8)	Brass
17 Glass Door Panel (1)	⅛", cut to fit
18 Rubber Bumpers (2)	⅜" Dia.

To make the door frame, first use your Roman ogee bit to soften the inside edge, then turn to a 1/8" edge-beading bit to both shape the outer edge and create the groove for the brass inlay (left). Later, you can cut the rabbet on the table saw or router table.

Form the binning strips by taking two passes with a beading bit and then cutting the rabbet with a straight bit.

⑨

Binning Strip: Full-size

The small frame is similar to the case frame, without the beading detail.

⑫

Small Frame Molding: Full-size

my trusty computer, I could do the same thing. I used my flatbed scanner to scan all the items for possible inclusion, created a document with a border (representing the back of the cabinet), imported the scans and slowly started moving them around until a design revealed itself. A commendation referring to "D" Day, July 10, 1943, took center stage, and the medals and photos found their spots from there. With a full-size pattern in hand and the approval of all, I was headed to the shop to start making some reddish sawdust.

Building the Case

I made the case from beautiful straight-grained cherry. Before I made any cuts, I selected the nicest looking wood for the most visible parts. The case sides,

top and bottom (pieces 1 and 2), were ripped to width and then a 1/4" groove was cut into them to receive the back and hanger strip (pieces 3 and 4). Remember that the sizes of the pieces in the *Materials List* will build a display case that fits my dad's stuff. Yours may need to be adjusted to house your own treasures.

Using my 10" chop saw and an 80-tooth blade, I mitered the case frame: first the sides and then the top and bottom. Miters are a pretty fussy joint, so take your time and be accurate. I like to pre-sand every piece to 600 grit before glue-up. It really doesn't take that much time, and I find that cleanup and finishing are much easier with this approach.

Next, cut the plywood back to size and select a piece of solid cherry for the hanger strip. The hanger strip is rabbeted so it laps the plywood back and has 1/4" lips that extend into the grooves in the case pieces (see *Elevation Drawings* for details). Once the piece is milled, take a moment to rout three keyhole slots (see *Hanger Strip Detail,* page 22). Next, dry-assemble all of the parts, and, when they fit perfectly, glue and clamp them together. I like polyurethane glue for a project this size.

Start with three small dabs of glue in one of the grooves, then add glue to one mitered edge and wet the other with a damp sponge brush. Pop the back and hanger strip into the groove, then quickly do the same to the other side. With the sides glued to the back assembly, place the assembly into a framing clamp, with the corner brackets adjusted loosely enough so you can slip the top and bottom frame pieces in, mitered ends covered with glue. Tighten the clamp toggles to pull it all together. Adjust the joint parts as necessary.

Making the Door Frame

The door frame needs to be just a bit bigger than the case so it can be opened without a knob. As I mentioned earlier, the selection of attractive wood is the key to a nice-looking display case. Again, start by ripping a long piece of door frame stock to its proper width. Then turn to the router table to form the edge details and groove for the inlay (see *drawings*). The brass gives just the right accent to the case. Miter the stock to create the door sides, top and bottom (pieces 5 and 6). Use the same gluing sequence as you did earlier with the case for gluing up this frame—it should go even easier. After allowing the glue to dry, remove the assembly from its clamps and clean up all the surfaces, nooks and crannies.

If your stock shows some evidence of figure like mine did, rub down the surfaces with boiled linseed oil cut to

50% with turpentine. The grain will really stand out under the oil! Let it dry for 24 hours and then hit it with an initial coat of spray lacquer. You'll want to spray on at least two more coats, but sealing all the wood before attempting to glue the brass inlay in place helps make cleanup a breeze.

Adding the Brass Inlay

I had heard that the thin accent brass strips (pieces 7) cut easily, but holding them proved to be the real challenge. I made a little jig to use on my chop saw, but when I tried to make the cut… "schwing," the blade's teeth caught the inlay and sucked it right out of my jig. Yikes! I had to go get another piece of inlay and figure out how to cut it. A nipper turned out to be the best answer.

After practicing a couple of times on my slightly mangled scrap, I got pretty good at scribing a 45° line with a .05 mm mechanical pencil and my 6" try square, then nipping right on the line. A mitered portion of my scrapped jig allowed me to hit the brass a couple of times with a fine tooth file and perfect the miter. After cutting one end, I would lay the brass in the frame's groove; mark its proper length, plus a hair; nip; then file until the fit was perfect. Hope my learning curve helps improve your luck on these cuts.

Since I was planning to apply a couple more coats of lacquer, I selected cyanoacrylate glue for installing the brass. It was easy, and there was virtually no clean-up to worry about. A quick swipe with some brass cleaner and just a little polishing with a soft cloth

had the brass looking good to go. Starting in a corner and applying just a tiny drop every five to six inches did the trick. Use three drops along the top, press in that section of inlay, and then apply four drops along each side— holding the last drop back from the corner because the next piece starts there.

Creating a Customized Interior

The interior of my father's case is designed specifically to fit the collection of memorabilia he brought home from WWII. It is not likely to be exactly what you might want to build, but the approach I used may be useful as you design your own case. I used two sizes of mounting blocks (pieces 8) for medals, binning strips (pieces 9) to

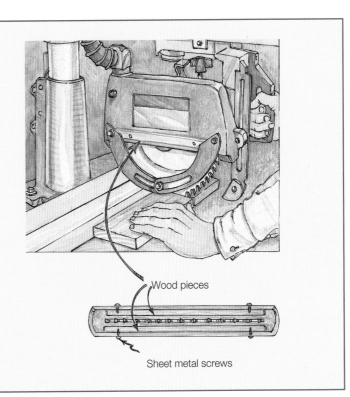

Wood pieces

Sheet metal screws

QuickTip

Add Suction to Your Radial Arm Saw

Without a good source of dust collection, fine dust created by saws and other machinery in a basement shop will float around in the air and get into your heating system, where it eventually will find its way to every room in the house. One tool that often has an inadequate system for channeling dust is a radial arm saw. If your saw has a wide blade shroud, much of it's dust-collection efficiency will be lost around the blade, even when connected to a dust collector or vacuum. Here's a simple solution to improve the suction: install a piece of wood inside the shroud with a kerf that fits around the blade, similar to a table saw's insert plate. A smaller blade opening will boost dust collection efficiency considerably.

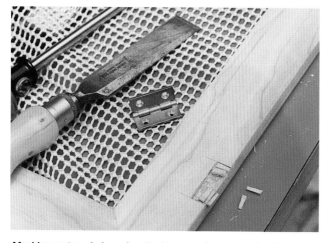

Marking out and chopping the hinge mortises was a hand-powered operation. The author's wheeled scriber and a sharp chisel made short work of the three-step process.

create clear divisions and free-floating foam core (piece 10) and photo matting (piece 11) to best show the old photos. I also milled and glued up a small frame (piece 12) of golden-hued white oak with a unique curly quartersawn grain to hold one of my dad's commendations. The wild grain made routing the molding's shape a little tricky, but it was well worth it for the look it created.

The entire contents of the case are held in place with a couple of different sizes of wedges (pieces 13) that run across the top of the case. This was a key design feature, since tightly holding the contents in place by friction allowed me to ship the case empty and put it all together at my parent's house. It also helped me create separate areas with the red, white and blue fields complementing the medals.

I folded red and blue velvet around the three medal mounting blocks and pinned it, and then my wife, Liz, sewed it up in the back. It was nice the way the smoothly finished wooden pieces and the velvet-covered blocks fit together— but it took me a couple of attempts cutting the plywood,

Right after completing my dad's commendations case, I flew home for the occasion of my mom's 75th birthday party. While there I mounted his case on the wall, and that night Dad decided to share some war stories with the family—among them, the event that earned him a commendation. Dad was a radio man on an LCI (Landing Craft, Infantry) during the invasion of Sicily. He had just come from the tail end of the invasion of North Africa. His craft had dropped their rangers on the beach when word arrived that LST 158 (a Landing Ship Tank) had been hit and was on fire. In spite of the risk of exploding

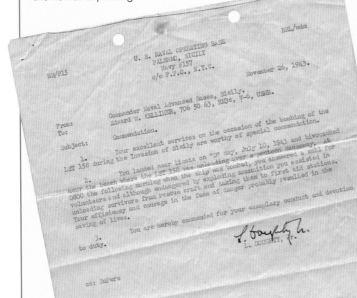

ammunition, Dad volunteered to help unload survivors from rescue crafts.

As his boat raced toward LST 158, a German submarine surfaced. "We exchanged machine gun fire," my Dad said, "but they must have thought we weren't worth a torpedo," because after the machine gun exchange they submerged and took off. The seas were rough, and although some lives were saved, many others were lost.

"It was "D" Day," Dad said, "so the Commander of Naval Advanced Bases was there. He sent his lieutenant down to get my name."

There was one other commendation that my dad had—for the invasion of Anzio. It was a lot more crinkled up and didn't really fit this case—so I left it in a plastic bag behind the medal mount panel. I have a feeling there are a lot of commendable acts that don't get framed appropriately. I'm glad I had the opportunity to frame Dad's.
— John Kelliher

wrapping and pinning the velvet on it, and fitting the frame with the two medal mounts, before I was satisfied with the final fit.

A Few Final Details

When I went to form the mortises (see *drawings*) for the hinges (pieces 14) and catch (piece 15), I ran into my first small challenge (every project has at least one!). I had to cut some of the hinge screws down in length, as they were lining up right behind the groove with the brass strip. A heavy wire cutters made quick work of chopping the screws down to size.

I used brass retainers (pieces 16) to hold the panel in place, which meant I could ship the case without the glass (piece 17) installed.

I wrapped up the finishing process by spraying the case with two more coats of lacquer. The lacquer serves both as a finish for the wood and a clear coat over the brass strips. After some careful packing and a prayer or two, I put it into the hands of the shipping company and it was on its way.

Two weeks later, when I arrived home for my mom's 75th birthday party, it was easy to have the glass cut locally and equally easy to install it. I hung the

case in its pre-designated spot and settled in to hear the stories behind some of those medals and pictures (see *tint box*, above). I don't know that I've ever seen my dad that proud or grateful for an audience.

by Simon Watts

This beautiful hall mirror *proves that "simple" doesn't have to mean "without style."*

HALL MIRROR FOR BEGINNERS

Projects don't have to start from dozens of parts to form beautiful objects in the end. This hall mirror, made from four sticks of mahogany, a piece of mirror glass and a few wooden retainers proves the point. The mirror would make a handsome accent in any decor and is easy to tackle if you are a beginning woodworker with modest tools.

The author used lap-jointed corners secured with copper nails and set off by decorative copper diamonds, materials he had on hand.

"MIRROR, MIRROR ON THE WALL ..."

This mirror differs from the usual run because the glass is actually mounted on the surface of the frame instead of being set in a groove or rabbet. This means you don't have to miter the corners of the frame at 45°—often a sore trial for the novice woodworker.

Instead, the glass is held in place by small, L-shaped wooden retainers fastened to the sides with brass screws. As a result, this is a great project for beginners...it looks good and can be completed in a weekend with simple hand tools.

Choosing the Shape and Size

The first step in this project is to decide where it's going to end up. Measure your space and then determine the overall size of your mirror. (If you'd prefer not to make a custom size, follow the *Material List* dimensions on page 30 to build the mirror shown here.) A square frame is one possibility, but if you go for a rectangular frame, I suggest making the width about two thirds of the length.

I also strongly suggest using ¼" plate glass, not the thinner variety, because it's dead flat and thus a more faithful reflector. Have the glass cut to size and all four edges polished smooth. To prevent moisture from being absorbed and marring the reflective surface, be sure to carefully seal all four edges with clear nail polish or lacquer.

The frame shown here is made of ¾" mahogany salvaged from an old boat. Darker woods like mahogany or walnut seem to define the glass better.

Cut the four lap joints on the stiles and rails (pieces 1 and 2) as shown in the *Technical Drawings* (see pages 32

Material List

		T x W x L
1	Rails (2)	¾" x 2½" x 14"
2	Stiles (2)	¾" x 1½" x 19⅜"
3	Mirror (1)	¼" Cut to fit
4	Retainers (4)	½" x ⅜" x ⅞"
5	Back (1)	⅛" x 13½" x 18"
6	Strap Hangers (2)	Steel
7	Decorative Accents (4)	Optional

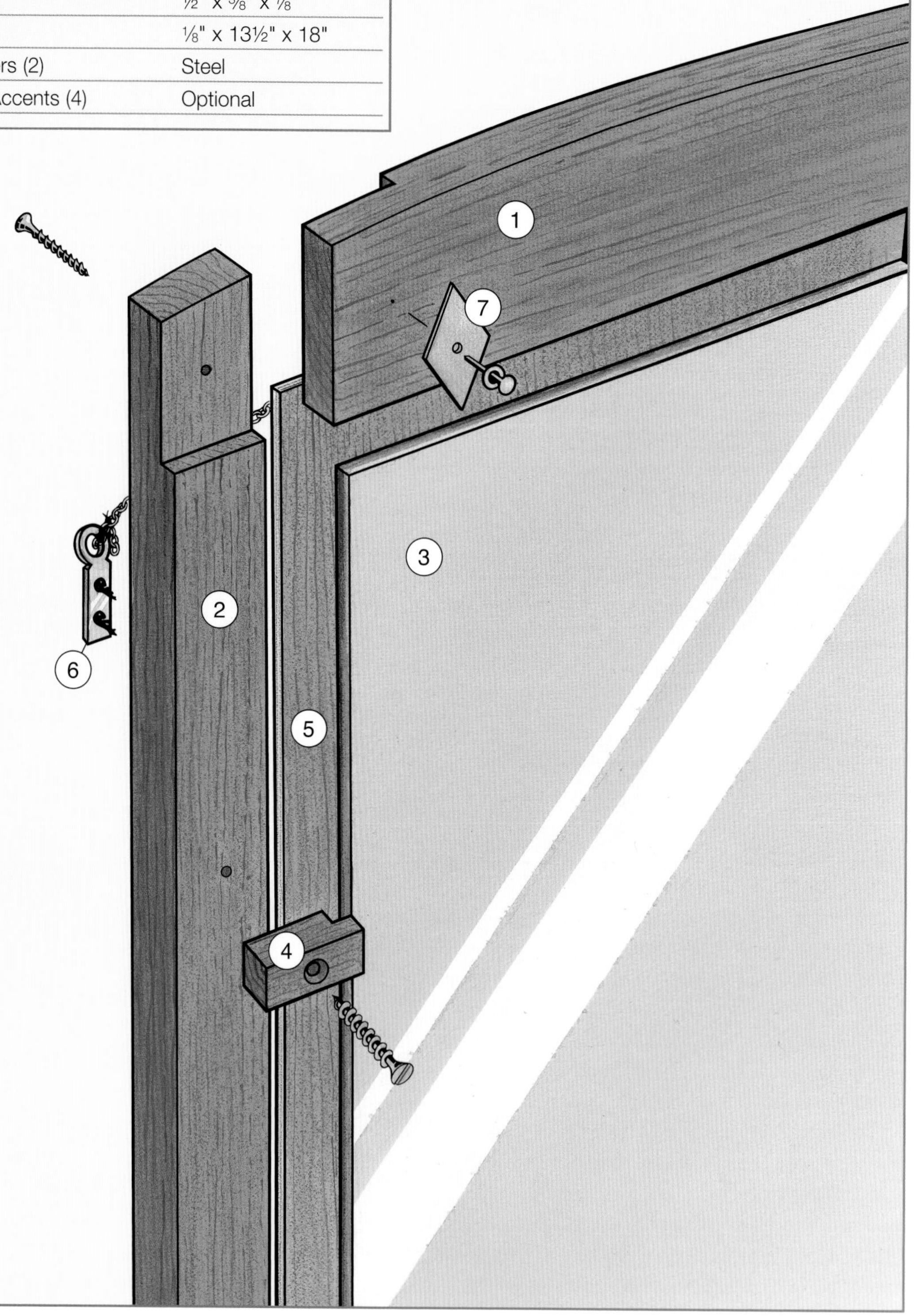

and 33), making a ¼" offset to match the thickness of the glass (piece 3). If you're a new woodworker without a full shop, you can cut these joints by hand, but if you have access to a shop, these lap joints are readily cut on a table saw.

Fastening the Corners

Fasten the four corners with rivets—copper nails peened over saucer-shaped copper washers—and cut the decorative diamonds out of a copper sheet metal: these are nautical supplies I had handy. You could come up with

a different motif or simply glue the lap joints with Titebond® glue or another yellow glue equivalent and countersink a small screw from the back. Shape the gentle curve of the rails after you've joined the frame. Next, form the retainers (pieces 4) out of the same wood as the frame, using a fine-cutting hand saw.

It's not strictly necessary to put a back (piece 5) on this frame, but it makes for a more finished job and protects the back of the reflecting surface from being accidentally

scratched. If you do this, use ⅛" plywood and countersunk ½"-long, #6 brass screws so they won't mar the wall.

Finishing Up

Topcoat the project with your favorite clear finish. Finally, having come this far, be sure to use quality strap hangers (pieces 6), available at hardware stores, to properly support the weight of the mirror.

QuickTip

Innovative Clamp Pads

Positioning a pad between the jaw of a bar clamp and the assembly you're building can be tricky. Trying to keep the clamps in position—especially when you're at the other end of a large cabinet—can be downright frustrating. These three-spoke pads solve both problems at once. Two of the three spokes become the stand's legs (they even allow for uneven surfaces), while the third spoke automatically centers itself as a hands-free pad between the metal of the clamp jaw and the workpiece being glued up.

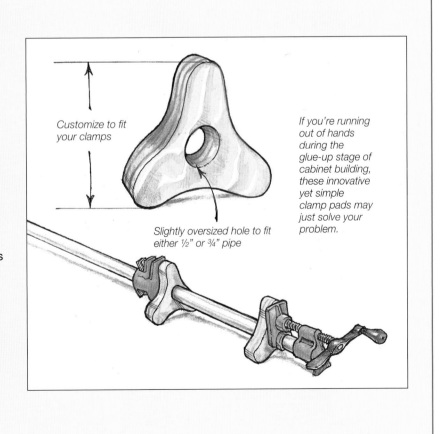

Customize to fit your clamps

Slightly oversized hole to fit either ½" or ¾" pipe

If you're running out of hands during the glue-up stage of cabinet building, these innovative yet simple clamp pads may just solve your problem.

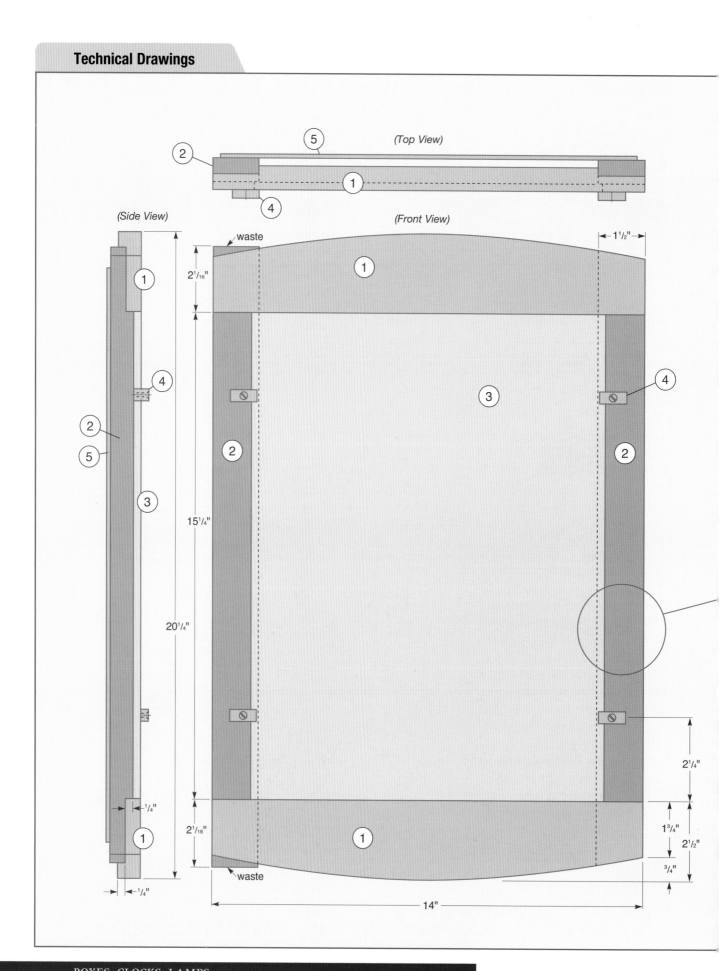

(Top View)

(Side View)

(Front View)

waste

2¹/₁₆"

15¹/₄"

20¹/₄"

2¹/₁₆"

waste

1¹/₂"

2¹/₄"

1³/₄"

2¹/₂"

³/₄"

14"

¹/₄"

¹/₄"

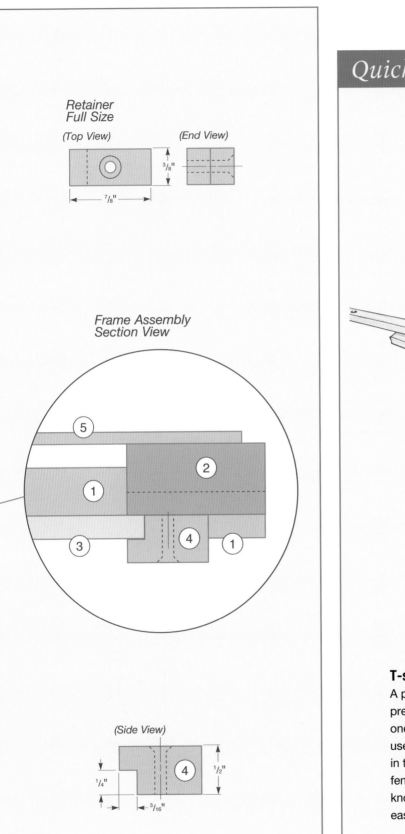

**Retainer
Full Size**

(Top View) (End View)

$^{3}/_{8}$"

$^{7}/_{8}$"

**Frame Assembly
Section View**

⑤
②
①
④
①
③

(Side View)

④

$^{1}/_{2}$"

$^{1}/_{4}$"

$^{3}/_{16}$"

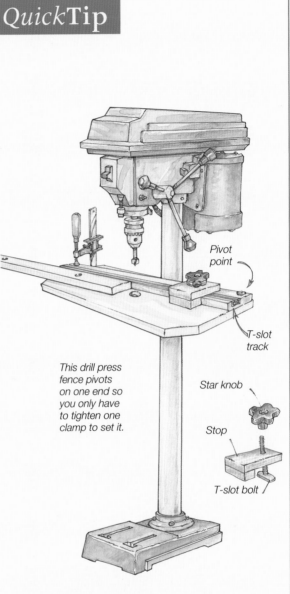

*Quick*Tip

Pivot
point

T-slot
track

*This drill press
fence pivots
on one end so
you only have
to tighten one
clamp to set it.*

Star knob

Stop

T-slot bolt

T-slot for Instant Stops

A pivot-style fence mounted on your drill
press is faster and easier to adjust than
ones that rely on C-clamps. For stops,
use T-slot hardware: bolt heads ride
in the track that is incorporated in the
fence. Attach stops to the bolts with star
knobs. They are infinitely adjustable and
easily removed.

by J. Petrovich

OCTAGONAL MIRROR

Miters depend on end grain-to-end grain glue joints, which can be weak and subject to failure. Dividing your miters in two to build an octagonal shape creates twice as many opportunities for trouble. Our author solved the challenge by painstakingly tuning his saw's miter settings and adding decorative splines at every miter.

A mirror's frame should always complement its use. This particular frame, for instance, was designed for a small entry. After years of trying a variety of pictures and "wall hangings", I came to the conclusion that a mirror was the best answer for this space. It brightened the area, gave depth to the adjoining living room and seemed more friendly to visitors.

Designing the mirror was open-ended. The size was determined by the space available, but the style, material and shape were a matter of preference. I wanted a complex shape, flat stock

and the usual "California roundover." The result is a design that, while it is quite clearly angular, suggests an oval. Joining the members of the frame with exposed splines adds another bit of complexity and interest. The job could have been done with biscuits in much less time, but the subtle accent that the splines add enhances the geometry.

Preparing and Machining the Stock

Constructing the mirror frame is relatively straightforward. This mirror is made of cherry, but any number of

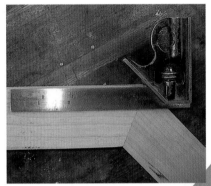

Two 22½° miters will add up to 45°. The author used his try square to check the accuracy of the frame's miters.

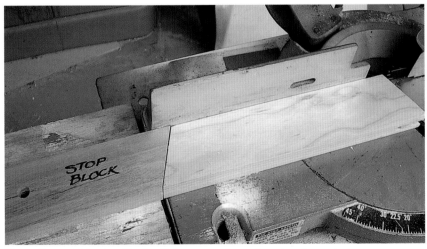

The author cut his stop block with the same miter as the mirror frame stock.

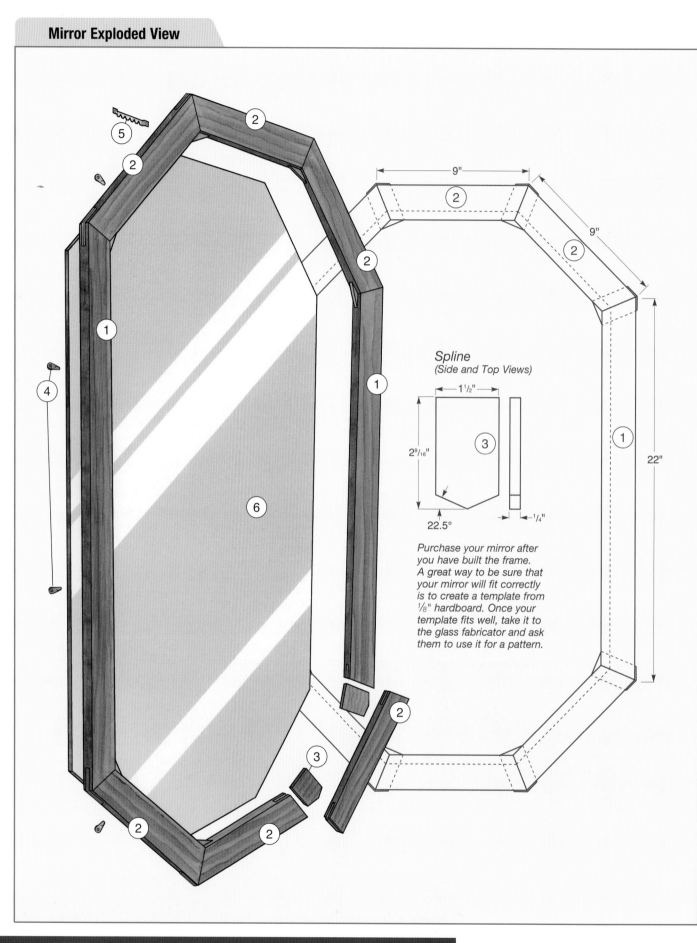

Spline
(Side and Top Views)

Purchase your mirror after
you have built the frame.
A great way to be sure that
your mirror will fit correctly
is to create a template from
1/8" hardboard. Once your
template fits well, take it to
the glass fabricator and ask
them to use it for a pattern.

Material List

		T x W x L
1	Sides (2)	¾" x 2" x 22"
2	End Segments (6)	¾" x 2" x 9"
3	Splines (8)	¼" x 2⁹⁄₁₆" x 1½"
4	Retainers (6)	Plastic
5	Hanger (1)	Steel
6	Mirror (1)	Cut to fit

Mirror Frame Joinery

(End View)

(Front View)

(Side View)

⁵⁄₁₆" ½" ¼" ¾" ¼"

other woods will work as well. If you are purchasing lumber for the frame and do not have a thickness planer, be certain to measure the stock for consistent thickness, side to side and end to end. Cutting the mortises for the splines is done on the table saw and is dependent upon a consistent thickness. If you are planning to run the stock

through a planer, plane all the stock at the same time using the same thickness setting to ensure consistency.

Once you've surfaced the material, rip the stock to width. The design here calls for frame members to be finished at 2". To this, add an additional ⅛". The extra material will be removed later, after mitering and mortising.

Next, the stock needs to be cut to length and mitered. Merely setting the miter gauge for the table saw or setting the arm on a miter saw to 22½° will not likely produce miters with sufficient precision. An error of ½° multiplied by the eight joints of the frame will guarantee that the last joint won't come close to closing up. If you have a

When cutting the frame segments, *you must not only miter them at exactly 22½°, but also cut them precisely to length as well. With 16 critical mating surfaces, accuracy is important.*

Simple Fluting Technique for Dowels

Flutes are cut into dowels to allow excess glue and pockets of trapped air to escape as the dowel joint is clamped shut. Several manufacturers offer pre-fluted dowels, and they're a good choice for all concealed dowel joinery. In a pinch, it's also easy to add fluting to smooth doweling. Just drag a length of dowel sideways across one tooth of a circular saw blade. Make sure the blade is secured (as in a vise), and keep your hands away from the teeth. Two flutes are usually more than adequate. Another option is to tap a dowel between the sawtooth portion of pair of pliers while gripping the dowel firmly in the jaws.

protractor head or similar device, use it to adjust the machine you are using. Use some scrap material to make adjusting cuts until you are satisfied with the tool's accuracy and the consistency of cuts.

If you do not have a protractor head and cannot borrow one, there is an alternative: Most try squares have a 45° shoulder somewhere on the body of the square. To use this method will require making two cuts on separate pieces and "trying" the resultant 45° miter that is produced when the two 22½° angles are brought together.

Cutting the Segments to Size

Of equal importance to the precision of the miters is accuracy in cutting the segments to length. As little as $\frac{1}{32}$" error will make assembly difficult and

Make a Jig to Cut Your Mortises

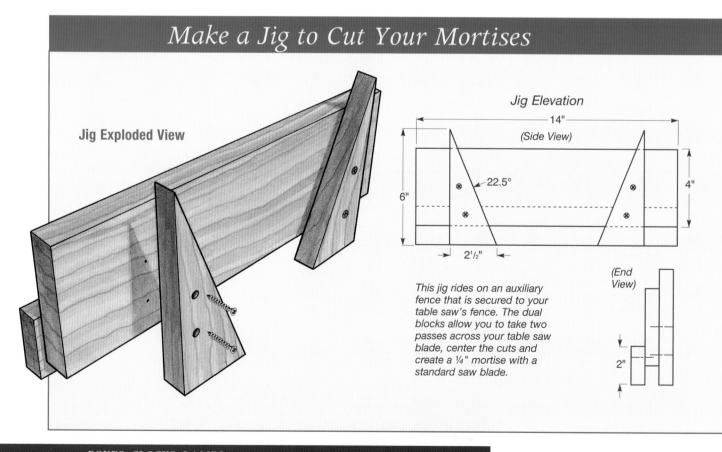

Jig Exploded View

Jig Elevation

14"

(Side View)

22.5°

6"

4"

2½"

(End View)

2"

This jig rides on an auxiliary fence that is secured to your table saw's fence. The dual blocks allow you to take two passes across your table saw blade, center the cuts and create a ¼" mortise with a standard saw blade.

less than satisfying. To this end, use a stop block. If you're using a miter gauge on the table saw, attach a face board to the gauge of sufficient length to accommodate a stop block screwed to it. If you are using a miter saw, mount the stop block to the support table. With either method, one end of the segment should already be mitered accurately prior to cutting it to exact length. Before each cut, check to be certain that the segment is snug against the fence and against the stop block. The stop block should also be mitered (see *photo* on page 35) to provide support along the mitered end.

If you are using a chop saw to cut the miters, you can take two actions to improve the quality of the cuts. First, allow the saw to come to full speed before entering the cut and allowing the blade to cut. Every wood cuts a bit differently. Maple, for example, is both hard and tough and requires a slower rate of feed. Your blade was designed to cut at a particular speed that, if exceeded, might degrade the quality of your miter. Secondly, use the same hand position and motion for each cut. An older or well-used saw (such as ours) may have small amounts of play in the pivot or slide. Consistency in motion will help eliminate the effect of that play.

How to Form Perfect Splines

After cutting the segments to length, lay them out on a flat surface to miter. Clamping several of the segments will make this dry-fit easier. If you are successful and the miters fit tightly, you're ready to cut the mortises. If not— if that last miter will not close—there are several possible solutions. First, try rearranging the segments. Despite your best efforts, some segments may be 22° or 23° instead of 22½°. (Mating a 22° to a 23° will result in the necessary 45°.) Once all segments mate properly, mark them.

If moving the segments doesn't work, check the segments for wind. (I spent 30 minutes flipping segments and checking miter angles only to discover that one of the long segments had a 1⁄16" wind end to end.) Cutting a new segment or diminishing the width of the frame is the only real solution here.

With all the segments cut to length and mitered, and after a successful dry fit, you are ready to cut the spline stock. Cut the splines so the long grain runs perpendicular to the miter. (Resist the temptation to make narrower splines

How do you cut 16 slots to form eight mortises in the exact center of your frame stock? Use a mortising jig. And if you don't have one, here's a simple design. This jig consists of four pieces of wood and rides on an auxiliary fence. The two triangular blocks are cut to match the 22½° angle of the frame miters. They extend past the edge of the center jig piece and, with a long block on the back, form a channel. This channel engages the auxiliary fence. Set up your cut using scrap wood, surfaced to the exact thickness of your frame pieces, and you are ready to make your mortises.

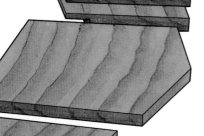

Two C-clamps *are used to bring each joint together. Scrap blocks protect the stock from marring.*

that are parallel to the miter. Each segment is a lever and will exert its force directly against the parallel grain. This configuration is just too weak.) To make the splines, start with a blank ¼" x 3" x 24"—even though the total length requirement is only 8 x 1½" plus the seven kerfs (or about 13"). The additional material is for safety. Trying to hold a 3" or 4" piece of material steady as you trim off a 1½" piece is dangerous.

Cutting the spline stock on the table saw is not advised. A band saw is a much better idea. If you are without a planer, use a hand plane and cabinet scraper to smooth and even both sides of the stock. For a job as small as this, a well-tuned hand plane is nearly as fast as the power tool and considerably more satisfying.

Mortises are cut on the table saw. If you own a mortising jig, use it. If not, you can rig your rip fence with an auxiliary board and clamp your material to a shop-made jig. (See the *sidebar* on the preceding two pages.) To set up and adjust the jig, use some scrap material the same thickness as the frame material. Miter this material to 22½° and mark it for the mortise using

the spline material. Next, raise the saw blade to full height and check it for perpendicularity. Even a slight deflection in the blade can produce a poor fit. Having satisfied yourself with the blade's adjustment, lower it to ¾". With the test material clamped to the sled, move the rip fence into position and lock it. By using ¼" splines and locating them exactly in the middle of the segment, you'll find that the spline's mortises will require only two passes on the saw. Make your first cut on one side, rotate the segment, and move it to the front block of the jig to make the second cut.

Test the mortise with the spline stock. The spline should move in and out of the mortise with light finger pressure. If the spline has any wobble in position, it is too loose. If the spline has to be forced or tapped into position, it is too tight. Adjust the fence accordingly, then re-cut the miter to prepare a fresh end. The need for a fresh end with an oversized mortise is obvious. However,

a fresh end is also necessary for an undersized mortise. Merely enlarging the mortise is not as exact as re-cutting the whole mortise. Attempting to enlarge an existing mortise will deflect the blade (albeit slightly) as one side of the mortise offers resistance and the mortise does not. Using an enlargement adjustment to cut a mortise on a fresh end will usually result in a mortise that is overly large.

Fitting the Splines

Once the mortising is complete, the splines should be cut to length. Be sure to test-fit the first spline. If it's a little long, trim it with a low-angle block plane. Once you are satisfied with the fit, cut the rest, using a stop block to ensure uniformity.

The segments are cut to length, mitered and mortised. The splines are cut but not trimmed. Now is the time to rip the segments to final width. Remember that they're ⅛" oversize. The mortising process will produce some tearout, but trimming 1/16" from both edges should serve to clean up these blemishes. Select the inside or outside to rip first, then flip the stock over and rip the other side. Trust us, removing the entire 1/8" from one edge of the segment will ruin it.

The final dry fit is a good time to begin organizing for glue-up. Lay out the frame segments and splines, which should be proud of the edges. With the splines in place, mark them for trimming—parallel with the outer edge and straight on the inner edge. A thick steel rule snugged against the edge of the frame leaves about the right amount of reveal. As you disassemble the frame to trim the splines, mark them to correspond with the mortise they'll secure, then smooth and bevel them with a block plane.

Making a Rabbet

Before final assembly, cut the rabbet for the mirror and smooth the edges of the frame. It's easier now, before the splines are in place. A pass or two with a sharp plane should do the job.

Glue-up is a matter of organization and forethought. Lay out all your glue, paper towels, clamps and so forth before opening the glue. I used white glue for assembly because it allows more working time than yellow glues.

Remember, the purpose of glue is merely to immobilize the joint. Glue that squeezes out is a pain to clean up. A dot here and there is best left to harden an hour or two rather than wiping it up with a towel. Wiping leaves a ghost that will neither accept stain nor oxidize with time.

Use C-clamps for the final assembly. One clamp on either side of the miter (16 total) will be enough for the job. Use blocks to prevent marring the face of the frame.

After removing the clamps, check for spots of glue and use a chisel to pop them off. The face of the mirror is now ready to be smoothed. Use a hand plane and scraper, followed by light hand-sanding to avoid cross-grain scratch marks. When you're done, you can bevel the edges of the frame with a small block plane.

Finishing

Finishing is a matter of taste. The frame shown here is made of cherry. I applied a coat of tung oil and placed it in direct sunlight for three days. Cherry darkens naturally in sunlight. The three days also gives the oil a chance to polymerize. For a topcoat, three thin coats of wipe-on poly will build to

a nice finish. When the finish cures, rub the surfaces with 0000 steel wool and rub on a coat of paste wax. Use a clean, soft cloth to buff the wax until the surfaces are silky smooth. The final look shows the texture and character of the wood but is also smooth and easy to dust.

Always wait to order your mirror until after the frame is done. Make a cardboard pattern of the exact shape you want the glass to be, and take it along when you order the glass.

by Rick White

PRAIRIE-STYLE LAMP

Starting with some beautiful quartersawn oak and art glass, and a bit of fine woodworking also known as "white magic"...Rick White's craftsmanship shines through. The angled, wood-framed shade makes this a relatively challenging project, especially if angle-cutting isn't your strongest suit. However, several jigs outlined here will make the process much easier.

If you've been a regular reader of *Woodworker's Journal* through the years, you know that I am a big fan of the Arts & Crafts movement. So is a large percentage of our readership, and it's not surprising why: Arts & Crafts styling has a timeless quality to it. Major figureheads of Arts & Crafts movement also believed in using tools—and most of us are in favor of turning on our table saws whenever it's going to make things easier.

"Prairie" is actually a subcategory of Arts & Crafts, made famous by the architect Frank Lloyd Wright. The wood and overall design of this Prairie-style Lamp reflect classic design aspects of the Prairie movement as well as the typical rectilinear, geometric base of Arts & Crafts pieces.

I wanted an authentic look for the lamp, so I called on our expert finisher Michael Dresdner for suggestions on how to stain it. For the shade, I used Kokomo-brand stained glass (from Gaytee Stained Glass; www. gayteestainedglass.com, 888-872-4550), the same brand Gustav Stickley and

Figure 1: *Make sure your rip fence is positioned opposite the direction the blade tilts when making the first two chamfers on the base molding.*

his buddies used to specify. The results have produced a lamp that looks great in my house on the Minnesota prairie—or in anyone's bungalow.

Starting with the Base

I'll break this project into three sub-assemblies: the base, the column and the shade. Even though you will tackle each subassembly separately, it's important to select all your material in advance to ensure you don't get bad grain matches once you start bringing the project together. As always, I strongly recommend you have all your

hardware on hand prior to turning on your saw. You may have to do a little fine tuning if your hardware is odd-sized, and the time to deal with that is before you make your first cut.

Start work on the base by cutting the molding, panels and spacer (pieces 1 through 4) to overall size. Form a long piece of molding on your table saw (see *Figure 1*), which you will miter around the panel subassembly later. Glue the spacer to the lower panel and trim this subassembly to size, referring to the *Technical Drawings* on pages 50 and 51 to establish the proper angle for these cuts. Center the top panel on top of these pieces, but hold off on gluing it in place for just a moment.

Hold the mitered molding in place with a web clamp, and test the fit of the top panel. Trim it until it fits in perfectly, and then glue and clamp the molding and top panel to the bottom panel and spacer.

Turn to your band saw to resaw some highly figured ¾₆"-thick veneer (piece 5) to cover your base and, while

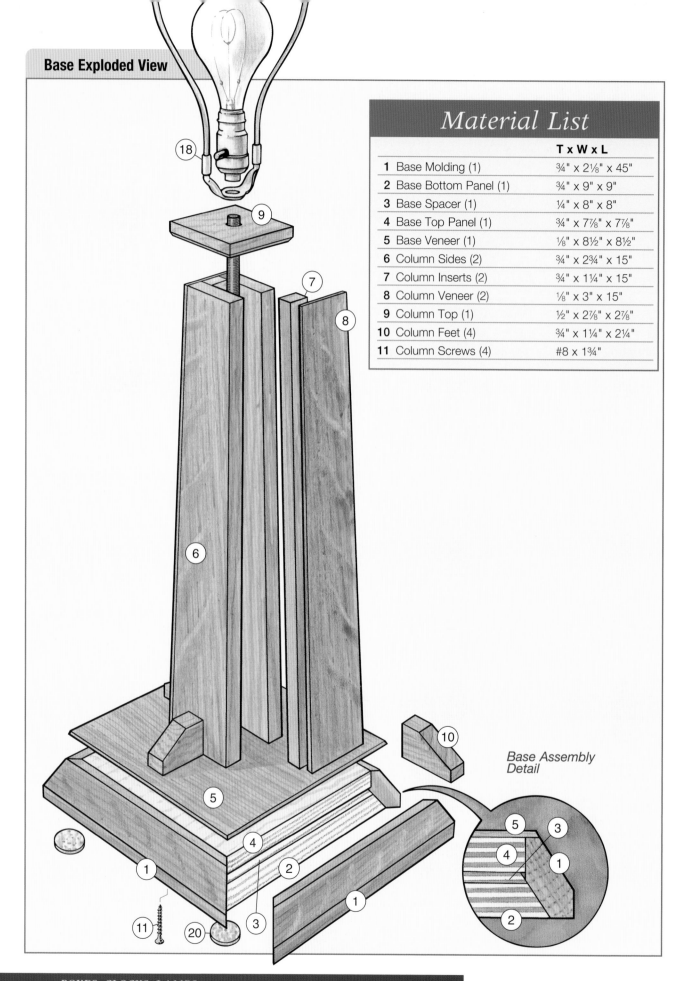

Material List

		T x W x L
1	Base Molding (1)	¾" x 2⅛" x 45"
2	Base Bottom Panel (1)	¾" x 9" x 9"
3	Base Spacer (1)	¼" x 8" x 8"
4	Base Top Panel (1)	¾" x 7⅞" x 7⅞"
5	Base Veneer (1)	⅛" x 8½" x 8½"
6	Column Sides (2)	¾" x 2¾" x 15"
7	Column Inserts (2)	¾" x 1¼" x 15"
8	Column Veneer (2)	⅛" x 3" x 15"
9	Column Top (1)	½" x 2⅞" x 2⅞"
10	Column Feet (4)	¾" x 1¼" x 2¼"
11	Column Screws (4)	#8 x 1¾"

Base Assembly Detail

you're at it, slice the veneer for the column. To get to the right thickness safely, I recommend using a slave board underneath the veneer to support it during planing. Set your blades to remove about 1/32" with each pass and bring these pieces to exactly 1/8" in thickness. Set aside the column veneer for now, and then book-match, glue and clamp the base veneer to the base, carefully trimming to pick up the angle of the molding. (I used a belt sander for this.)

Moving Up to the Column

The dimensions of the column sides and inserts (pieces 6 and 7) are provided in the *Technical Drawings*. Start this step by cutting the sides and insets to length and forming the angles on their tops and bottoms. Now dig up your tapering jig to form the taper on each edge of these pieces. I used up a few scrap pieces of plywood to ensure that these taper cuts were right on the money.

When the four pieces fit together nicely, glue and clamp them together and sand the joints smooth. Trim the column

---

QuickTip

Sharpening Stone Options

Choosing sharpening stones presents three basic options: oil, ceramic and waterstones. Take your pick. That choice has become easier for woodworkers in recent years with huge improvements in the quality and variety of waterstones. They are cleaner to work with than oilstones and don't permanently spot the wood. A diamond waterstone costs a little more, but it will remain flat and true with minimum maintenance (an occasional cleaning), give service life proportional to its cost, and is available in a wide range of sizes and grits. It can even be used to flatten your worn-out oilstones!

Making Molding on the Table Saw

Ribbons of quartersawn flake are visible on only one aspect of any given piece of lumber. Form the lamp's base molding to take advantage of the best-looking figure and flake, following the process at right for best results. Look to the Technical Drawings for establishing proper saw blade settings.

The first and second cuts are made on the left side of the saw blade, as shown in the photo on page 48.

First cut

Second cut

Move your fence to the other side of the saw blade to complete the molding, this time holding it flat to the tabletop.

Third cut

Fourth cut

It took Rick a while to work out the angled shoulders for the frames' mortise and tenon joints. On the Technical Drawings, you will find elevations for the jig (pictured below) that will make this step easy for you. Its design allows you to cut both the mortise and the tenon. Test the open mortise and tenon joints on appropriately dimensioned scrap lumber.

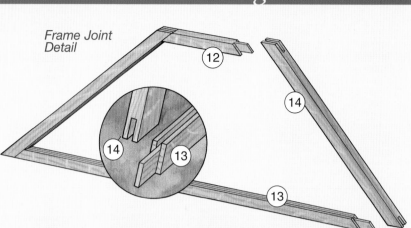

Frame Joint Detail

Figure 2: *Before cutting the rails and stiles to length, use a dado blade to plow a groove. This will make it easier to create the rabbets for the glass after you assemble the frames.*

Figure 3: *With the same dado blade in your table saw, use our jig to help chop the mortises and slice the tenons on the ends of the frame's stiles and rails.*

veneer strips (pieces 8) roughly to size, then glue and clamp them over the insert pieces. Once again, take your time trimming this veneer, keeping the corners nice and square.

Now turn to the *Technical Drawings* and mill the column top and feet (pieces 9 and 10) to size. Keep an eye on grain orientation, particularly for the feet. The *Exploded View Drawing* on page 44 will help you decide. Now bore a 1"-diameter stopped hole in the base's center, followed by a through hole to accommodate the lamp hardware (see *Technical Drawings*). Drill another through hole in the column top and glue it in place. Now you're ready to

attach the column to the base, using two screws (pieces 11) to hold the subassemblies together. Leave the feet to the side for now.

Making the Shade

The elegant simplicity of the shade's appearance is produced by some sophisticated woodworking. The shade is four frames that are joined by modified mortise and tenon joints, mitered at the corners and capped with a slotted top piece.

Begin by cutting the shade frame top and bottom rails as well as the shade frame stiles (pieces 12 through 14) to size. To achieve the best

appearance, slice these pieces from the same piece of well-figured (nice quartersawn flake) white oak. While the pieces are still in sticked-up form, put a dado head in your table saw and plow a groove down their inside edges, as shown in *Figure 2*. Move to your miter saw and cut the stiles and rails to their appropriate lengths while chopping the correct angles on their ends. (see the *Technical Drawings*).

Build the jig shown in the *tint box*, above, to help form the angled mortise and tenon joints. You can find elevations of the jig on page 51 of the *Technical Drawings* as well as details for the three other jigs you'll need to complete this

Figure 4: *Use a rabbeting bit and a shop-made jig to safely and accurately rabbet the back of the shade frames. Homemade jigs are the key to success with this Prairie project. See the details for making this jig in the* drawings *on page 139.*

project. Once the jig is ready, use it to plow out the mortises and slice the cheeks of the tenons. Simply adjust the dado head (the same one used earlier to plow the grooves) to the proper height. Then it's a matter of clamping the stiles and rails in place and removing stock from the center of the stiles and the outside faces of the rails, as shown in *Figure 3*. (As always, testing the setup with scrap lumber is a good idea.) Dry-fit the stile and rail subassemblies and, once you are happy with the fit, glue and clamp them together.

With that task complete, create a routing jig like the one shown in the *photo*, above, using the details provided in the *Technical Drawings*. This is a two-level jig that holds the frames securely as you rout the rabbet for the glass into their back faces (see *Figure 4*). When you have routed all the rabbets, use a sharp chisel to extend the rabbet into the corners of the frames.

Beveling Away

Two new jigs are required to miter the joining edges of the shade frames. These jigs allow you to make essentially the same cut, but on opposite sides of the frame. It's a simple operation to do with these jigs but nearly impossible without them. The jigs hold the frame's stiles exactly parallel to the saw blade while you

slice 31° chamfers on their edges. See the *sidebar* on the next page for more details.

Assembling the Shade Frames

Now for the fun part: Once the miters are cut, it's time to assemble the shade frames. I hinged three of the four joints with clear packing tape. Next, apply yellow glue, fold the frame together, and tape the fourth joint. Then use whatever combination of web, squeeze, hand and any other clamps you can think of to complete the clamp-up. (Just be absolutely sure the glue-up is square!) Cut the shade cap (piece 15) to size and test-fit it to the shade frame subassembly. When it fits well, lay out the ventilation slots and the location of the two-step boring at the cap's center. Step over to your drill press and remove most of the waste from the ventilation slots with a drill bit. Then bore the stopped and through hole to accommodate the lamp harp's mounting bolt. Move to a scroll saw and clean up the ventilation slots. Glue the shade cap in place. After the glue cures, sand the shade carefully through the grits.

Adding More Details

A few more steps and you are on the home stretch. Rip a length of shade frame retaining stripping (piece 16) to use for securing the shade glass (pieces 17) into the rabbet

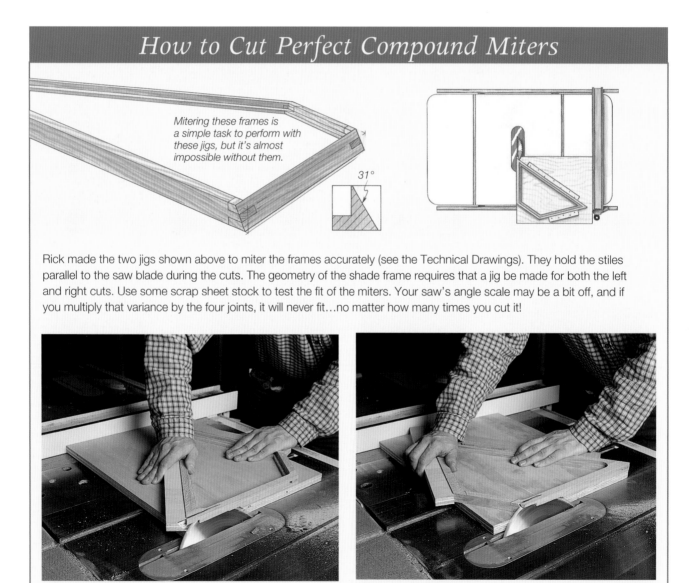

How to Cut Perfect Compound Miters

Mitering these frames is a simple task to perform with these jigs, but it's almost impossible without them.

31°

Rick made the two jigs shown above to miter the frames accurately (see the Technical Drawings). They hold the stiles parallel to the saw blade during the cuts. The geometry of the shade frame requires that a jig be made for both the left and right cuts. Use some scrap sheet stock to test the fit of the miters. Your saw's angle scale may be a bit off, and if you multiply that variance by the four joints, it will never fit…no matter how many times you cut it!

The first jig miters the left side of the frames.

The second jig miters the right sides.

Material List

		T x W x L
12 Shade Frame Top Rails (4)		¾" x ⅞" x 6⅞"
13 Shade Frame Bottom Rails (4)		¾" x ⅞" x 20⅛"
14 Shade Frame Stiles (8)		¾" x ⅞" x 13¼"
15 Shade Cap (1)		½" x 5¾" x 5¾"
16 Shade Frame Retainer Stripping (1)		¼" x 44" Quarter round
17 Shade Glass (2)		Cut to fit. Kokomo brand
18 Lamp Hardware Kit (1)		Brass kit with 7½" harp
19 Hardware Cap Cover (1)		⅝" x 1" x 1"
20 Cork Feet (8)		¹⁄₁₆" x ⅝" Dia.

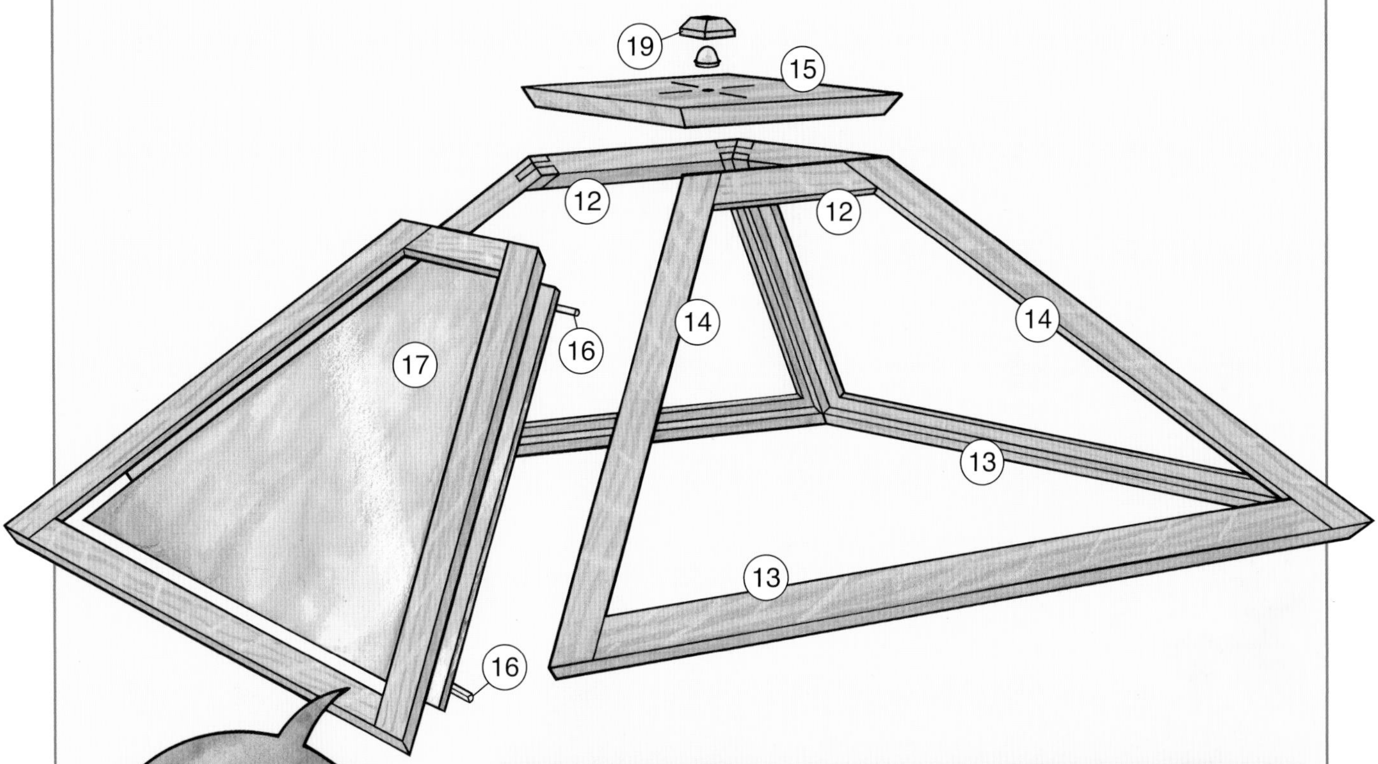

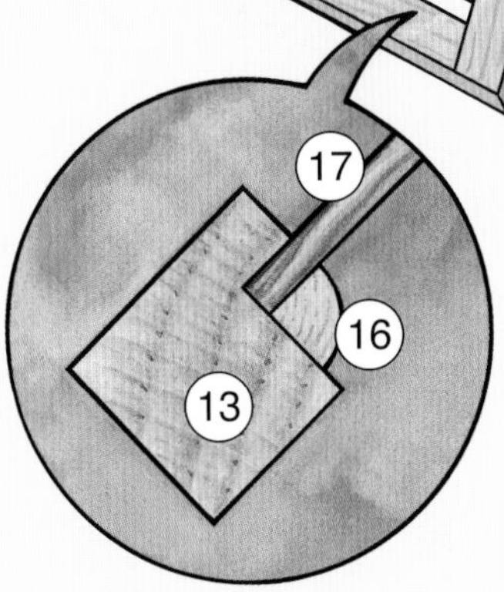

Retaining Strip Detail

you routed earlier. You'll need to buy supplies for holding the lamp socket in place and wire it for a wall plug. To enhance the appearance of the shade, create a pyramid-shaped hardware cap cover (piece 19) and epoxy it to the metal retaining nut that holds the shade on the lamp harp you buy. Mount the lamp hardware in the lamp. When it all fits correctly, take it back out until you are done finishing.

Just a note of caution: Do not order your glass until you have completed making the shade. Make a template for your glass from heavy card stock, and use it to have your art glass cut to final size and shape.

Finishing Up

Michael Dresdner recommended that I finish this lamp by fuming it with strong ammonia in a sealed plastic tent.

Fuming was a common Stickley finishing technique. If you do the same, be sure to remove the metal lamp hardware first or you'll discolor the metal. You could also stain this project conventionally. Either way, follow up with a topcoat of satin varnish. Install the glass with the retaining strips and apply the self sticking cork feet (pieces 20). Re-install the hardware, attach the electric wires and screw in a light bulb.

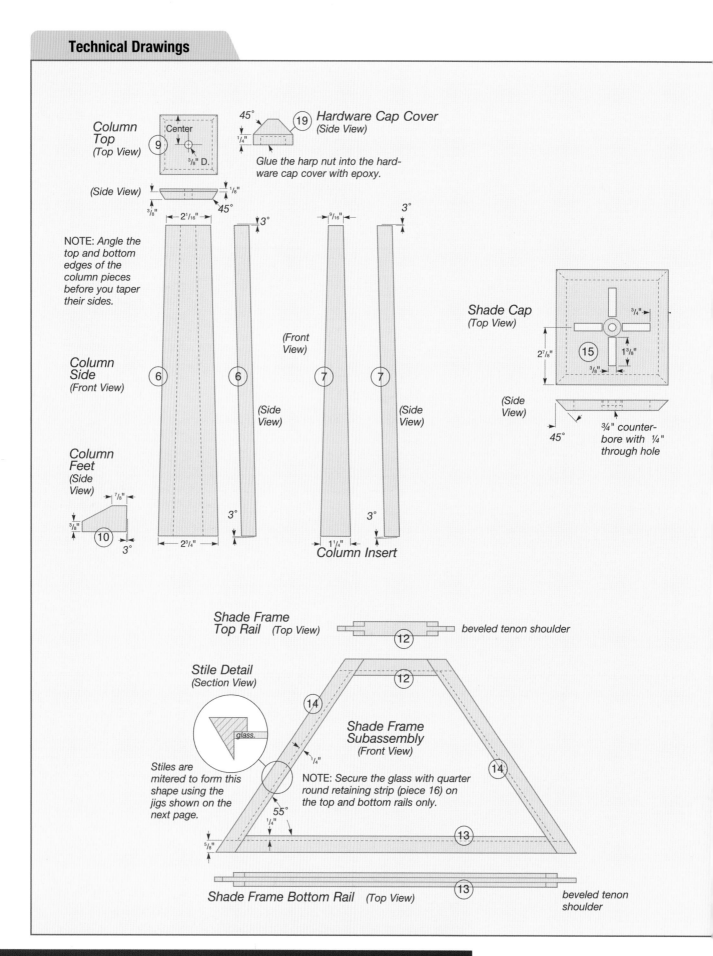

Column Top (Top View) ⑨

Center

³/₈" D.

Hardware Cap Cover (Side View) ⑲

45°

¹/₄"

Glue the harp nut into the hardware cap cover with epoxy.

(Side View)

¹/₈"

³/₈"

45°

2¹/₁₆"

NOTE: Angle the top and bottom edges of the column pieces before you taper their sides.

Column Side (Front View) ⑥

⑥

3°

(Front View)

⁹/₁₆"

⑦

3°

⑦

(Side View)

(Side View)

Shade Cap (Top View) ⑮

³/₄"

2⁷/₈"

1³/₈"

³/₈"

(Side View)

45°

³/₄" counter-bore with ¹/₄" through hole

Column Feet (Side View) ⑩

⁷/₈"

³/₈"

3°

2³/₄"

3°

3°

1¹/₄"

Column Insert

Shade Frame Top Rail (Top View) ⑫

beveled tenon shoulder

Stile Detail (Section View)

⑫

glass.

⑭

Stiles are mitered to form this shape using the jigs shown on the next page.

Shade Frame Subassembly (Front View)

¹/₄"

NOTE: Secure the glass with quarter round retaining strip (piece 16) on the top and bottom rails only.

⑭

55°

¹/₄"

⁵/₈"

⑬

⑬

Shade Frame Bottom Rail (Top View) ⑬

beveled tenon shoulder

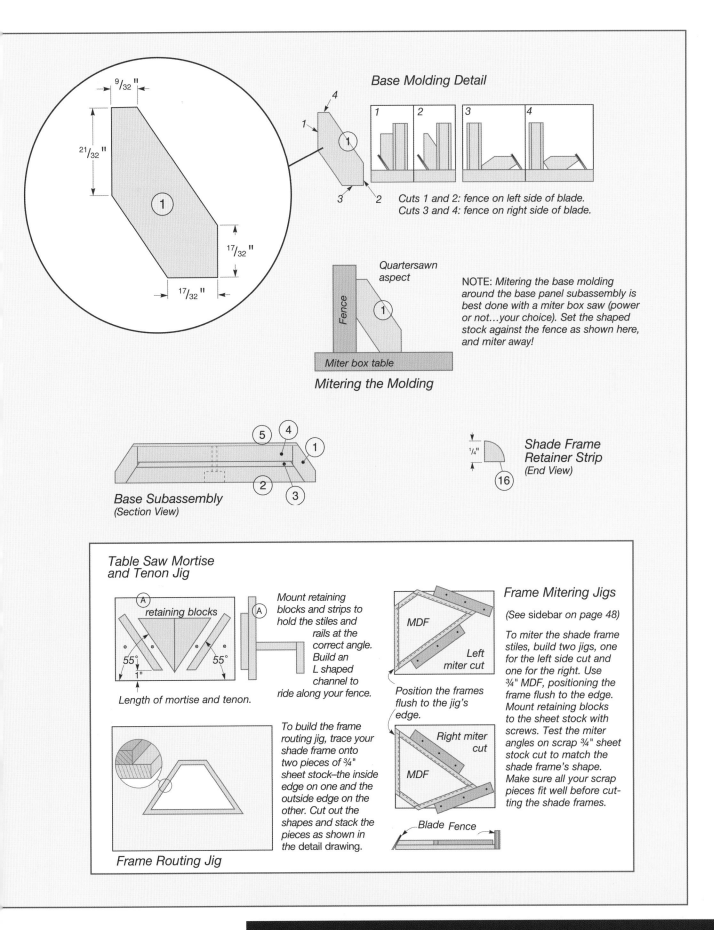

Base Molding Detail

$^{9}/_{32}$ "

$^{21}/_{32}$ "

1

$^{17}/_{32}$ "

$^{17}/_{32}$ "

4

1

3

2

1

2

3

4

Cuts 1 and 2: fence on left side of blade.
Cuts 3 and 4: fence on right side of blade.

Quartersawn
aspect

Fence

1

Miter box table

Mitering the Molding

NOTE: *Mitering the base molding around the base panel subassembly is best done with a miter box saw (power or not…your choice). Set the shaped stock against the fence as shown here, and miter away!*

5 4 1

2 3

Base Subassembly
(Section View)

$^{1}/_{4}$ "

16

Shade Frame Retainer Strip
(End View)

Table Saw Mortise and Tenon Jig

(A)

retaining blocks

(A)

55°   55°

1"

Length of mortise and tenon.

Mount retaining blocks and strips to hold the stiles and rails at the correct angle. Build an L shaped channel to ride along your fence.

To build the frame routing jig, trace your shade frame onto two pieces of ¾" sheet stock–the inside edge on one and the outside edge on the other. Cut out the shapes and stack the pieces as shown in the detail drawing.

Frame Routing Jig

MDF

Left miter cut

Position the frames flush to the jig's edge.

Right miter cut

MDF

Blade Fence

Frame Mitering Jigs

(See sidebar on page 48)

To miter the shade frame stiles, build two jigs, one for the left side cut and one for the right. Use ¾" MDF, positioning the frame flush to the edge. Mount retaining blocks to the sheet stock with screws. Test the miter angles on scrap ¾" sheet stock cut to match the shade frame's shape. Make sure all your scrap pieces fit well before cutting the shade frames.

by Rick White

BIRD'S-EYE MAPLE LAMP

When designing a production project, you need to streamline the building set-ups and use jigs as much as possible. However, you don't have to compromise quality or appearance for the sake of efficiency. This lamp project with decorative inlay is both attractive and quick to build.

I've had lots of requests over the years for projects that can be sold at local craft shows. While there are plenty of good designs to choose from, the real key to this kind of woodworking is knowing how to streamline your production techniques. A project has to be appealing, but if you're going to succeed in this market it must also be easy to mass-produce. To accomplish this you need to take full advantage of jigs and shop shortcuts, testing them until they deliver consistently perfect results on a prototype.

This bird's-eye maple lamp provides a great example of how production techniques used by professionals can drastically reduce the time it takes to turn out a project. In this case, your first lamp, including the jigs and plywood prototype, will take the better part of a weekend to complete. But once the jigs are ready and you work out a few shop shortcuts, you should easily be able to make ten or more lamps in that amount of time.

Starting with Angle Jigs

Get started on this project by making the set of angle-cutting jigs shown in *Figures 1 and 2*. You'll need two pieces of ¾" plywood about 14" long and 10" wide. To make the first jig, set your miter gauge at exactly 4°. Now cut the

angle along one edge, stopping about 2" from the end. Back your stock out and, without changing the miter gauge angle, turn the panel and cut off the waste to form a notch. Follow the same procedure for making the second jig, but reset the miter gauge to 8° in the opposite direction. The opposing angles ensure that the miters on the lamp sides will end up facing each other. One addition to the second jig is a 1"-wide by ¼"-thick strip glued and nailed along the angled edge. This taller strip creates a better contact point for supporting the angled edge of the side pieces.

To test your jigs, make a prototype using four pieces of ¾" plywood cut to the side (pieces 1) dimensions shown in the *Material List*. Now, with the 4° jig riding against the table saw's rip fence, tilt the blade 45° and set your fence to cut ½" off one edge of each side piece. Once these cuts are made, put the 8° jig in position, flip your workpieces end-for-end and set the rip fence to leave 3½" of material at the top end of each side. Now cut the second angled edge.

Dry-assemble the four prototype pieces to ensure that the jigs are accurate and that your 45° blade setting is true. Continue recutting until your prototype is right on the mark and then apply yellow glue to the miters. Use two

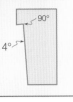

Figure 1: *Use jig "A" to cut the first edge of the lamp sides. For safety, set the fence so the blade tilts away from it.*

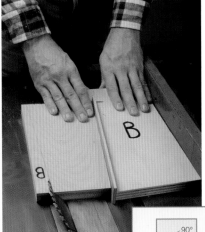

Figure 2: *Jig "B" angles the opposite way from the first jig and is used for cutting the second edge on each of the four sides.*

Router Fluting Jig

To make the fluting jig, start with a piece of ¼" hardboard about 10" wide by 22" long. Use a copy machine to enlarge the jig pattern on this page and glue it to the hardboard with spray-mount adhesive. Follow the outside lines of the pattern to cut the hardboard to its square size. Now clamp the template to a piece of plywood that's just slightly smaller than the hardboard. Chuck a ⅝" straight bit in your plunge router, set to cut ⅜" deep. Attach a straightedge guide to your router base and rout the center groove.

Next, use your table saw and the two angle jigs shown in *Figures 1* and *2* to rip the edges of the jig (following the dotted lines on the pattern). Then go back to your plunge router set-up and rout the outside flute grooves.

Add the cleats to the jig, positioning them as shown above. Glue the top and one side cleat first, and when the glue sets, flip the assembly over to countersink several screws. Now use the prototype to position your other two cleats, and secure them in place for a snug fit.

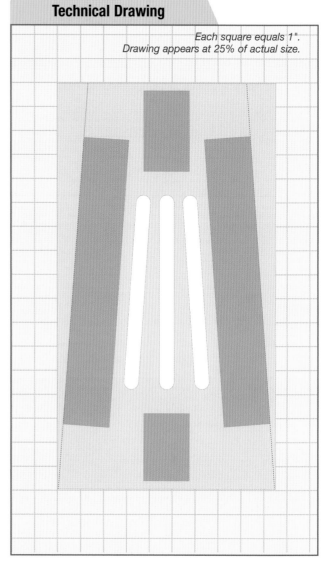

Figure 3: *The fluting jig should fit tightly over the side assembly. The weight of the router will hold the jig in place as you cut the flutes.*

Each square equals 1".
Drawing appears at 25% of actual size.

Building the Fluting Jig

The fluting on the lamp sides is another good example of a technique that lends itself to a jig. Without a jig you'll spend a lot of time setting up alignment guides and stop blocks. Build the jig carefully and methodically, making sure every cut is perfect to guarantee the accuracy of your routing on the lamp sides later.

Making the hardboard fluting jig is described in the *sidebar* on this page. To help you get it exactly right, we've included a jig pattern (above) that you can enlarge and glue to your template material. Once the jig is completed, you simply clamp the side assembly to the edge of your workbench, lay the jig over one side and template-rout the three flutes, as shown in *Figure 3*. Use a ½" core box bit with a rub collar and set the depth to make your flutes ³⁄₁₆" deep. Be sure to start each cut in the middle of the jig, then move toward the ends at a steady pace. Don't allow the router bit to linger in

band clamps to draw the pieces together, tapping lightly on their ends to make sure they line up on the bottom. If everything fits perfectly, you're ready to move on to the real lamp.

Cut each of the sides to the length and width indicated in the *Material List*, and follow the procedure you just developed with prototypes to glue up the first lamp base. After the glue dries, use a scraper and sandpaper to remove any excess, being careful to avoid rounding the sharp mitered edges.

Lamp Base Exploded View

Cove Detail

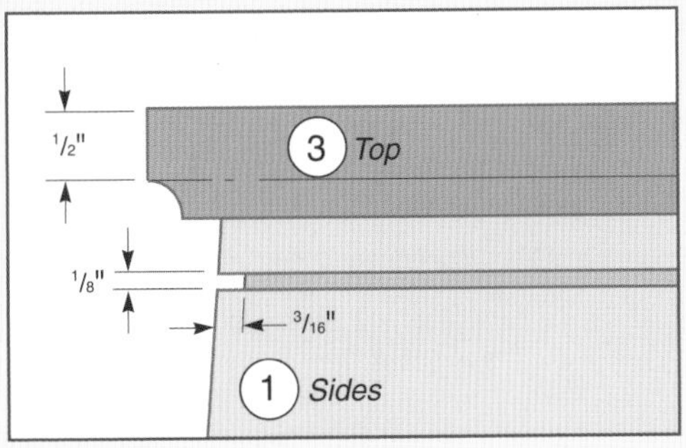

1/2"
3 Top
1/8"
3/16"
1 Sides

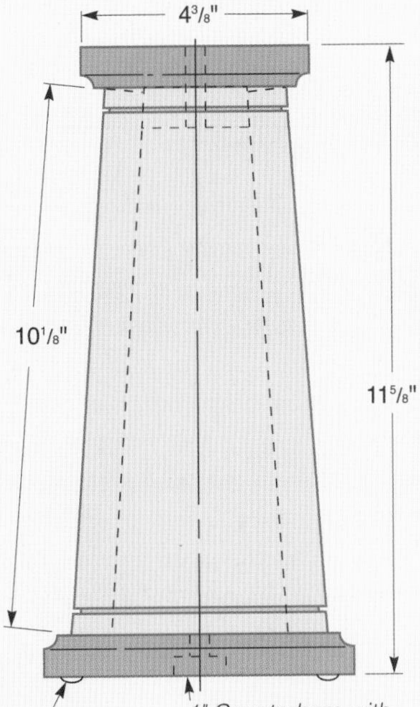

4 3/8"
10 1/8"
11 5/8"
Blum cushions
1" Counterbore with a 3/8" through hole

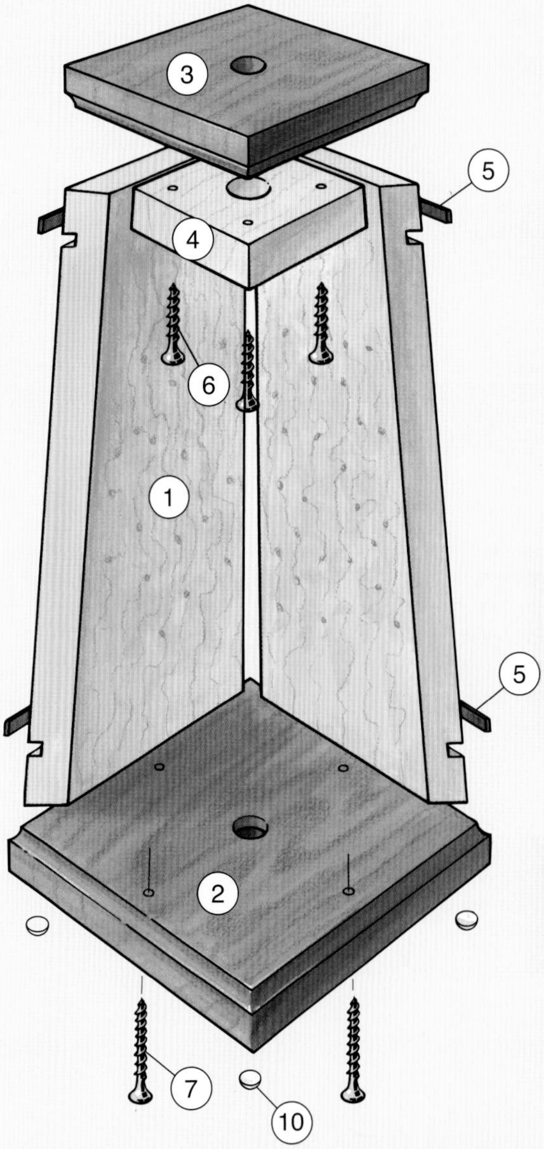

3
4
5
6
1
5
2
7
10

Material List

	T x W x L		T x W x L
1 Sides (4)	¾" x 6" x 10⅛" (maple)	**6** Screws (4)	#8 x 1¼" (wood screws)
2 Base (1)	¾" x 5⅞" x 5⅞" (cherry)	**7** Screws (4)	#8 x 1½" (wood screws)
3 Top (1)	¾" x 4⅜" x 4⅜" (cherry)	**8** Lamp Wiring Kit (1)	11" harp with 12" shaft
4 Glue Block (1)	¾" x 1⅞" x 1⅞" (plywood)	**9** Lamp Shade (1)	12" (purchase locally)
5 Veneer Strips (8)	1/28" x ⅛" x 6" (dyed ash)	**10** Stick-on Pads (4)	⅛" x ½" Dia.

Figure 4: *To guarantee a consistent angle on your table saw blade, tilt it against the side assembly. This will reestablish the 4° angle used previously on the jigs.*

Figure 5: *With the side assembly held squarely against the blade, slide your miter gauge up to one side to set it for trimming the bottom edges of the base flat.*

one spot, especially at the ends of the flutes, or you'll burn the wood. Be sure to test the routing jig on your plywood prototype to get comfortable with this operation.

By the time you've completed 12 cuts on the prototype you should have the feel for it. Go ahead and rout the 12 flutes on the sides of the actual lamp now. If you do get some burn marks at the ends of your router cuts, you can easily remove these chars by using a ¼" core box bit and turning it by hand, as if it were a scraper. Cleaning up the burn this way won't change the sharp look of the flute cuts as might happen if you use sandpaper.

Adding the Top, Base and Glue Block

Cut the cherry base (piece 2) and top (piece 3) to the dimensions provided in the *Material List*, and then rout a cove along the bottom edges of the top and the top edges of the base. Use your router table, centering the fence on a ½"-radius core box bit and raising the bit ¼". These are small pieces you're cutting, so use a push block to keep your fingers clear. After making the cuts, lightly sand both pieces to remove any burn marks, but be careful to maintain the crisp lines. Lay out the center points on these parts, then drill a 1"-diameter counterbore in the bottom of the base followed by a ⅜"-diameter through hole. Drill a ⅜" hole through the top.

Now make a glue block (piece 4) to fit inside the lamp body. In order to get the best gluing surface from the glue block, its edges should be angled to match the slope of the lamp sides. Getting the blade to tilt exactly 4° could slow you down, but here's a shop shortcut to keep things moving at a production pace. Raise your blade all the way up and stand your trusty prototype next to it. Tilt the blade until it lies flush against one of the sides (see *Figure 4*). The blade angle is now

*Quick*Tip

Straight and Narrow on Angle-Setting

Setting table saw blade angles can be tricky if you measure off the blade. Here's a simple set-up device to improve your accuracy. Drill a ⅝" hole through a piece of extruded aluminum that's about 16" long. Remove your saw blade and bolt this straightedge to your saw arbor. Now you've got an elongated reference edge for setting angles. Use a large drafting triangle held against the straightedge for dialing in square or 45° blade settings. Switch to a preset bevel gauge for establishing other blade angles. Keep this device near your saw so it's easy to find every time you change blade angles.

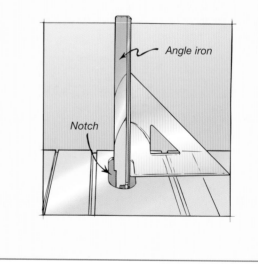

consistent with the side angles, and you don't have to spend extra time measuring or making test cuts.

Now draw a line on your miter gauge fence exactly 2⅛" from the near side of the blade, and use a "C" clamp to hold a piece of scrap wood flush with the line. Press your glue block material up to the scrap and cut your piece to size. While testing the fit you'll notice that the tops of the glued-up sides angle in slightly. You want the glue block to be flush with the outside edge; otherwise, when you screw it to the top, it will push the sides apart. Hold a square across the top, then trim the block until it touches the straightedge. Once the block fits correctly, drill a ½"-diameter hole through its center and a 3⁄16" screw hole at each corner. Turn the lamp assembly upside down and glue the block into position.

Trimming and Detailing Made Easy

The bottom cut and the two wrap-around banding kerfs on the sides don't lend themselves well to a jig, but there are other ways to reduce your set-up time in the shop. The three *photos* on these two pages show you how to quickly set up both the miter fence and blade angle for these operations. In fact, your blade angle *(see Figure 4)* should still be at the correct angle from cutting the glue block.

Like the top end of the lamp assembly, there's an angle on the bottom edge of the sides. This time, however, the angle must be flattened because the inside edges are slightly higher than the outside edges. If this isn't done, a reveal will show when the sides are attached to the base. To make this cut, raise the blade 1" and butt the side assembly up to the blade as shown in *Figure 5*. Now loosen the miter gauge and slide it up to the side assembly. The miter gauge will turn to the correct angle as it contacts the side, which, for your purposes, is 4°. Test your set-up on the prototype and then trim the bottom edge of each side. Next, reset the blade height to 3⁄16" and mark your miter gauge fence to cut kerfs for installing the decorative banding ⅜" from the top and bottom ends of the sides. Again, use a "C"-clamp and stop block to hold a scrap piece flush with your marks, as shown in *Figure 6*. Make test cuts first, then cut your lamp assembly.

Now cut the ⅛"-wide black inlay strips (pieces 5) about 1⁄16" longer than the saw kerfs, apply glue to their backs, and press them in place. A small file will take care of the overhanging inlay in quick order.

Final Machining and Assembly

To secure the top to the sides, turn the lamp assembly upside down, slip the top underneath, square it to the sides and use an awl to mark your drilling locations through the glue block. Drill ½"-deep pilot holes into the top at each awl mark

Figure 6: *Keep the blade and miter gauge angled to cut saw kerfs for installing the decorative inlay. Clamp a stop block on the miter gauge to ensure that the kerfs will line up all around the base.*

with a ⅛" bit. Now use 1¼" screws (pieces 6) and a long-shanked screwdriver to fasten the top to the glue block. Don't glue the top down since it has to float with seasonal expansion and contraction.

The last assembly step is to attach the base to the sides. Make sure it overhangs evenly on all four sides, clamp the parts together, then drill four ⅛"-diameter holes through the base and into the sides, maintaining the 4° angle. Switch to a 3⁄16" bit to open up the holes in the base (for expansion) and countersink these holes so the screw heads sit flush with the surface. Secure the base to the sides with 1½" screws (pieces 7), leaving the bottom unglued so it can move freely.

Finishing Up

I used a lacquer finish on this lamp to bring out the bird's-eye maple details. Danish oil or clear shellac would look good, too.

One source for the electric parts for this lamp is Cherry Tree Toys (800-848-4363; www.cherrytreetoys.com). Their lamp kit can be installed in about five minutes and includes all the parts necessary to complete the project. A square shade makes a fitting top to this lamp base. Add some stick-on rubber or felt pads underneath the lamp base to keep it from scratching other furniture and provide a bit of room for the lamp cord to slip past.

Well, you've completed your first lamp. Label your jigs clearly and store them in a safe place. Next time, try making three or four lamps at once. Then you'll really see how jigs and shop shortcuts can save you time—which, ultimately, puts more money in your pocket.

by John Nelson

SCROLL-SAWN NIGHTLIGHTS

Looking for something to interest the kids when they can't sleep or to reassure them during a late-night thunderstorm? These simple scroll-sawn nightlights are also a good project for introducing older gradeschoolers to the basics of woodworking. Tighten up a fresh scroll saw blade and let your imagination go.

These nightlight projects are a lot of fun and simple to complete, and they make great gifts. You can make yours from scrap wood or even metal. Stack a few of the same designs together when cutting them out to really speed up the process. If you are introducing kids to the shop, I recommend starting out with ⅛" plywood. As you might guess, kids love this sort of project, particularly since they get to actually operate a power tool! (Scroll saws, if approached properly and with adult supervision, are one of the safest power tools around.)

Even if a child does not do the actual cutting, they can paint or decorate the cutouts as they choose: from a single color (like the flocked frog) or painted with a lot of detail. If you have some attractive leftovers from other projects, you could use a clear finish to show off the wood grain.

Starting Out

Using one or more of the full-size patterns shown on the next two pages, get started on your nightlights by making copies at a local library or copy center. (Permission is hereby granted for your personal use.) Select your material and cut the metal, plastic or ⅛"-thick plywood to overall size. If you are going to stack-cut the parts (as shown in the *photo* on page 61), carefully tape three or four pieces together along the edges. Do not try to cut stacked pieces that add up to more than ½" thick as a group—it's too much for a scroll saw. If you want to make your nightlight out of a thin metal such as aluminum or copper, simply sandwich three to four sheets between two pieces of ⅛" thick plywood and cut out as usual.

Take your paper pattern and attach it to the top piece of the stack with spray adhesive. (Take care to apply adhesive to the paper pattern, not the wood.) If the pattern has interior cutouts, drill a ⅛"-diameter starter hole for the blade at each interior cut. Make all your interior cuts first. Then, starting on one edge, form the piece's outside shape by following the pattern. If you're cutting stacked pieces, it's very important that you keep everything together as you cut. Don't hesitate to stop and re-tape if necessary to keep everything properly aligned. Once your pieces are cut, use a block of wood with sandpaper wrapped around it to lightly sand away any burrs or splinters from the front and back surfaces.

Finishing Up

If you are going to leave the wood looking natural, simply brush or spray on a topcoat of a clear satin or gloss

**Full-size
Patterns**

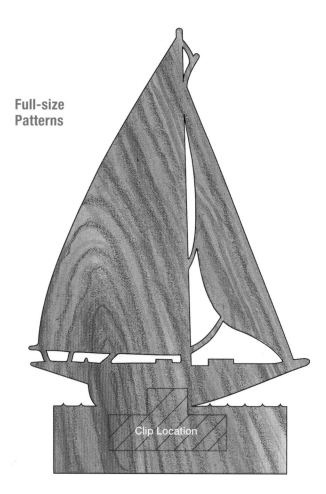

Clip Location

Clip Location

finish. If you are going to paint your nightlight one color (such as black), using a can of spray paint is an easy application method. For fancier paint schemes, apply a light primer coat and hand-paint to suit. Finish up by adding a light, clear topcoat of your choice to seal in the paint.

Attach the plastic clip to the back surface of the project (five-minute epoxy works well) where indicated on each of the patterns above. Snap the clip onto the nightlight, add a bulb, and you're done! A wonderfully simple project.

One final tip: On the cat, horse and boat patterns, you might want to hide the lightbulb by gluing a piece of non-stick baking liner paper (parchment paper) across the back surface. (Refer to the *photo* on the next page.) You can get this liner from a grocery or kitchen supply store. This hides the bulb and lends a nice "glowing" effect. Do not use regular paper, as it could overheat.

*Quick*Tip

Magnetic Blade Organizer
Here's a simple organizer for scroll saw blades. Whenever you install a blade, attach the relevant number tag to your saw. Then it's always easy to tell what size blade is in the saw. When you change blades, stick the used blade to the magnet in front of the correct hole, so it doesn't get mixed up with brand new blades.

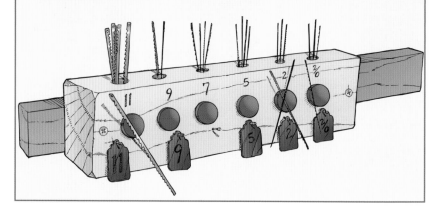

Clip Location

Clip Location

Stacked cutting is a great way to speed up the process of creating these nightlights. For best results, don't stack parts thicker than about ½".

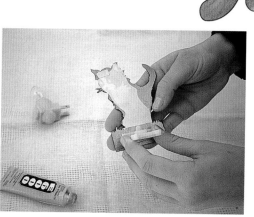

Use epoxy to attach the nightlight's clip to the scroll sawn design. Five-minute epoxy will do fine.

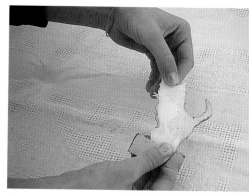

Use parchment paper to line the back of see-through lights to help hide the light bulb.

by Michael McGlynn

ARTS & CRAFTS WALL LAMP

Built in the Greene and Greene tradition, this beautiful wall lamp features stained-glass panels, a dyed mahogany framework and classic ebony accents. It takes only a small amount of stock to build, so you can spend a little extra on high-quality glass to complete the project properly.

Expose ³⁄₁₆" of the dado head cutter, *then relieve the front face of the plate. Since the length of this dado exceeds half the length of the workpiece, leave a stub at the end to keep the wood from tipping into the blade as the dado gets wider.*

Although the origins of this lamp lie in the ornate oil lamps that graced the walls of manors and elegant homes, this version is designed as an electrical fixture in a 21st century home. In a sense, it effectively demonstrates the transition of the Arts & Crafts movement itself, which connected two centuries, rural crafts and high technology.

For stock selection, I used mahogany for the major lamp components and ebony for the plug and spline details. The Greene brothers made extensive use of these two woods in their designs, so the combination is a fitting choice here. You won't need much of either material. You could also use quartersawn white oak with walnut accents if you prefer, to achieve an Arts & Crafts effect.

Making the Wall Bracket Plate

The wall lamp is mounted using a simple, L-shaped wooden bracket, and this is the first subassembly you need to make. Rip and crosscut the wall plate (piece 1) to the dimensions shown in the Materials List on page 65. Note that these dimensions are ¼" longer than the final dimensions of the plate. That excess will allow you to remove material from the front face, creating a stepped effect—it

suggests a classic Greene and Greene brother's "cloud lift" detail.

To create that look, install a dado head in your table saw and make sure your miter gauge is truly set to 90°. Make a series of repetitive cuts as shown in the photo above, saving the last ¼" stub at the bottom to keep the piece from tipping down into the blade as you work. Mill the entire dado, then turn the piece over, install a standard crosscut blade and remove the bottom ¼" stub to finish up the step. Use a Forstner bit to drill two 1"-diameter holes in the back of the plate,

one stopped and the other all the way through (see the Wall Plate Elevation Drawings on page 65 for details), then chuck a ¾" straight bit in your router to plow a groove between these holes (make several passes). The groove forms a relief area for the power cord that will pass through the top hole of the plate.

Next, lay out and chop the two ³⁄₈"-square mortises in the plate for the mounting screws (refer to the Drawings). The screw heads will be covered by square plugs—accents that are repeated throughout this project.

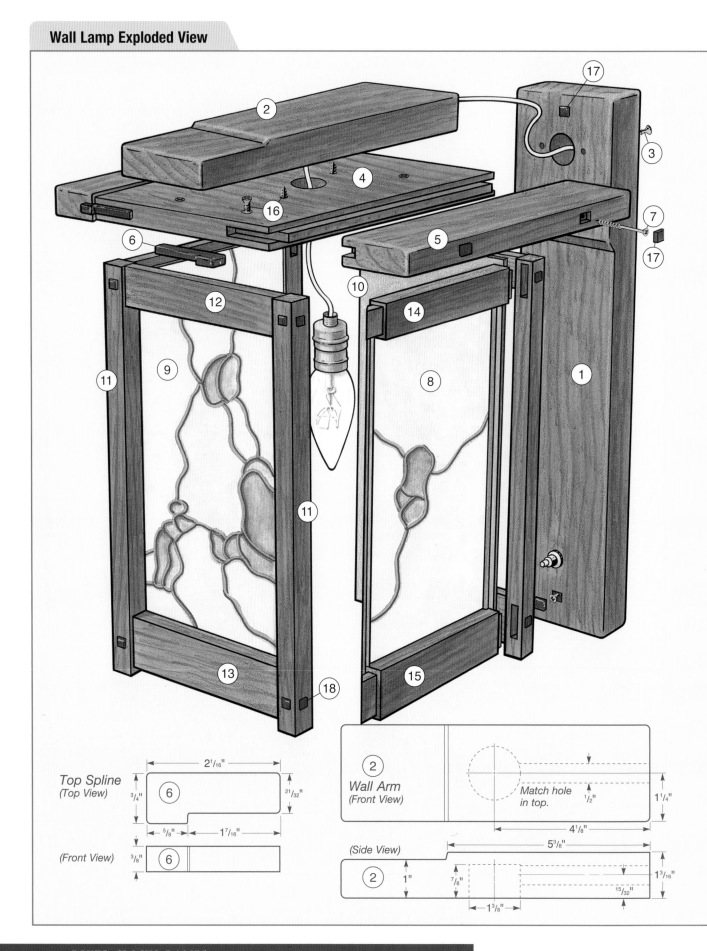

Top Spline
(Top View)

$2^1/_{16}$"

$^3/_4$" 6 $^{21}/_{32}$"

$^5/_8$" $1^7/_{16}$"

(Front View) $^3/_8$" 6

2
Wall Arm
(Front View)

Match hole in top. $^1/_2$" $1^1/_4$"

$4^1/_8$"

(Side View) $5^3/_8$"

2 1" $^7/_8$" $1^3/_{16}$"

$^{15}/_{32}$"

$1^3/_8$"

Frame Style
(Front View)

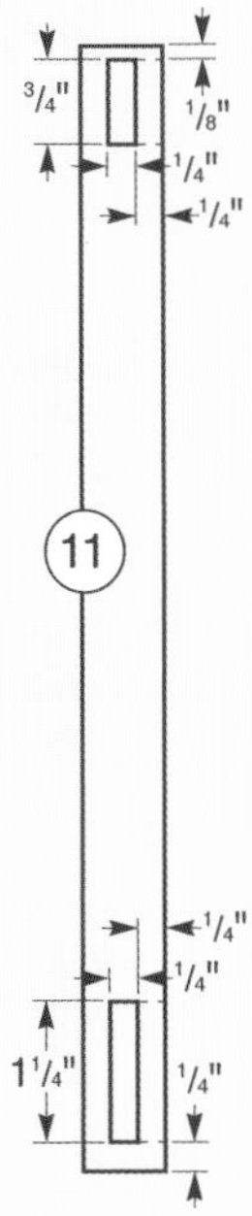
3/4"
1/8"
1/4"
1/4"
11
1/4"
1/4"
1 1/4"
1/4"

Endcaps, Splines and Top Subassembly Detail
(Top and Side View)

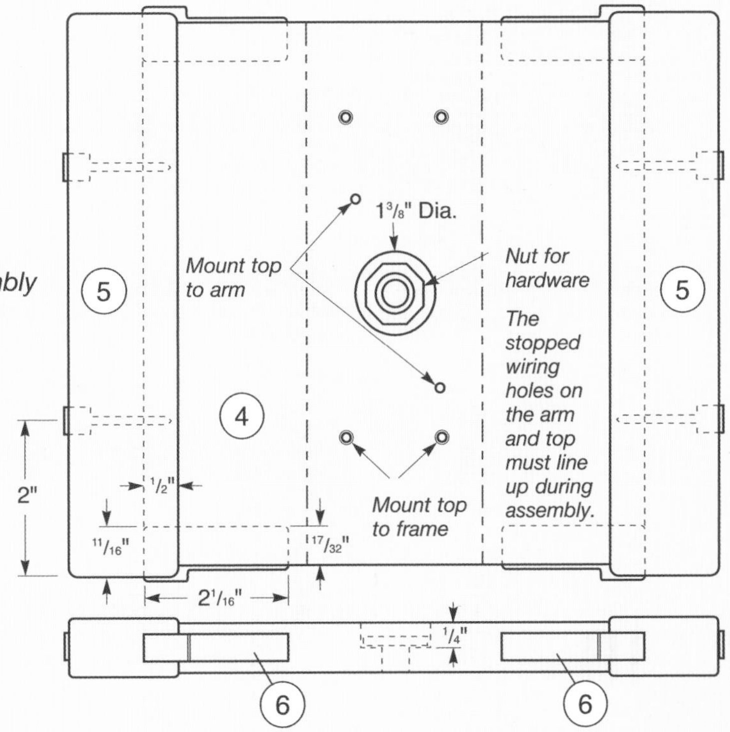
1 3/8" Dia.
Mount top to arm
Nut for hardware
The stopped wiring holes on the arm and top must line up during assembly.
5
4
5
2"
1/2"
11/16"
17/32"
Mount top to frame
2 1/16"
1/4"
6
6

Material List

	T x W x L
1 Wall Plate (1)	13/16" x 3 7/8" x 14 1/2"
2 Wall Arm (1)	13/16" x 2 1/2" x 8 1/4"
3 Screws (2)	#10 x 3"
4 Top (1)	11/16" x 7 7/16" x 7 3/16"
5 Top Endcaps (2)	13/16" x 1 9/16" x 7 3/4"
6 Top Splines (4)	3/8" x 3/4" x 2 1/16"
7 Endcap Screws (4)	#6 x 2"
8 Stained-Glass Sides (2)	1/8" x 3 3/4" x 9 1/4"
9 Stained-Glass Front (1)	1/8" x 4 1/2" x 9 1/4"
10 Colored Glass Back (1)	1/16" x 4 1/2" x 9 1/4"
11 Frame Stiles (4)	3/4" x 3/4" x 10"
12 Upper Front and Back Rails (2)	1/2" x 1" x 5 7/16"
13 Lower Front and Back Rails (2)	1/2" x 1 1/2" x 5 7/16"
14 Upper Side Rails (2)	1/2" x 1" x 4 11/16"
15 Lower Side Rails (2)	1/2" x 1 1/2" x 4 11/16"
16 Frame/Top Screws (6)	#6 x 1 1/4"
17 Large Plugs (6)	3/8" x 3/8" x 1/4"
18 Small Plugs (16)	1/4" x 1/4" x 1/4"

Wall Plate
(Front and Side View)

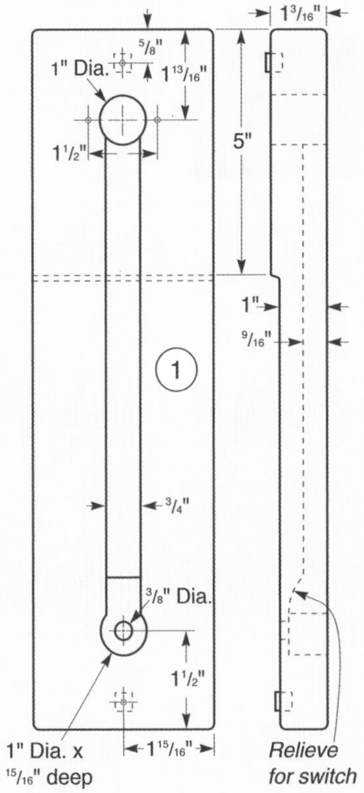
1 3/16"
5/8"
1" Dia.
1 13/16"
1 1/2"
5"
1"
9/16"
1
3/4"
3/8" Dia.
1 1/2"
1" Dia. x 15/16" deep
1 15/16"
Relieve for switch

Screws attaching the arm and plate should barely slip through the holes in the plate. The holes in the arm are about half their diameter.

The last milling operation is to drill a through hole for the On/Off push button switch and the cord. Buy the switch before you size this hole so the switch fits correctly, and drill it at the location shown on the *Drawings*.

Building the Wall Bracket Arm and Assembly

The arm for the bracket (piece 2) is cut from stock the same thickness as the plate. It, too, is stepped, so return to the dado head for your first milling operation. Since the lower step is less than half the length of the arm, there's plenty of stability in the workpiece for safe dadoing, so no need to leave a stub on the end this time around. Simply nibble away the waste, using your miter gauge as a guide.

The thick end of the arm is attached to the plate with two screws (pieces 3). Refer to the *Drawings* for their locations, then drill your pilot holes, countersinking them for the screw heads. Now use your 1⅜" Forstner bit to form the stopped hole on the underside of the arm for the wiring. Assemble the

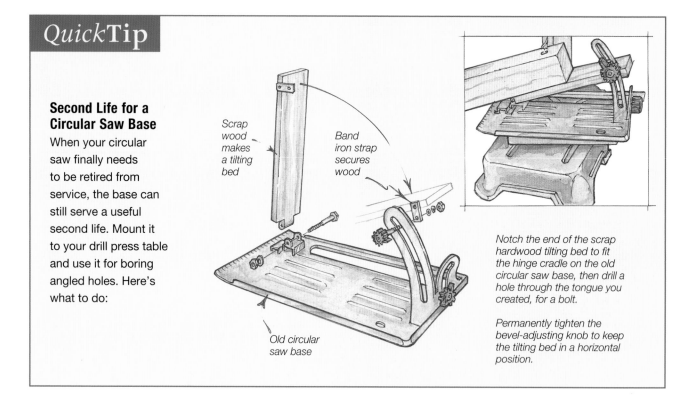

*Quick*Tip

Second Life for a Circular Saw Base

When your circular saw finally needs to be retired from service, the base can still serve a useful second life. Mount it to your drill press table and use it for boring angled holes. Here's what to do:

Scrap wood makes a tilting bed

Band iron strap secures wood

Old circular saw base

Notch the end of the scrap hardwood tilting bed to fit the hinge cradle on the old circular saw base, then drill a hole through the tongue you created, for a bolt.

Permanently tighten the bevel-adjusting knob to keep the tilting bed in a horizontal position.

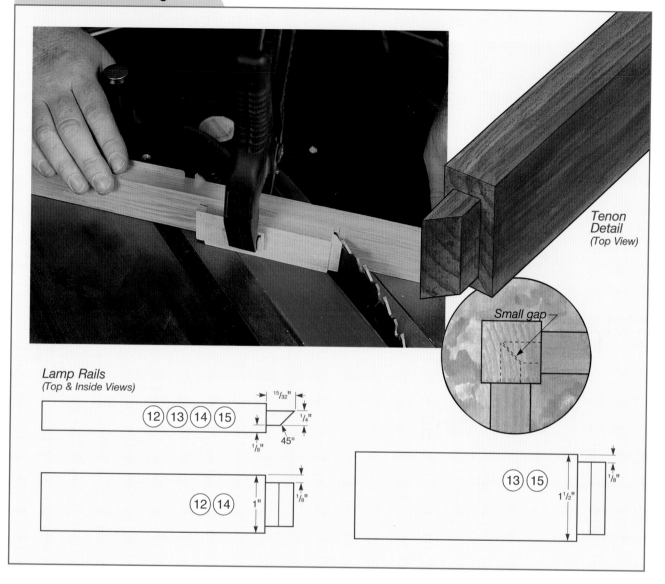

Tenon Detail (Top View)

Small gap

Lamp Rails (Top & Inside Views)

12 13 14 15

15/32"

1/4"

1/8"

45°

12 14 1"

1/8"

13 15

1 1/2"

1/8"

two parts without glue to test their fit, then remove the screws.

Chuck an extra-long bit in your drill press to bore the ½"-diameter wiring hole that extends to the access hole you just made. Stand the arm against a tall fence on your drill press table and clamp it in place to ensure this deep hole passes straight through the arm.

Adding Greene and Greene Styling

One hallmark of the Greene and Greene style was a soft, rounded edge treatment that added an exotic look to simple joinery. Admittedly, it's

a tiny detail but one that really adds authenticity to the overall design. The goal here is to just break the sharp edges and corners with curves, not to make the piece look over-routed.

Chuck the smallest radius roundover bit you can find—⅛" works beautifully—in your router and gently round all but the back edges of the plate. Then mill all edges of the arm except the face that is joined to the plate. Use a fine-cut file and sandpaper to soften the transitional steps in both pieces, but make sure you don't leave scratches across the grain.

Forming a Top with Breadboard Accents

Asian in influence, the oversized top of this lamp is pure Greene and Greene. The top of our lamp (piece 4) is a simple board topped with a pair of breadboard endcaps (pieces 5). These are narrow but slightly thicker boards with their grain across that of the top. The endcaps are grooved and joined to matching tenons with two screws each.

Start by installing a ⅜" dado head in your table saw and mill a groove in one long edge of each endcap (see *Drawings* for dimensions). Stay with the dado head

Clean up the mortises *for the ebony splines in the top with a sharp ⅛"-wide chisel.*

to create the tenons on the ends of the top. Dry-fit the endcaps to the top to check their fit. Next, drill slightly oversized pilot holes through the endcaps to allow for wood movement. Chop square mortises to fit the ebony plugs that will later cover the screw heads. Return to the drill press and bore the stepped hole at the center of the top.

The Greene brothers used ebony accents to add stylized elements to their pieces. Typically, as with this lamp, these were exposed splines or screw plugs. Band-saw the four splines (pieces 6) to the shape shown in the *Drawings*, then lay out and chop their mortises in the endcaps and the sides of the top.

Break the exterior edges of the top and endcaps with sandpaper and assemble the endcaps to the top with screws (pieces 7): these are driven through oversized predrilled pilot holes. Don't glue the endcaps in place: the screws will allow for wood movement.

Stained-Glass Framework

The three decorative stained-glass panels (pieces 8 and 9) and the back panel (piece 10, a less expensive sheet of amber-colored glass), are protected and framed by a mahogany skeleton. Begin its construction by cutting the four stiles (pieces 11), the four front and back rails (pieces 12 and 13) and the four side rails (pieces 14 and 15) to the sizes outlined in the *Materials List*.

Lay out the four mortises in each stile, according to the dimensions and locations shown on the *Drawings*. Chop these mortises by drilling out most of the waste, then paring the edges of each with a sharp chisel. Cut the tenons on the rails using your saw's miter gauge and a sharp dado head (see *Drawings*), and then switch to your crosscut blade to form the miters on the ends of the tenons, as shown in the *photo* on page 67.

Next, locate and lay out the 16 small square mortises in the stiles, and chop these with a sharp ⅛"-wide chisel. The plugs that will fit these mortises are decorative. Dry-fit the rails to the stiles. When everything fits, break all the long edges of the styles and rails, but leave the ends as they are. Glue and clamp the framework together.

Applying the Dye

I used a water-based aniline dye to stain the mahogany to a rich, deep brown. Start the finishing process by sanding all the mahogany elements of your lamp with 120-grit paper, then raise the grain with a damp sponge. After it dries, sand with 220 grit. Add a small drop of dishwashing soap to the dye to break the surface tension and help the dye penetrate properly.

Apply the dye generously to the wood with a foam brush and wipe it off immediately with clean, soft paper towels to ensure even coverage. Be sure to wear disposable surgical gloves to keep from staining your hands. If the dye goes on too heavily in some places, use a paper towel dampened with distilled water to draw out some of the dye.

Finishing and Final Assembly

Pull on a fresh pair of gloves (your skin moisture can leave blotches on the dyed surfaces) and begin the assembly process by screwing the wall plate to the arm. Position the top on the arm by matching up the 1" holes at their centers. Drill pilot holes (see the *Drawings* for locations) through the underside of the top into the arm, then remove the top and drill pilot holes through the top side of the top for attaching the frame. After countersinking these holes, screw (pieces 16) the framework assembly to the top. Attach the top to the arm with two more of these screws.

Spray the assembled lamp with three coats of satin lacquer, sanding between coats with 600-grit paper.

Make the decorative plugs (pieces 17 and 18) by crosscutting them from lengths of appropriately sized square sticks of ebony. Polish their top faces to gently break their edges before you crosscut and epoxy them into their mortises. Secure the glass panels in place with more epoxy. Next, install the On/Off switch and the lamp receptacle, and complete the wiring.

Be sure to use a small (40 watt) bulb and locate your lamp where it will serve both to light up a dark area and act as a wonderful accent piece that illuminates your woodworking skills.

Floating Ebony Splines

Contrast, texture and shape are all created once the floating ebony splines are placed into the lamp's breadboard top. Cut them to shape on the band saw, then test their fit in the clamped-up top. The section of the splines that extends into the breadboard endcaps must float freely within the mortise. When you're satisfied with the fit, break all the exposed edges of the splines with sandpaper and polish them to an ultra-smooth finish.

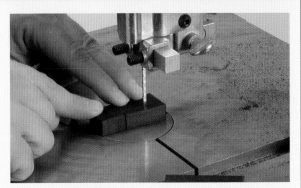

Start with a band saw to form the decorative splines, then complete their organic shape using files, scrapers and sandpaper.

Mahogany and ebony pieces surround the stained-glass panels in this wall lamp. It is simply made, yet rich in details—the legacy of the Greene brothers' designs.

by Michael McGlynn

FRANK LLOYD WRIGHT TABLE LAMP

This table lamp is modeled after a print stand designed by the master architect. Although its size allows you to build it from leftover material, its design is true to the original and evokes the best of the Prairie School.

With any artistic or architectural movement, pieces of furniture come to evoke its essence. Examples are the Stickley Morris chair, representing the Arts and Crafts period, or just about any piece by Ruhlmann representing the Art Deco movement. Within the Prairie School, a number of pieces, mostly by Frank Lloyd Wright, would qualify as hallmarks of the movement. This lamp is based on one such classic: Wright's Japanese print stand.

Wright was a major collector and dealer of Japanese prints, and he designed his original print stand to display some of them. Variations of his print stand show up many times throughout his career; there is even a floor lamp version.

I built this table lamp for a client who has a long-standing affection for Wright and his furniture style. The hardest part of this design was figuring out the lamp part and what to use for a shade. In the end, I used Lumacite™ material left over from an interior shoji style door. Lumacite is an acrylic material that comes in a number of different patterns; it's also quite expensive. As an alternative, you can also use Plexiglas™ with rice paper glued to the outside and achieve a similar result.

One nice thing about this lamp is that it is made out of a lot of small pieces. You may be able to make the entire thing out of scraps you already have in the shop.

A down side to being constructed with pieces this small is they will want to warp every which way (especially the slats). Any warping of the slats will throw off the symmetry of the lamp. To help prevent warping, and for a pleasing grain pattern, choose pieces of wood that are as close to rift or quartersawn as possible.

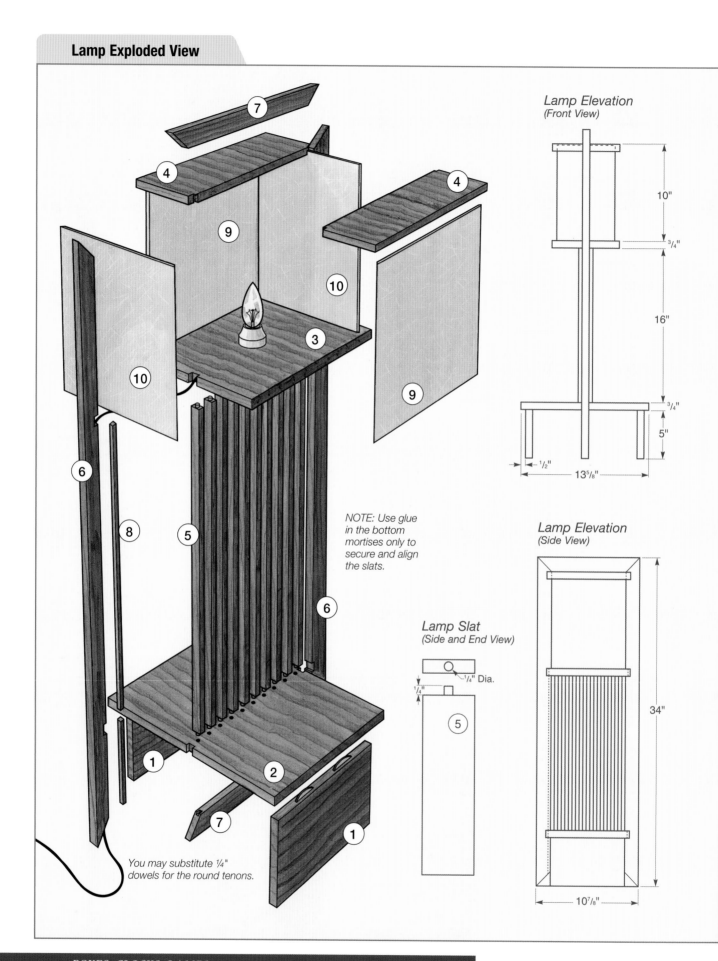

Lamp Elevation
(Front View)

10"

³/₄"

16"

³/₄"

5"

¹/₂"

13⁵/₈"

Lamp Elevation
(Side View)

34"

10⁷/₈"

Lamp Slat
(Side and End View)

¼" Dia.

¼"

5

NOTE: Use glue in the bottom mortises only to secure and align the slats.

You may substitute ¼" dowels for the round tenons.

Platform
(Top View)

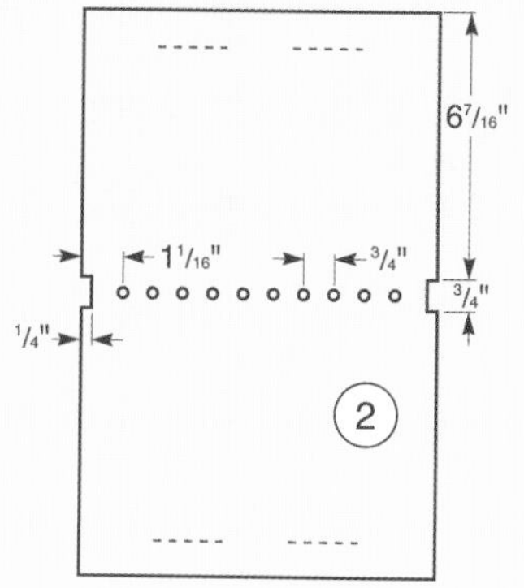
6⁷⁄₁₆"
1¹⁄₁₆"
³⁄₄"
³⁄₄"
¹⁄₄"
2

Lamp Base
(Top and Side Views)

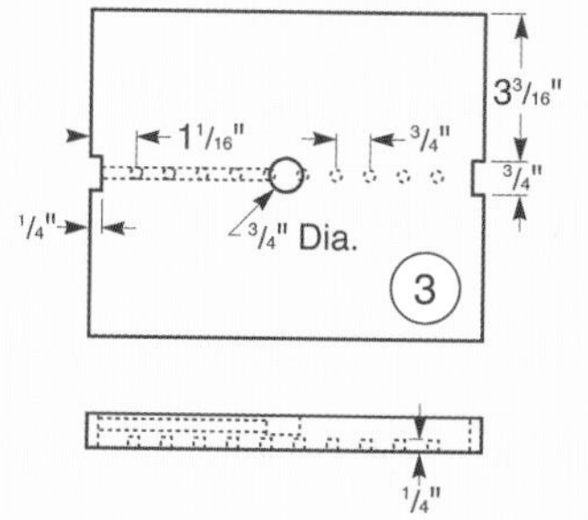
3³⁄₁₆"
1¹⁄₁₆"
³⁄₄"
³⁄₄"
¹⁄₄"
³⁄₄" Dia.
3
¹⁄₄"

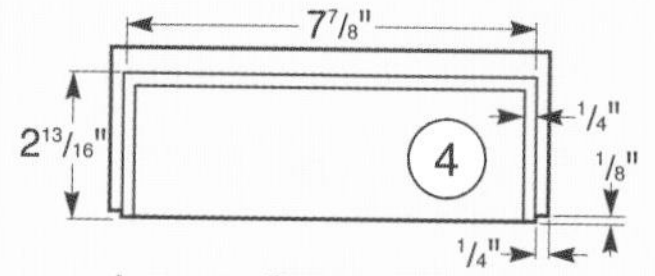
7⁷⁄₈"
2¹³⁄₁₆"
¹⁄₄"
¹⁄₈"
¹⁄₄"
4

Lamp Cap
(Bottom View)

Frame Assembly
(Front View)

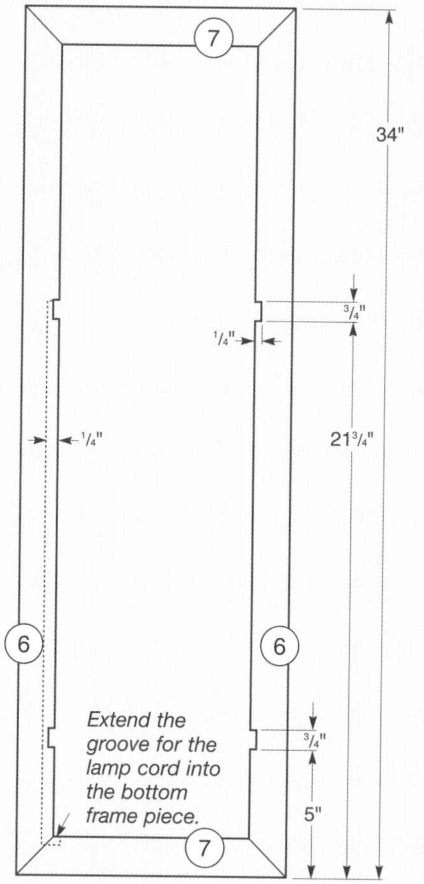
7
34"
³⁄₄"
¹⁄₄"
¹⁄₄"
21³⁄₄"
6
6
Extend the groove for the lamp cord into the bottom frame piece.
³⁄₄"
5"
7

The author uses 3M packing tape to "clamp" the mitered corners of the frame assembly.

Material List

		T x W x L
1	Legs (2)	¾" x 5" x 7⅞"
2	Platform (1)	¾" x 8⅞" x 13⅝"
3	Lamp Base (1)	¾" x 7⅛" x 8⅞"
4	Lamp Caps (2)	¾" x 8⅞" x 3⁵⁄₁₆"
5	Slats (10)	⅜" x 1½" x 16½"
6	Frame Sides (2)	⅝" x 1½" x 34"
7	Frame Top & Bottom (2)	⅝" x 1½" x 10⅞"
8	Wire Cover Strip* (1)	¼" x ¼" x 24"
9	Shade Front & Back (2)	³⁄₁₆" x 7⅞" x 9⅞"
10	Shade Sides (2)	³⁄₁₆" x 6⅛" x 9⅞"

**Trim to fit.*

Getting Started

Once you've selected your wood, mill the pieces oversize, let them acclimatize to your shop for a few days, then mill them to final dimension. With the spindles, be extra careful and use three steps, with two adjustment and flattening sessions. Start with several more spindles than you'll actually need, because there will probably be a few that will develop twists or warping and won't be acceptable here.

Due to my "use-of-scrap methodology" here, the legs, platform, lamp base, and lamp caps (pieces 1 through 4) are all made of glued-up stock. Glue up one length of material, plane it down, sand the faces and cut it into the six respective pieces. This also assures that the grain and color will be well matched on all the parts.

After milling the pieces to size, use water to raise the grain and sand them to 220 grit when the surfaces dry. As you are breaking the edges, it is important to keep in mind that some edges, such as the top of the legs, are not rounded over in any way. Mark the sharp edges, if need be, to avoid sanding where you shouldn't.

Building the Center Section

This lamp is a bit of a puzzle in that it has to be assembled in a particular order for everything to come together properly. The first step is to build the center section.

Before you start the assembly, several joints need to be cut: the slat tenons, the mortises (and a lamp mounting hole) in the platform and lamp base, and the half-lap joints on the platform and lamp base. In addition, the lamp base needs to be drilled for the cord. See the *Elevation Drawings* on page 72 and 73 for the construction details.

With regards to the slats (pieces 5) and their tenons, I machined the

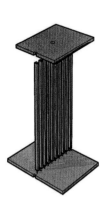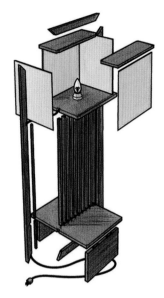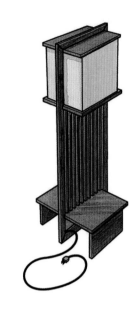

This lamp is a bit like a puzzle. It has to be assembled in a particular order for all the pieces to come together correctly.

¼"-long, round tenons on the ends of the slats with my multi-router machine. A round tenon works well because its corresponding mortise is simply a drilled hole. An alternative here is to make floating tenons from ¼" dowels.

After cutting your tenons, lay out and carefully drill the platform and lamp base for their corresponding mortises. For appearance's sake, keep this in mind: on the platform the holes go in the good side, and on the lamp base they go in the lesser side.

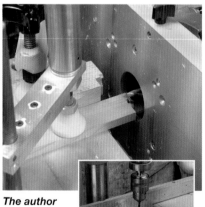

The author used a multi-router *to create round tenons on the slats. These fit the holes drilled into the platform and base.*

Cutting the half-lap joints is the next step. These joints are exposed, so it is important to take your time laying out and cutting them. It's imperative to have a piece of the frame material handy when doing this step. To prevent blowout, cover the joint area with masking tape, then mark out the joint on the tape using a sharp pencil. Starting in the center of the joint, take multiple passes on a table saw, using your miter gauge with a fresh scrap fence attached to further avoid grain tearout. As you get close to your edge markings, check the joint with the frame material. By taking fine passes, you'll get a tight, sliding fit.

One of the cool design details of this lamp is how the cord is hidden. Drilling a long hole like this through the long dimension of a board is not for the faint of heart. As can be seen from the *drawings*, this hole is slightly offset from the center to avoid the tenon holes. I used a ¼" x 10" auger bit while holding the piece on-edge in a vise. Take your time: drilling through the face at this point may make you say things that require a trip to the confessional.

Assembling the center section is another exercise in patience. To ease their insertion, bevel the ends of all

the tenons with sandpaper, and dry-fit them before attempting final assembly. Then put a drop of glue in each of the platform mortises and insert the slat tenons into the mortises. Square up each slat before going on to the next.

Don't glue the top end tenons; the glued bottom joints provide all the alignment necessary. Installing the lamp base onto the tenons is quite difficult; you have to line up all the tenons almost simultaneously. Start at one end and slowly work to the other until all the tenons are engaged in their holes. Then simply tap the base home. Once you've completed the center section, attach the legs to the platform with biscuits.

Assembling the Frame

To begin the frame (pieces 6 and 7), cut all four miters on the upright frame pieces. Laying out and cutting the half-lap joints in the uprights is the next step, and this is where having the legs already attached comes in handy. Set the lamp on a flat surface, insert the uprights into the half-laps and, with the bottom miter touching the surface, carefully scribe the half-laps onto the uprights. Then form the joints carefully on the table saw.

The second half of the hidden wire process requires routing a groove down the middle of an upright. This groove extends from the bottom mitered end to the top edge of the top lap joint (see *drawings*). MIll a piece of stock (piece 8) to hide the wire in the groove.

Before the uprights can be installed on the center section, the cord must be installed and hidden. I used 10' of standard 16-gauge lamp cord. Lay the wire in the groove (make sure 12" stick out of the top) and use Super Glue to secure the covering strips (cut it into two pieces to avoid impinging on the lap joints). When the glue cures, sand the filler strip flush.

Threading the wire through the lamp base (piece 3) is the only tricky part about attaching the uprights. Place a dab of wood glue on each lap joint and glue the uprights in place with a couple of bar clamps. Take your time and carefully fit the frame's top and bottom miters. Prior to gluing in place, cut a groove in the end of the bottom frame member that meets the cord so it can exit easily.

Find that Packing Tape

After years of trying all sorts of miter clamps, I still prefer 3M packing tape for assembling miter joints. It has a bit of stretch to it that snaps back once it's applied, giving the tape a helpful "memory" for drawing joints tightly closed. Put glue on the miters and, with two to four strips of tape, close the joints. When the glue dries, scrape or sand away any glue squeeze-out.

Construction of the shade (pieces 9 and 10) is quite time-consuming. In order for the shade to look uniform all the way around, you should miter and glue the pieces together, as described in the *sidebar* above.

The last step is to machine the retainer grooves in the shade caps, as shown in the *Elevation Drawings*. Rout them in several passes on the router

Making a Lumacite Shade

Cut the shade pieces to size and miter the joining edges using a chamfer bit on your router table. Use 3M packing tape to miter-fold the shade together. Align the pieces, apply Super Glue accelerator to the joints and roll the shade into a cube. Apply a last bit of tape at the open corner. Place two wooden frames (to hold the lamp shade square as the glue cures) on the ends of the cube. Now apply Super Glue to each corner joint from the inside (with that joint pointing down). Allow the glue to cure for one minute and move on to the next joint.

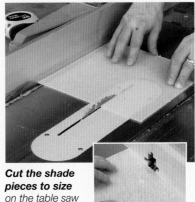

Cut the shade pieces to size on the table saw and miter their edges on the router table.

Miter-roll the shade pieces into a cube using 3M packing tape as your hinge. Tape the last open joint closed, then apply a bead of Super Glue along the inside of each joint to bond the parts.

table. Fit the caps carefully so that when they are in place the shade can't move.

Prior to finishing, go over the lamp in a meticulous fashion, easing edges and looking for any missed glue squeeze-out. Sand everything up to 220 grit, clean off all the dust and apply your choice of finish.

The last order of business is to install the socket, switch and two-prong plug. I used a basic, compact, screw-on porcelain socket. The switch is a standard in-line rocker style.

This lamp is a great introduction to the elements of Prairie School style and at the same time requires a pretty high level of attention to detail to get it to turn out right. Have fun!

by John English

IRISH PARLOR CLOCK

In today's electronic world, an elegant wooden wall clock makes more of a statement than ever. It ties us to a simpler past, when parlors were reserved for distinguished household guests and time was measured by handmade clock movements. This project has the added appeal of a charming family story passed along by John English, an Irishman and former editor with *Woodworker's Journal*.

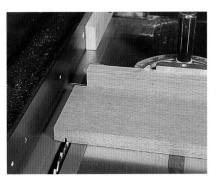

Figure 1: *No need to set up a dado head: you can use a standard saw blade to make the small dadoes on the inside faces of the sides.*

A couple of years ago in the ancient Irish market town of Arklow, an uncle of mine had a client who decided to retire. Uncle Joe, who supplied bottled propane to hardware stores, drove to Arklow and began helping his customer clear out some stock so the store could be listed with a realtor. He was out back, counting gas cylinders, when he spotted the original version of this project. Its veneer was peeling off, and the carcass was riddled with woodworm.

Joe knew immediately he had discovered something special. Though the carcass was decrepit, the clock's solid-brass movement had been exceptionally well built with thick, hardened gears and a great deal of hand-fitting. Knowing that, and being aware of my love of clocks, Joe asked me to build a new home for the wonderful Westminster movement. I enjoyed the task so much that I ordered a brand-new movement and built this second clock as soon as I rebuilt the first. It's now telling the time at my sister's home in Dublin.

A Few Modifications First

I decided to forgo veneering and build the new clock entirely out of solid stock. Since my sister's home is furnished throughout with mahogany

pieces, I also switched from oak to Honduras mahogany. You can build the clock case from any wood you like.

Building the Carcass

The measurements in the *Material List* on page 79 can be used both to purchase stock and to cut all the pieces to rough size. With that done, the first milling step is to cut ¼" square dadoes *(see Figure 1)* across the case sides (pieces 1) at the locations shown on the *Elevation Drawing* on page 80. These dadoes are small, so this operation can be completed in two passes with a standard blade.

Stay at the saw to cut a rabbet in each side for the back (piece 2), as shown on the *drawings*. The back is set in ¼": the reason will become obvious when you mount the movement.

The ends of the carcass top and bottom (pieces 3) are also rabbeted *(see Figure 2)*, creating tongues to fit in the dadoes you just milled. Take your time making these cuts, dry-fitting them several times to ensure a perfect fit.

Glue and clamp the sides to the top and bottom, making sure everything is both square and flat. (For parts orientation, refer to the *Exploded View* on page 78.) Attach the back with ¾" pin nails every 6" along the perimeter, then set the carcass aside to dry.

Building the Crown Subassembly

The crown of the clock rests on a plate (piece 4) that will eventually be screwed to the carcass. The radii on its front corners and the profile of the crown front (piece 5) can be found on the *Elevation Drawing* on page 81. Cut both to shape on your band saw, then miter both ends of the crown front and one end of each crown side (pieces 6).

Dry-fit these parts to the plate, then locate biscuits on the mitered joints. Keep the biscuits toward the insides of the miters. When everything lines up, glue and clamp them together. Glue the entire subassembly to the plate.

After the glue cures, use a belt or disk sander to shape the glued-up mitered corners to the radii on the plate.

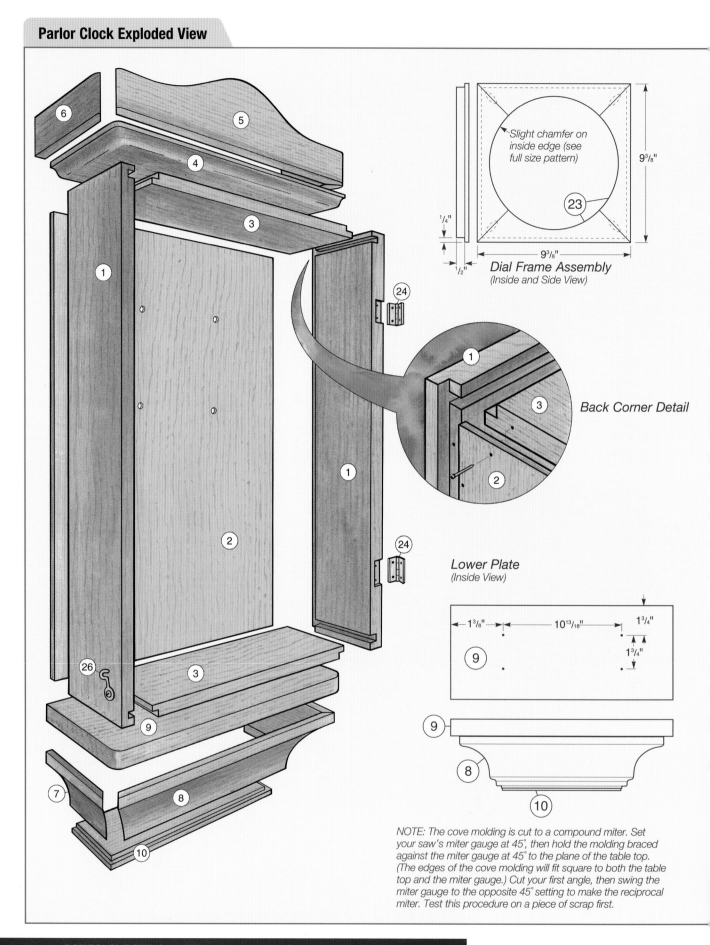

Slight chamfer on inside edge (see full size pattern)

9³/₈"

9³/₈"

¹/₄"

¹/₂"

Dial Frame Assembly
(Inside and Side View)

Back Corner Detail

Lower Plate
(Inside View)

1³/₈" 10¹³/₁₆" 1³/₄"

1³/₄"

NOTE: The cove molding is cut to a compound miter. Set your saw's miter gauge at 45°, then hold the molding braced against the miter gauge at 45° to the plane of the table top. (The edges of the cove molding will fit square to both the table top and the miter gauge.) Cut your first angle, then swing the miter gauge to the opposite 45° setting to make the reciprocal miter. Test this procedure on a piece of scrap first.

Material List

		T x W x L
1	Case Sides (2)	3/4" x 4 1/8" x 23 3/4"
2	Case Back (1)	1/4" x 11 3/16" x 22 11/16"
3	Case Top & Bottom (2)	3/4" x 4 1/8" x 11 1/4"
4	Upper Plate (1)	1" x 5 13/16" x 14 1/4"
5	Crown Front (1)	1" x 3 1/2" x 13 1/2"
6	Crown Sides (2)	1" x 1 3/4" x 5 1/2"
7	Side Cove Moldings (2)	3/4" x 4 3/8" x 4 7/8"
8	Front Cove Molding (1)	3/4" x 4 3/8" x 12 3/16"
9	Lower Plate (1)	1" x 5 9/16" x 13 9/16"
10	Cove Molding Plug (1)	1/2" x 2 5/16" x 7 1/8"
11	Door Stiles (2)	3/4" x 1 5/16" x 23 5/8"
12	Center Door Rail (1)	3/4" x 1 7/16" x 9 3/8"
13	Top Door Rail (1)	3/4" x 1 7/16" x 9 3/8"
14	Bottom Door Rail (1)	3/4" x 1 7/16" x 9 3/8"
15	Biscuits (8)	R3 Ryobi style
16	Door Molding (2)	3/4" x 1" x 23 5/8"
17	Door Stile, Small 1/4 Rnd. (2)	1/4" x 1/4" x 23 5/8"
18	Door Muntins (2)	3/4" x 5/8" x 12 13/16"
19	Bottom Side Panes (2)	Glass, cut to fit
20	Bottom Center Pane (1)	Glass, cut to fit
21	Stop Molding (1)	1/4" x 7/16" x 90"
22	Top Pane (1)	Glass, cut to fit
23	Dial Frame Segments (4)	3/4" x 2 1/4" x 9 3/8"
24	Door Hinges (2)	Brass, 1 1/2"
25	Dial Frame Turnbuckles (4)	Brass
26	Door Catch (1)	Brass hook and eye

Start with a coarse-grit belt to remove most of the waste, then refine the corners with less aggressive belts, finishing with 220 grit. Move to a drum sander chucked in your drill press to clean up the top edges, then mill the ogee at the bottom of the upper plate's edge with a piloted ogee bit in your router table.

Attach the crown to the carcass with screws driven up from the inside the top, through pre-drilled and countersunk pilot holes.

Making a Mitered Compound Cove

In a technique common among nineteenth-century clock case builders, the bottom of the clock is dressed up with three pieces of wide molding. These moldings (pieces 7 and 8) are mitered and glued together before they're attached to the lower plate (piece 9). Their profile is shown on page 81.

Cut the molding's main cove on your table saw (see *sidebar* on page 81), then reset the saw and rip the

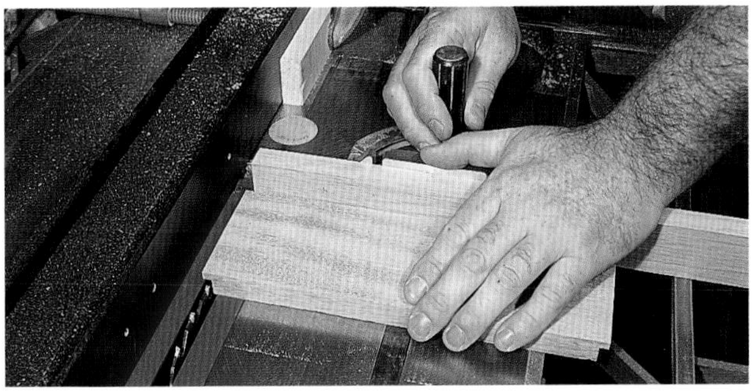

Figure 2: *Tongues on the top and bottom fit into dado slots in the sides. Create them by milling rabbets on the opposing edges.*

edges to the correct angles. Mill the decorative groove with a core box bit in your router table *(see Figure 3)*, then sand the entire molding. A sanding drum works great as a manual sanding block to clean up the main cove (see *inset photo*).

Round the front corners of the lower plate and sand, then miter the cove molding. Now pin nail and glue the molding segments to the lower plate. Attach this subassembly to the carcass with screws, then rabbet the edges of the cove molding plug (piece 10) before gluing and clamping it in place (see *Elevation Drawing* on page 81 sidebar).

Forming the Built-up Door Stiles

Begin building the door by rabbeting one edge of each door stile (pieces 11) and both edges of the center rail (piece 12), following the dimensions shown on the *Door Assembly Drawing*, page 80. This saw setup can also be used to cut rabbets on the inside bottom edge of the top rail (piece 13) and the inside top edge of the bottom rail (piece 14).

Again referring to the *Drawings*, use the saw's miter gauge to create tongues on both ends of each rail. After dry-fitting, glue and clamp the stiles and rails together. Make sure to check for squareness, and be gentle with the clamp pressure. That extra turn or two on the clamp screws could distort the door out of flat, which will make it fit poorly.

Now use biscuits (pieces 15) to attach the door molding (pieces 16) to the outside edge of each stile. This molding is

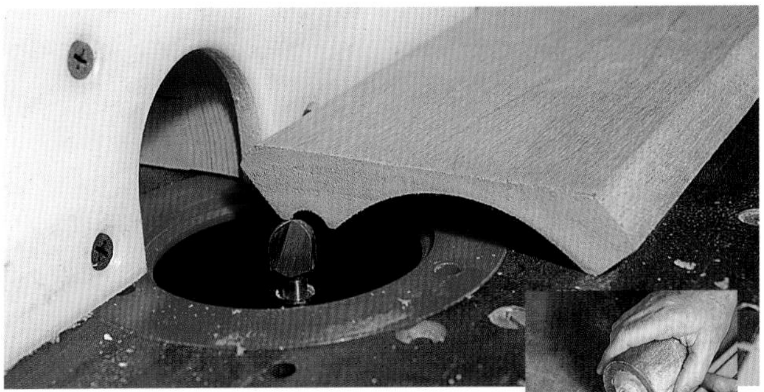

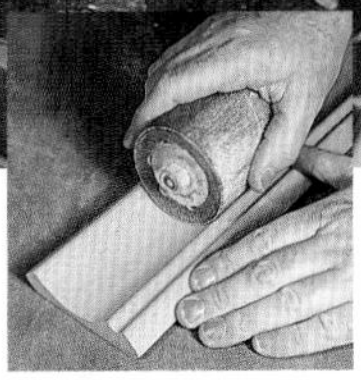

Figure 3: *Use a core box bit to rout a decorative groove into the lower edge of the crown molding, then clean up the main cove (right).*

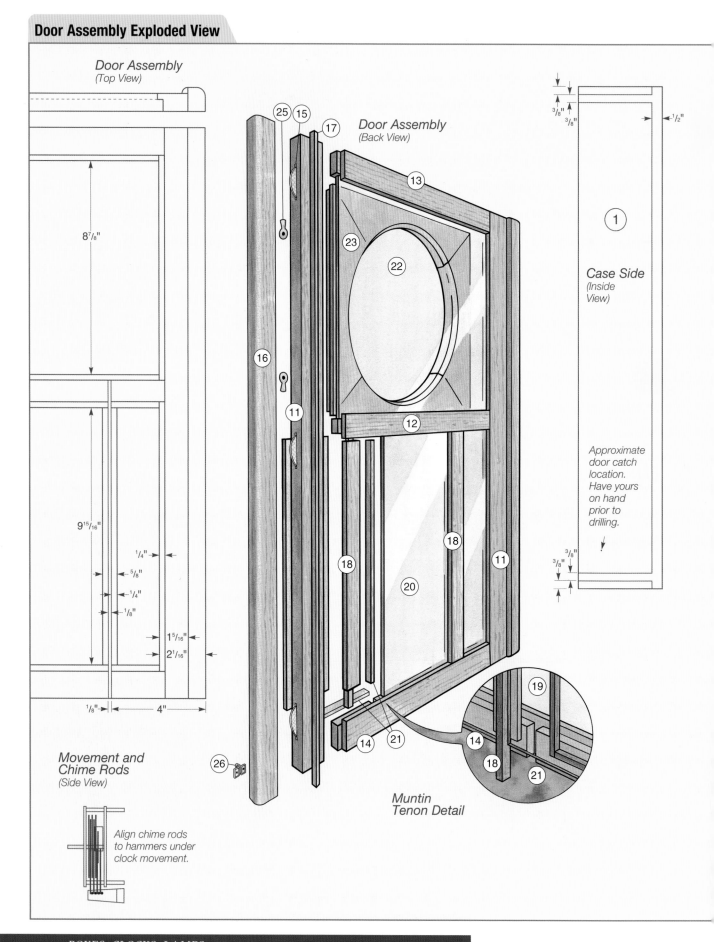

Door Assembly
(Top View)

$8^7/_8$"

$9^{15}/_{16}$"

$^1/_4$"
$^5/_8$"
$^1/_4$"
$^1/_8$"

$1^5/_{16}$"
$2^1/_{16}$"

$^1/_8$"   4"

Door Assembly
(Back View)

Case Side
(Inside View)

$^3/_8$" $^3/_8$" $^1/_2$"

Approximate
door catch
location.
Have yours
on hand
prior to
drilling.

$^3/_8$" $^3/_8$"

Muntin
Tenon Detail

Movement and
Chime Rods
(Side View)

Align chime rods
to hammers under
clock movement.

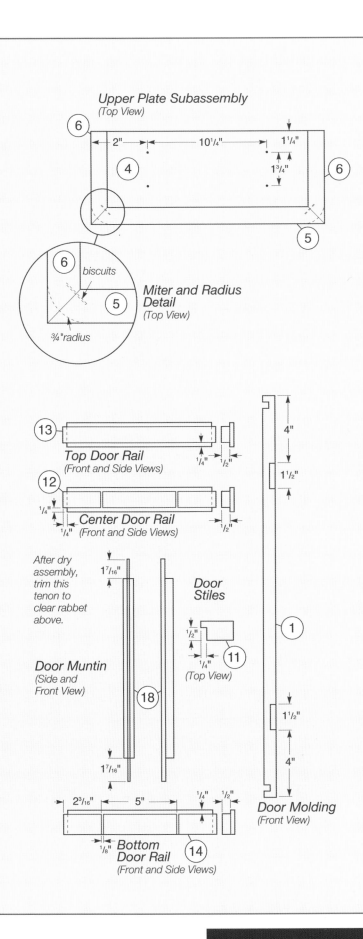

Upper Plate Subassembly
(Top View)

6

2" 10¹/₄" 1¹/₄"

4

1³/₄"

6

5

6

biscuits

Miter and Radius Detail
(Top View)

5

³/₄"radius

13

Top Door Rail
(Front and Side Views)

¹/₄" ¹/₂"

12

¹/₄"

Center Door Rail
(Front and Side Views)

¹/₄" ¹/₂"

4"

1¹/₂"

After dry assembly, trim this tenon to clear rabbet above.

1⁷/₁₆"

Door Stiles

¹/₂"

¹/₄"

11

(Top View)

1

Door Muntin
(Side and Front View)

18

1¹/₂"

1⁷/₁₆"

4"

2³/₁₆" 5" ¹/₄" ¹/₂"

¹/₈" **Bottom Door Rail**
(Front and Side Views)

14

Door Molding
(Front View)

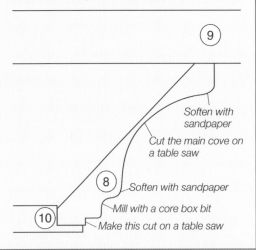

Clamp two scrap auxiliary fences to your table saw 4¹/₈" apart and at 45° to the blade. Center them on the blade (front to back). Use a fine-toothed blade for best results, and set the blade height to ¹/₁₆". Test your set-up on scrap. Raise the blade ¹/₁₆" for each pass until the cove shown below is formed. Use a push-pad to guide the wood: never pass your hands over a spinning blade.

Cove Molding Subassembly

9

Soften with sandpaper

Cut the main cove on a table saw

8

Soften with sandpaper

Mill with a core box bit

10

Make this cut on a table saw

first shaped on the router table with a ⅜"-radius roundover bit as shown in *Figure 4*. Once secure, attach the small quarter rounds (pieces 17) to their inside edges, (see *Figure 5* and the *Elevations* on the previous page).

Milling the Door Muntins

A pair of thin muntins (pieces 18) divide the bottom half of the clock door into three glazed segments. The safest way to make the muntins is to form them on the edge of a wide board *(see Figure 6)*, then trim them to size *(see Figure 6 Inset)*.

These muntins are set into dadoes cut in the door's center and bottom rails. Locate these dadoes on the *Door Assembly Elevation*, page 80, then cut them on the table saw, as shown in *Figure 7*. Keep in mind that the top rail isn't dadoed like the others.

Use your saw's miter gauge to trim tenons on the ends of the muntins to fit into these dadoes, following the dimensions shown in the *Muntin Tenon Detail* on page 80. When everything fits, glue and clamp the muntins in place.

Forming Glass Retainers

The three lower panes of glass in the door (pieces 19 and 20) are secured by a simple stop molding (piece 21) ripped off the edge of a wide board and mitered to fit the glass openings.

The large pane of glass in front of the dial (piece 22) is kept in place by a separate, removable frame made up of four mitered segments of square stock (pieces 23) that are biscuited and glued together before being milled to accommodate the dial. Hold off on this assembly until you locate the dial in the door.

Figure 4: *The outside edge of the large door molding is shaped on a router table with a ⅜"-radius roundover bit.*

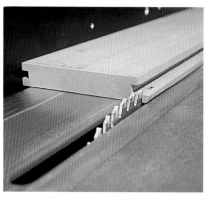

Figure 5: *The safest way to make the small quarter round molding for the door edges is to form it first with a router on the edge of a wide board, then rip it to width as shown here.*

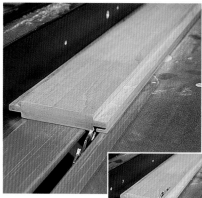

Figure 6: *Machine the muntins from larger pieces of lumber in a two-step process.*

Lining Up the Dial with a Template

Getting the dial to line up properly in the door is critical for visual balance. In fact, if it's even slightly off it will be noticeable. So I strongly recommend creating a template from ¼" plywood to help. Rip and crosscut the template to fit the rabbets in the upper door opening, and carefully center the clock dial on the template *(see Figure 8)*.

Use it to outline the large circular hole. Cut the dial hole with a jigsaw or scroll saw, then clean up the edges with a drum sander chucked in the drill press. Be very particular—the quality of this work will be quite obvious later on.

Finishing and Hardware

You're now ready to sand and finish the entire project. I used four coats of clear satin polyurethane to bring out the mahogany's luster in my clock. Sand between coats with 400-grit paper, then use a tack cloth to clean up before the next coat. When your finish is dry, set the clock on its back and position the door on the carcass. Locate and install the hinges (pieces 24) next. Each hinge will require a single dado in the front edge of the carcass stile, as shown on the Door Elevation Drawing: this eliminates the need to chop any mortises in the back of the door. Drill pilot holes for the hinge screws, and fasten the door to the carcass. Then temporarily tack the dial template into the rabbets in the back of the door.

Milling the Dial Frame

With the location of the dial established, you can now make the frame that fits around it. Rip the four frame segments (pieces 23) to size, then miter them to the lengths shown on the Material List. Use biscuits to reinforce the miter joints, and join the parts with glue and clamps to create a square form that looks like a picture frame. Make sure this frame is flat and square as you tighten the clamps.

When the glue is dry, trim the outside of the frame to fit in the door rabbet, leaving 1⁄16" of play all round. Remember to shave a little off each

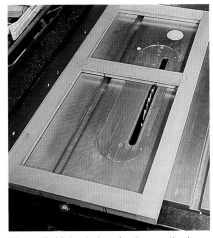

Figure 7: *Make dadoes for the muntins in the door frame subassembly. Remember that the top rail does not have dadoes.*

Figure 8: *A ¼" plywood template will help you place the clock face accurately.*

side so the mitered joints don't look off-center in the door. When the fit is perfect, center your plywood template on the frame, clamp it gently in place, and then draw a line for making the final circular cutout.

Make the cutout with a scroll or jig saw, then use a drum sander to clean up the edges. When you're satisfied with the fit, use a bearing-guided chamfering bit to relieve both the front and back edges of the cutout to give it a finished look. Cut a ⅜"-wide rabbet on the back edges of the dial frame, to bring it flush with the door.

Attach the dial to the movement according to the manufacturer's instructions, then remove the large square pane of glass from the door. Place the movement in the case (with the 12 at the top), then close the door. Gently reposition the movement until the dial is centered in the cutout (see *photo*, below).

Open the door and use a pencil to mark the movement's bolt locations on the plywood back. Then remove the movement and drill the holes. Secure the movement to the back with the nuts and washers provided by the manufacturer.

Install the chiming rods next, then attach the hands. Set the clock upright to install the pendulum, then follow the manufacturer's instructions to set the time and adjust the movement.

Apply finish to the dial frame, then secure both it and the glass with four tiny brass turnbuckles (pieces 25). Close the door and install the brass catch (piece 26) to the side of the clock case with a screw and a couple of pins, as shown on the *Exploded View Drawing* on page 78.

All that's left to do at this point is install the movement on the clock face (see *sidebar*, above.)

One final piece of advice: mechanical clock movements are very sensitive, so make sure the wall where the clock will hang is absolutely plumb and level. If it is, you'll enjoy years of reliable service from this reproduction of an Irish parlor clock.

by J. Petrovich

CRAFTSMAN CLOCK

Sloping sides, exposed box joints and a deeply overhanging top are all classic elements of Craftsman styling, even though our clock is an invented design. Select some heavily figured quartersawn white oak for your clock to add the crowning touch.

The styling of this clock is loosely based on designs from the Arts & Crafts period. Not a specific reproduction of any particular clock, the final look emerged from some sketches and a little recomposing at the bench.

I actually made two versions of this mantel clock: one from leftover teak flooring, and the other from four old bed slats cut from quartersawn white oak. While teak was not typically used during the Arts & Crafts movement, that clock fits right into my Scandinavian style dining room.

Design Issues to Consider First

Clock construction necessarily begins with selecting the clock face and movement first, then sizing the carcass and face frame to fit. I hand-painted the face shown here. If you'd rather buy a face, you may need to resize some of the part dimensions in the Material List to fit the face you buy (see page 91). As far as the clock movement goes, today's quartz movements are an excellent choice. They require little maintenance beyond a yearly battery change. They're also quite accurate, adaptable and inexpensive.

The face frames of this clock are central to its design and construction. They establish the angle of the case sides, serve as the hinge frame for the doors and display the best qualities of the wood selected. For these reasons the joinery needs to be clean and predictable. If the rails and stiles are not flush and true, the clock's small scale leaves little room for correction.

To join the face frames and doors, we'll use thin loose tenons. The carcass sides have decorative box joints at the the top, and shallow hidden dadoes accept the carcass bottom. Basic joinery makes for a beautiful clock case.

Preparing Stock

Begin work by taking all the stock required for the clock down to a consistent ½" thickness. Surfaced material bought at the lumberyard may vary by up to ¹⁄₁₆". If you do not have access to a thickness planer, you should keep this in mind.

With the dimensioned stock in hand, decide where to best use the most attractive pieces. Then cut the face frame rails and stiles (pieces 1 through 3) for the front and back

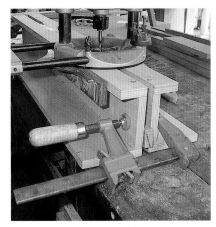

Two "L"-shaped fixtures *can hold the door and face frame components securely for routing the skinny face frame mortises.*

frames. They should be cut to exact length at this time, but don't cut the tapers for the stiles just yet. That task is more easily dealt with after joining.

It's a good idea to mark where all the pieces will mate. Use matching numbers at the joints and an arrow that points to the inside plane of the face frame to keep everything clear.

Milling Skinny Mortises

TIme to lay out the start and stop marks for the mortises. Because the stock is just ½" thick, we'll use ⅛" thick loose tenons

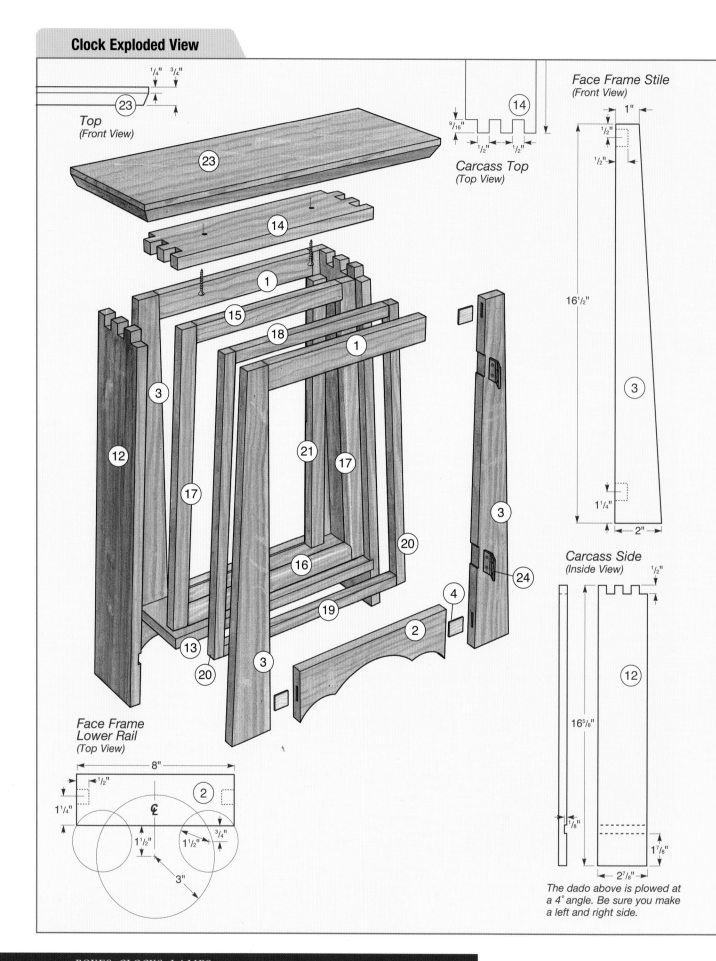

Top
(Front View)

Carcass Top
(Top View)

Face Frame Stile
(Front View)

Carcass Side
(Inside View)

Face Frame
Lower Rail
(Top View)

The dado above is plowed at
a 4° angle. Be sure you make
a left and right side.

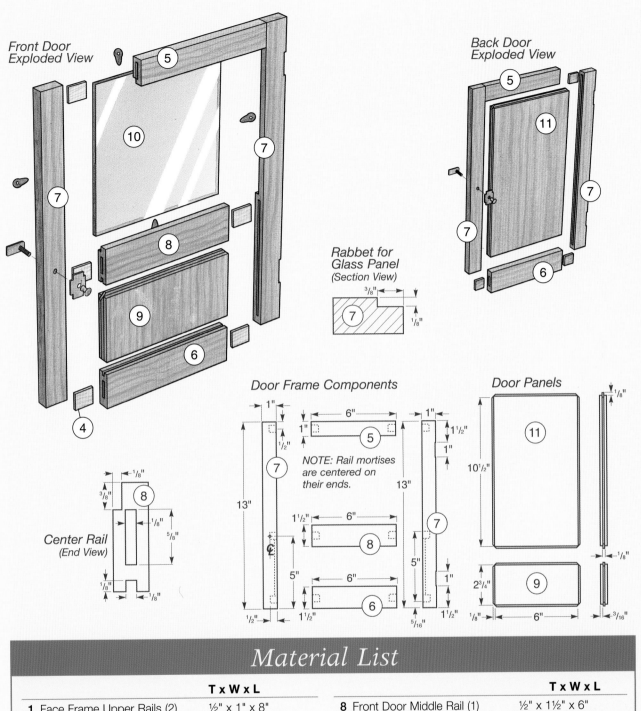

Front Door Exploded View

Back Door Exploded View

Rabbet for Glass Panel (Section View)

3/8"

1/8"

Door Frame Components

1"

6"

1"

1/2"

1 1/2"

1"

NOTE: Rail mortises are centered on their ends.

13"

1 1/2"

6"

13"

5"

1/2"

1 1/2"

6"

5/16"

1 1/2"

Center Rail (End View)

1/8"

3/8"

1/8"

5/8"

1/8"

1/8"

Door Panels

1/8"

10 1/2"

1/8"

2 3/4"

1/8"

6"

3/16"

Material List

		T x W x L
1	Face Frame Upper Rails (2)	½" x 1" x 8"
2	Face Frame Lower Rails (2)	½" x 2½" x 8"
3	Face Frame Stiles (4)	½" x 2" x 16½"
4	Loose Tenons (18)	⅛" x ⅝" x 1"
5	Door Upper Rails (2)	½" x 1" x 6"
6	Door Lower Rails (2)	½" x 1½" x 6"
7	Door Stiles (4)	½" x 1 1/16" x 13"

		T x W x L
8	Front Door Middle Rail (1)	½" x 1½" x 6"
9	Front Door Lower Panel (1)	½" x 6¼" x 3"
10	Front Door Glass Panel* (1)	⅛" x 6⅝" x 6⅝"
11	Rear Door Panel (1)	½" x 6¼" x 10¾"
12	Carcass Sides (2)	½" x 2⅞" x 16⅜"
13	Carcass Bottom (1)	½" x 2⅞" x 10¾"
14	Carcass Top (1)	½" x 2⅞" x 9⅞"

Purchase after door frame is made.

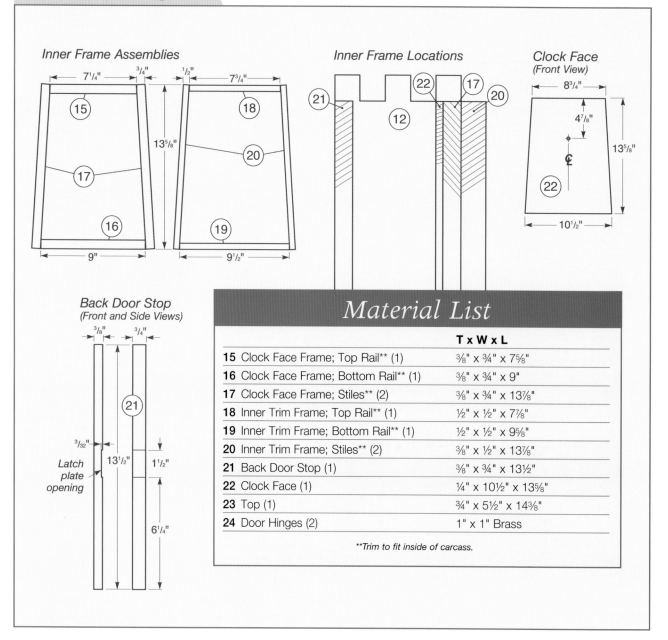

Inner Frame Assemblies

Inner Frame Locations

Clock Face
(Front View)

Back Door Stop
(Front and Side Views)

Latch plate opening

	Material List	
		T x W x L
15 Clock Face Frame; Top Rail** (1)		⅜" x ¾" x 7⅝"
16 Clock Face Frame; Bottom Rail** (1)		⅜" x ¾" x 9"
17 Clock Face Frame; Stiles** (2)		⅜" x ¾" x 13⅞"
18 Inner Trim Frame; Top Rail** (1)		½" x ½" x 7⅞"
19 Inner Trim Frame; Bottom Rail** (1)		½" x ½" x 9⅝"
20 Inner Trim Frame; Stiles** (2)		⅜" x ½" x 13⅞"
21 Back Door Stop (1)		⅜" x ¾" x 13½"
22 Clock Face (1)		¼" x 10½" x 13⅝"
23 Top (1)		¾" x 5½" x 14⅜"
24 Door Hinges (2)		1" x 1" Brass

**Trim to fit inside of carcass.

(pieces 4). Thin mortises will allow for ³⁄₁₆" of material on either side of the tenon. To hold and register the stock during routing, make a simple routing jig like the one shown in the *photo* on the previous page. A pair of "L" shaped fixtures will allow room beneath the guide/support member for clamping. Clamp the whole assembly into a bench vise for stability. Be certain to mark one side of the fixture for registration. This is important as it provides a fixed distance from the same edge.

Use a ⅛" up-spiral plunge bit and a gentle feed rate to cut the mortises. While the bit is not removing much material, the bit itself is somewhat slender and fragile. Plunge the "stop" cut first, followed by the "start" cut, then clean out the material in between, plunging no deeper than ⅛" per pass.

Forming Loose Tenons
Dimensioning the loose tenons is relatively simple at the table saw. Use stock wide enough that the tenons can be ripped safely and cleanly from the outside of the blade. The loose tenons should fit into the mortises with no more than finger pressure.

Once the loose tenons are cut to size and the face frames dry-fitted, lay out and cut the front and back door stock (pieces 5 through 11). There are rabbets for the glass panel and grooves for the back door panel to cut and plow. Refer to the *Elevation Drawings* on page 87 for construction details. We used a ⅛" slotting bit with a bearing at the

To help form the box joints, *attach a simple fence with a registration key to your miter gauge. Always test your cuts on scrap. This setup will generally require some fine-tuning for proper alignment.*

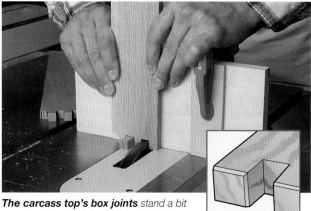

The carcass top's box joints *stand a bit proud and are slightly chamfered for a decorative touch.*

router table to cut the channel for the door frame panels. Because the panels are flush with the frames, make the cuts as close to the centers of the ½" stock as you can. After slotting the pieces with all registration marks facing down on the table, flip the pieces and run them through the slotting bit again to center them. Make the door assemblies

½2" oversize—it's easier to plane them slightly for a snug fit than it is to get lucky with a glue-up that produces a clean and even reveal all around.

Building the Clock Carcass

Like the face frames and the doors, the carcass of the clock (pieces 12 through 14) is made from ½" stock. Box joints

are used at the top of the case—not so much for strength as for visual detail. Cutting the fingers a bit long on the carcass top allows them to protrude just a hair and to be slightly chamfered.

The bottom of the clock (piece 13) is joined to the sides with an angled dado joint. Remember when cutting the dado in each side that the angles

---

*Quick*Tip

Spin for a Drill Bit

Here's a drill bit holder design that makes it easy to pick out any bit with a spin. Mount a circular piece of plywood to a lazy Susan mechanism. Drill a series of stopped holes around the perimeter of the plywood first to match each bit diameter you own. Mark the plywood on the face and edge as well to indicate sizing. Now it's easy to find the right bit for the job with a spin of the wrist. You might even want to make several of these drill bit holders for each bit type you own—brad point, twist, Forstner, and so forth.

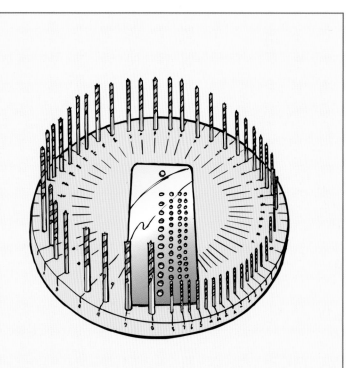

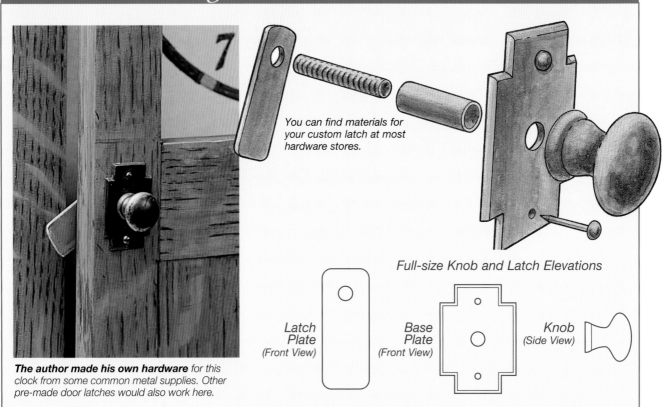

You can find materials for your custom latch at most hardware stores.

Full-size Knob and Latch Elevations

Latch Plate (Front View)

Base Plate (Front View)

Knob (Side View)

The author made his own hardware for this clock from some common metal supplies. Other pre-made door latches would also work here.

Door hardware is a matter of taste. For our author's first (teak) clock, he used a small brass knob treated with steel wool and gun bluing and a small magnet for a catch. This is a good option if you'd rather not make your own knob and latch. For this version of the clock, he wanted a custom fix to the catch situation. With a bit of threaded rod, a knob, a short length of tubing and some scraps of brass, he made a knob-operated catch. The tools required are common to most home shops. Solder the latch plate to the threaded rod, which screws into the knob. Use the brass tubing as a race so the knob/rod assembly can turn freely. The base plate is a small piece of brass trimmed and drilled for rod access and the mounting brads. Making your own hardware can be fun. But like the clock face, don't let it be an obstacle to building the project.

measure the same, but they are opposite in orientation.

Before moving on to assembly, mill the two interior frames (pieces 15 through 20) and test-fit them inside the carcass. (Make sure their combined width accommodates the shaft of your clock movement.) The bottom rail of the trim frame (piece 19) also serves as a door stop, but the back door stop (piece 21) stands alone and is glued to the inside of the rear face frame's stile.

Assembling the Parts

With the frames, doors and carcass all cut and jointed, mark the tapers for the sides of the face frames. Cutting them now, after mortising them, lessens the chances for a misstep. Use your band saw to make these cuts, then mount pairs of them together in a bench vise for cleanup and to ensure that the part sizes match. It's a good idea to generally stay a blade width or so off the layout line and plane down to

the mark. Once all four stiles are smooth and identical in angle, glue up the face frames.

After the face frames have cured, there is scrollwork to be done on the bottom rail. Deferring this work until after the face frame is glued provides a little extra support to the bottom edge of the rail where it meets the stiles. The face frames are now ready for sanding.

With the face frames, doors and case glued, the next consideration is the face of the clock (piece 22). I used a ¼"-thick panel of Masonite that I painted with gesso after cutting it to fit the opening of the case. (Gessoed panels are also available at art supply stores.) Onto this panel I laid out a clock face that I generated on the computer. After darkening the outlines of the numerals and the time rings, I carefully over-painted with gouache and drilled the center hole for the clock shaft.

Editor's Note: If you'd prefer not to go to the effort of making a custom clock face, you can simply purchase one instead. Several suppliers, including Klockit (www.klockit.com), offer inexpensive Arts & Crafts-style paper clock faces that can be used for this project. However, don't make the mistake of building the entire project before finding a face to fit it. Find and buy the face first, then adjust the *Material List* part dimensions as needed to suit the face you plan to use.

Once the clock face panel is complete it is ready to mount into the clock face frame, which is positioned directly behind the trim frame. Sink four screws through the panel and into the clock frame to mount the panel.

Painting the clock face's numerals *and dial details adds a degree of custom artistry you may want to try. Otherwise, you can buy a printed face and save yourself some effort.*

With the face mounted inside the case, the clock is ready to receive the face frames, both front and back. We found that it's much easier to glue one frame to the case at a time. Then mount the top (piece 23) to the case with two screws driven through the inside of the case's top and into the top piece itself.

To hang the doors, I used 1" x 1" hinges (pieces 24). I didn't like their bright brass look, so I rubbed off the protective finish and then darkened them with some touch-up gun bluing. Another option is to buy hinges with an antique brass or wrought-iron finish, which will look appropriate here.

Finishing Touches

Sand the entire clock up to 220 grit and then apply a golden highlighted stain. Three coats of medium-luster polyurethane with a light sanding between the coats will seal the deal. Use small glass retainers to secure the glass panel, and mount the quartz movement following the manufacturer's instructions. Now all you need is a suitable mantel and a cup of tea to enjoy watching the hours tick away.

*Quick*Tip

Understanding Moisture Content

The moisture content of wood is measured in terms of weight: the weight of the water versus the weight of the wood. On average, the ideal moisture level for stock you use for furniture and cabinetry should be around 7 to 10%; that is, the moisture in the wood should weigh 7 to 10% of what the wood weighs. Freshly cut green wood can have a moisture level as high as 200%. In that case, the moisture weighs twice what the wood alone weighs. The only way to accurately know how "wet" the wood actually is is to test it with a moisture meter, taking a reading from the center area of the board and in a few inches from an end. Since most of us don't own one of these rather expensive meters, you'll have to trust your lumber supplier. Most suppliers will readily tell you their standards for lumber dryness, and some will test the wood in your presence before you buy.

ARTIST'S PENCIL BOX

Here's a quick project you can make for an aspiring young artist. It recalls a time when even a set of pencils befitted a special wooden container. Our design will hold a collection of colored pencils and an eraser for carting along in a bag or backpack. It's a perfect way to put some attractive or exotic scrap wood to good use.

by David Larson

Years ago, colored pencils came in a wooden box instead of today's impossible-to-open plastic blister packages. A wooden box seemed to make the pencils more special. In fact, I still have a pencil box I received as a boy, which sits on my desk next to my computer to remind me of simpler times. Thinking about those cherished pencils one day, I realized what an ideal gift project it would make. A little time at the drawing board produced the project you see here—it's a fitting keepsake you could give to that budding artist in your life.

The key to making this pencil box is to construct it as one assembly and then rip it in half to separate the upper and lower compartments. This may seem strange, but it's actually a common box-making technique. The two units are then held together by a dowel, which allows them to swing apart when the top is slid back.

Cutting the Parts to Size
Get started on this pencil box by cutting a ¾" x 3" x 24" piece of stock and resawing it in half with your band saw. Plane the thin strips down to ⁵⁄₁₆" in thickness and cut the sides (pieces 1)

Figure 1: *Outline the bit's cutting area on the fence, then use the lines as starting and stopping points when routing the stopped grooves.*

to size from this stock. Next, plane some of this resawn stock down to ⅛" for the top, middle panel and bottom panel (pieces 2, 3, and 4), and finish up by machining some ½" material for the endwalls (pieces 5 and 6).

Now you can rout the grooves in the sides and endwalls. Chuck a ⅛" straight bit in your router table and rout the grooves for housing the middle and top panels, as shown in the *Side Panel Groove Locations Drawing* on page 95. Rout the grooves ⅛" deep, carefully setting your stock onto the bit at the starting point and lifting it off the bit when you reach the stopping line. Be sure to stop the front end of the top groove and both ends of the middle groove ¼" from the ends of the stock (see *Figure 1*).

Gluing Up and Splitting Apart
Gluing up is really quite simple—just be sure to use the glue sparingly or it will run all over the inside of your box. Spread glue in the middle grooves of the sides and endwalls and on the ends

of the endwalls. Slip the middle panel into the sides and add the endwalls, then, to help keep the assembly square, slide the top into place without glue. Next, spread glue on the bottom edges of the box, square up the assembly and clamp the bottom panel into position.

As the glue dries, drill two ⅛"-diameter x ½"-deep holes at each joint, as shown in the *Pin Location Detail* on the next page—be sure you avoid drilling into a groove. Cut short pins (pieces 7) and glue them into the holes to reinforce the weak butt joints. It will help prevent the sides from pulling away from the endwalls over time. Sand the dowels flush with the sides.

Now it's time to rip the box in half. Really, there isn't any mystery to this, but check your saw settings carefully to avoid cutting in the wrong place. Raise your table saw blade to cut through the box and clamp the fence ⅞" from the blade. With the top of the box riding against the fence, rip the box in two. (I've made allowances in the *Material List* for the loss of a ⅛" saw kerf.) Plane the edges

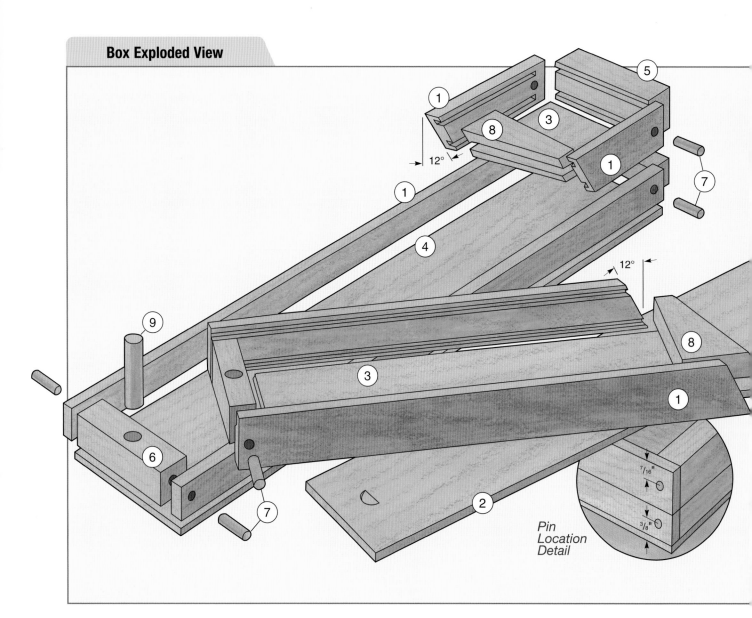

12°

12°

7/16"

3/8"

Pin
Location
Detail

QuickTip

Non-slip Floors with Walnut Shells

If you have painted, wooden floors in your workshop, you know that a little sawdust makes for a dangerously slick surface. What you may not know is that boatbuilders use crushed walnut shells in their paint formulations to create non-skid decks. Pick up some from a local paint store and add it to a can of floor paint, according to the proportions listed on the container. The walnut shells will add just the right amount of grit to improve traction. In case you're wondering, you can't do this with sand because it sinks right to the bottom of the can. Walnut shells will remain suspended in the paint.

to get a good fit, then cut a 5⁄16"-thick block for the divider (piece 8) and glue it into the upper compartment, as shown in the *Upper Compartment Drawing*, next page. Then stack the compartments and use a drill press to bore a ¼" hole down through the back endwall to install the hinge dowel (piece 9).

Cut the hinge to length and glue it into the lower compartment. Trim the dowel flush with the bottom of the box, then lay out the compound angle cut in the upper compartment, as shown above. Tilt your band saw table 12° and turn your miter gauge 12°, then pass the upper compartment through the blade. When setting up this cut,

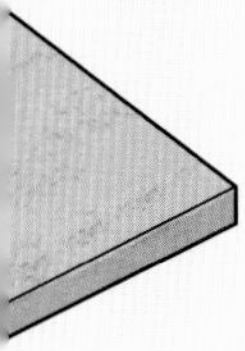

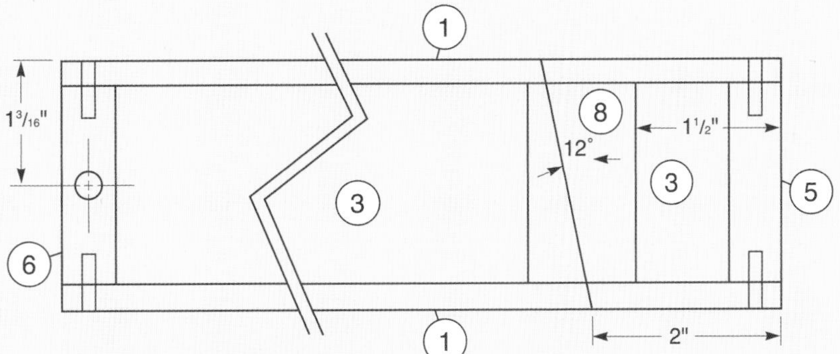

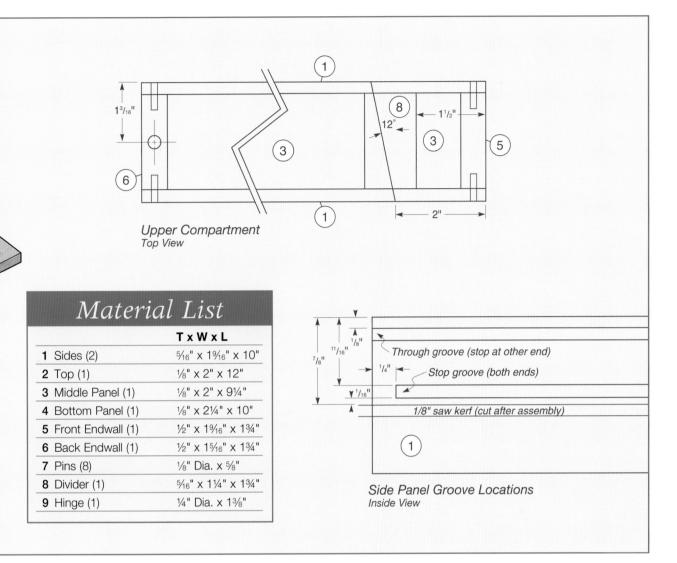

1
1 3/16"
8
12°
1 1/2"
3
3
5
6
1
2"

Upper Compartment
Top View

Material List

	T x W x L
1 Sides (2)	5/16" x 1 9/16" x 10"
2 Top (1)	1/8" x 2" x 12"
3 Middle Panel (1)	1/8" x 2" x 9 1/4"
4 Bottom Panel (1)	1/8" x 2 1/4" x 10"
5 Front Endwall (1)	1/2" x 1 9/16" x 1 3/4"
6 Back Endwall (1)	1/2" x 1 5/16" x 1 3/4"
7 Pins (8)	1/8" Dia. x 5/8"
8 Divider (1)	5/16" x 1 1/4" x 1 3/4"
9 Hinge (1)	1/4" Dia. x 1 3/8"

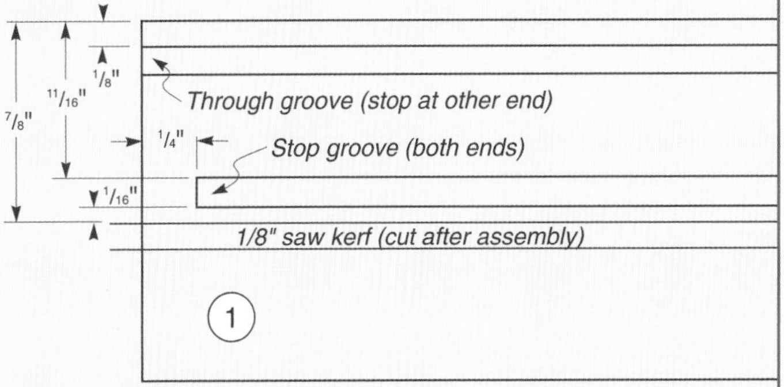

1/8"
11/16"
7/8"
Through groove (stop at other end)
1/4"
Stop groove (both ends)
1/16"
1/8" saw kerf (cut after assembly)
1

Side Panel Groove Locations
Inside View

try to achieve the correct angles, but realize that a little deviation won't matter in terms of how the top and bottom compartments seat together.

Stack the compartments again and you'll notice that, due to the saw kerf, the lower compartment is a little longer than the two upper sections combined. Glue the front part of the upper compartment to the lower compartment; then, after the glue dries, sand the ends flush.

Cut the top to length and chuck a 1/2" Forstner bit in your drill press. Tilt the drill press 25° and bore into the top just 1/16" to form the half-moon shaped finger pull.

Finishing Up

Apply a couple coats of oil finish to complete the pencil box. Once you've made it through your first box the next one will go much faster. This is such a fun project you'll no doubt make more.

Then fill it with a set of artist's pencils and give a special youngster a keepsake that will inspire memory.

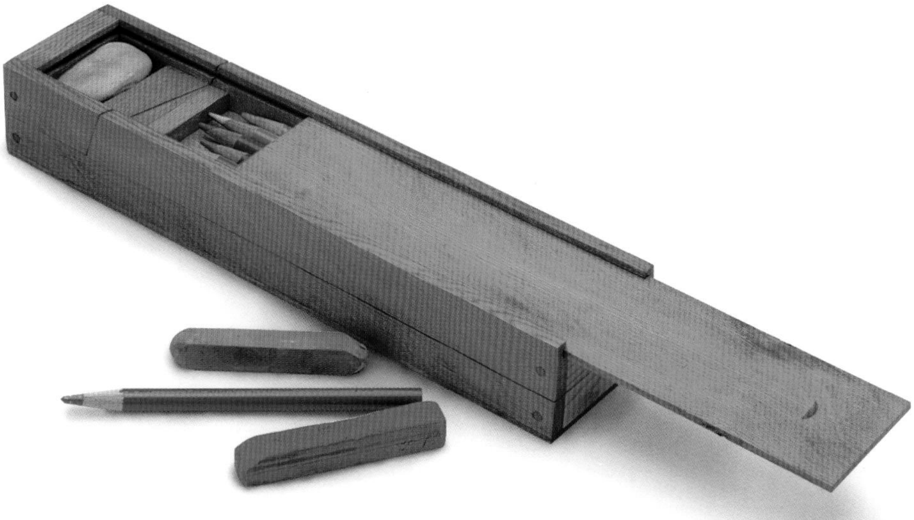

by Nina Childs Johnson

UNDELIVERED LETTER BOX

Originally a wedding present for a family member, this box traveled a circuitous path before it was finished. Here's one woodworker's tale of love lost and lessons learned through the process of designing and building this beautiful and intricate box. It illustrates the truth that woodworking often influences other aspects of our lives.

Sometimes, life is unpredictable. I originally designed this letter box for my brother, an English teacher who collects fountain pens. The request came from my sister-in-law-to-be as a wedding gift, three months in advance. We mutually decided that a box to hold his pens and ink would be just

right. Unfortunately, the relationship wasn't just right, and before I finished building the project, the wedding was cancelled. In any case, I pushed on with the project and, after careful planning and design, it was beautifully executed, as you can see. It's an intricate and somewhat ambitious project but one that's definitely within the scope of an intermediate-level woodworker's skills.

Reviewing Some Box Basics

Step one on virtually any box design is to select an attractive plank and cut it so the grain is continuous around the front, back and ends (pieces 1 and 2). With this particular box, the process calls for a little early planning. You need to be sure to allow for saw kerfs when determining the final height and length of the drawer front (piece 3). This, in turn, will affect the dimensions of the back and ends. For the drawer front's first cut, choose a place in the grain

pattern where a glue line will be least conspicuous. Then rip the front into three pieces, and crosscut the drawer front out of the middle. Next, glue these pieces back together (except for the drawer front). You'll want to make the drawer front slightly larger than the drawer opening (to allow for cutting dovetails later on), so move the two small pieces toward the center slightly. Then trim off both ragged ends, cut the back piece to match, and machine the two end pieces to the exact dimensions shown in the *Material List* on page 99.

To prevent the thin piece below the drawer opening from breaking, I recommend that you cut a piece of wood the same width as the drawer opening and tape it into the opening for the time being.

Once the sides are cut to final size and the inside faces are both flat and smooth, move on to laying out the dovetails. I was looking for a different

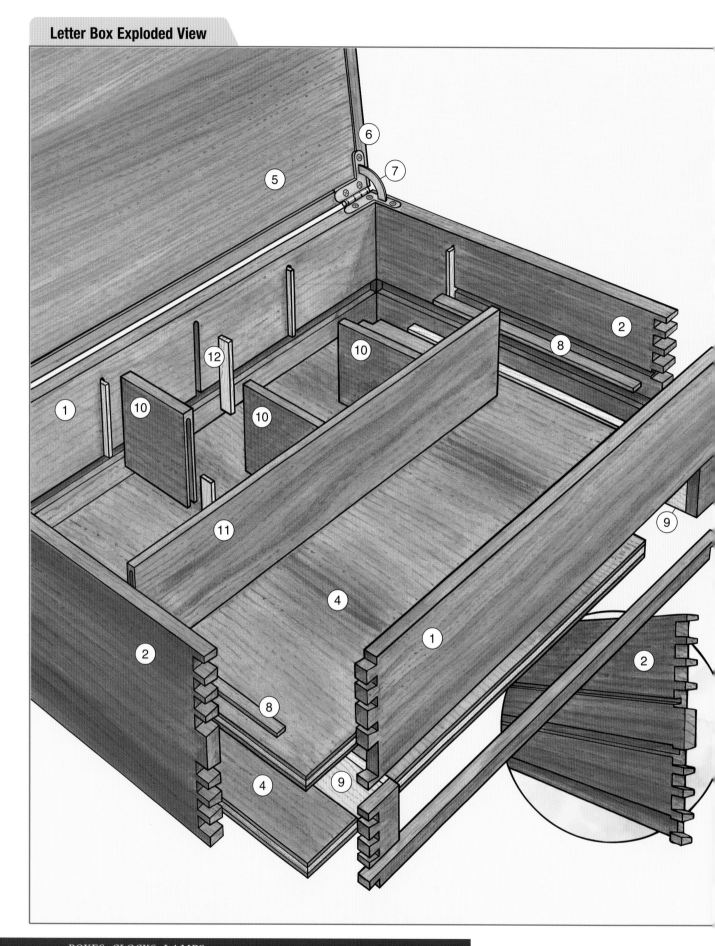

Material List

		T x W x L
1	Front and Back (2)	⅜" x 4⅝" x 13⅝"
2	Ends (2)	⅜" x 4⅝" x 10"
3	Drawer Front (1)	⅜" x 1⅜" x 11⅝"
4	Horizontal Dividers (2)	⁹⁄₃₂" x 13¼" x 9⁷⁄₁₆"
5	Lid (1)	⁹⁄₃₂" x 9⅜" x 13¹⁄₁₆"
6	Edge Banding (1)	⁷⁄₁₆" x ⅜" x 50"
7	Quadrant Hinges (2)	Solid brass
8	Tray Supports (2)	⅛" x ⁷⁄₁₆" x 6⅞"
9	Drawer Pocket Sides (2)	⅜" x 1⁷⁄₁₆" x 9¼"
10	Small Dividers (3)	¼" x 2⅛" x 2¹⁄₁₆"
11	Long Divider (1)	⁹⁄₃₂" x 2⅜" x 12⅞"
12	Splines (8)	⅛" x ¼" x 1⅞"

QuickTip

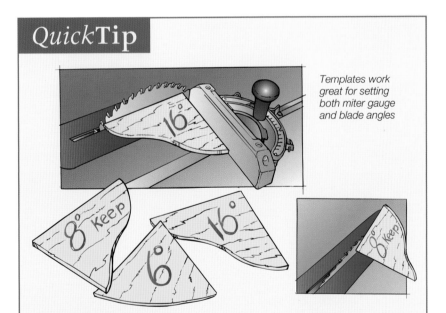

Templates work great for setting both miter gauge and blade angles

Table Saw Angles

Rather than look for a protractor or bevel gauge, or trust the arrow indicators, make a set of the angles you use most commonly to adjust your table saw blade and miter gauge. Scraps of ¼" plywood work fine for this. Make the set-up gauges large enough so they register the angles accurately. Then, keep them close to the saw so they're always at the ready.

rhythm than the usual rigid, uniform pattern of pins and tails, so I varied the size and spacing. (Look to pages 108 and 109 for more of these construction details.)

Making the Horizontal Dividers

This box has two levels: the upper for the ink and pen storage, and the lower for the paper drawer. This requires two horizontal dividers (pieces 4)—the lower one serves as the box's bottom. Since these pieces will be fully captured by the walls of the box, they need to be made out of plywood. It wouldn't do to have them expanding and contracting with the seasons. I made these panels from handmade veneers and ⅛" plywood (see the sidebar on page 101). I also made a third panel that would become the lid of the box (piece 5), with the application of thick, hand-made edge banding (piece 6). The lid is eventually attached to the box with quadrant hinges (pieces 7).

To capture the middle divider, rout grooves around the inside of the box, stopping the cuts before the dovetailed ends. Eventually, you'll rout slots for the supports (pieces 8) that hold the tray. You'll also install the drawer pocket sides (pieces 9) later. Next form a rabbet along the bottom of the two ends and back to capture the bottom divider. This way, the piece serves double-duty as the bottom of the drawer pocket. Don't cut this rabbet in the box front: the bottom will be glued flush with the drawer pocket opening.

Creating the Ink Dividers

Your next step is to go to the Technical Drawings on pages 106 and 108 in order to lay out the upper compartment. Cut the dividers (pieces 10 and 11) to size and mill the small slots in the ends of each piece for the splines (pieces 12). Next, cut the corresponding slots into the long divider and the interior walls of the box.

Building the Pen Tray and Slides

The pen tray is a simple lidless box consisting of sides and ends (pieces 13 and 14), a captured panel bottom (piece 15) and a fabric-covered pen carrier inset (pieces 16 and 17). Make the pen carrier by cutting a piece of ¾" plywood a bit smaller than the tray (allowing for the fabric) and dividing it up into eight sections. After testing several angles, I clamped a temporary fence on my table saw at an angle to the blade. After doing this, cut the outermost slots at both ends of the board first, then move the fence further away from the blade to mill the successive slots. To form each pair of slots, raise the blade in small, safe increments. Then lightly sand the grooves and apply the fabric with spray-mount adhesive. The pen tray should fit quite closely to its space. To facilitate removal (and gain access to the hidden compartment), add loops secured with tiny dowels (pieces 18 and 19) on the sides.

Because the pen tray is shallower than the compartment it sits in, it needs to be held up just a little from the floor. Use a ⅛" router bit and form grooves along the sides of the box to receive narrow supports.

Finishing the inside of the box will be much more difficult to do after it is assembled, so tape off the exposed pins and tails and apply several coats of your favorite finish to the inside surfaces of the box. I chose shellac.

Quadrant hinges *look simple, but they require hidden mortises for the support arms to hide in. For this box, some of the screws provided with the hinges will need to be cut down in length to fit properly.*

The front panel *of the box is sliced into five separate pieces in order to achieve a tightly fitting drawer front.*

Carrying Out the First Glue-up

You are now ready for glue. In this first stage, glue up the four sides of the box, making sure to include the middle horizontal divider. After the four corner joints cure, move on to the internal dividers. First, glue the splines into the sides of the box and then slide the dividers onto them. To aid in clamping the small dividers to the bottom of the compartment, make a clamp block thick enough so the clamp will reach around the sides of the box and put pressure on the underside of the horizontal divider. It's also time to glue in the supports for the pen tray. At this point all the interior work is done.

Making the Drawer

The next step is to build the drawer and its pocket. The drawer is sized to be a little bigger than a standard sheet of paper, with room for a finger to lift the paper out. You've already cut the drawer front to size, so go ahead and slice the stock for the back, sides and bottom (pieces 20 through 22). When creating drawers, it's a good practice to set the shoulders deeper than the thickness of the side material and file or plane off the excess after glue-up for perfect alignment. This time you need to be very careful because the front is so close to final size already. The front joints are half-blind dovetails, and the back corners are through dovetails. Make the drawer bottom a bit longer than the drawer so it can be trimmed later to serve as the drawer stop.

Contrary to the usual process, we'll build the drawer before completing the space for it to fit into. Once you establish that the drawer fits well through its opening, focus on its relationship to the drawer pocket sides. You'll want the sides of the pocket to provide slight resistance so the drawer

Handmade Plywood

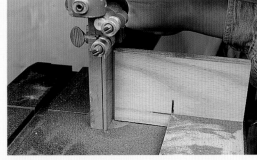

Resawing fat ⅛" veneer is the first step in creating handmade plywood. A point fence and a properly tuned band saw are essential.

Use a slave board clamped in place to aid in planing your veneer pieces smooth. They must all be uniform in thickness.

To book-match the veneer, select successive flitches and join two pieces with packing tape, glue and a heavy weight.

Making your own plywood gives you total control of your project's appearance. You're not limited to the commonly available species of plywood, and you can match the color and figure of the wood used on all aspects of your piece. As an example, our author book-matched the veneer she used on the top and bottom layers of this project's lid from successive flitches. When you open the box, the plywood appears to be a solid piece of book-matched narra lumber.

To apply these veneer pieces to the ⅛" plywood core, use the same series of steps you would for any standard veneering job. For added strength, however, use white or yellow glue instead of contact cement.

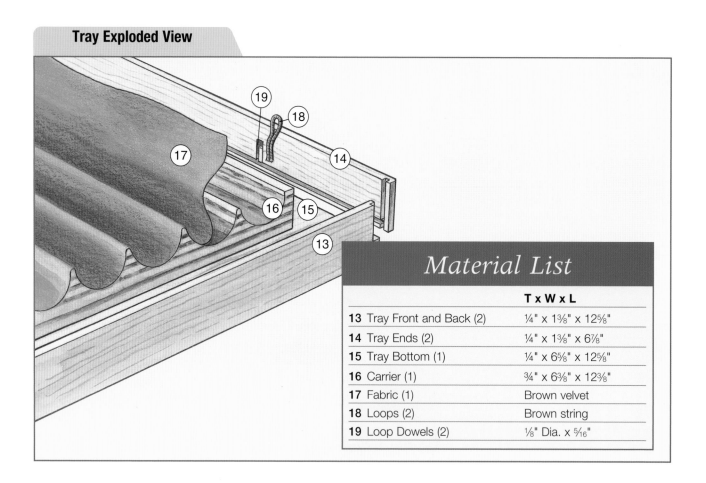

Material List

		T x W x L
13	Tray Front and Back (2)	¼" x 1⅜" x 12⅝"
14	Tray Ends (2)	¼" x 1⅜" x 6⅞"
15	Tray Bottom (1)	¼" x 6⅝" x 12⅝"
16	Carrier (1)	¾" x 6⅜" x 12⅜"
17	Fabric (1)	Brown velvet
18	Loops (2)	Brown string
19	Loop Dowels (2)	⅛" Dia. x ⁵⁄₁₆"

Great Results with Delicate Dovetails:
Five Tips from a Pro

Hand-cut dovetails are a sign of excellence in woodworking. Alas, practice is still the key to success, but here are a few of our best tips to help you to advance your skills.

1. Our author uses a Zona saw (a thin-kerf back saw, inexpensive—but effective). Slant the saw slightly back (towards you) so the saw reaches the line on your side of the stock first. Then level it up and cut to the line on the other side, being careful NOT to cut into the scribe line.

2. Cut all the same sides of the pins and tails at the same time in order to keep your posture in line with that angle, decreasing your chances of deviating (screwing up).

3. For chopping out waste, use a chisel block (shown at left) to keep the cuts vertical. The hardwood block is as long as necessary and has a sandpaper bottom to keep it from moving. The bottom also has one long edge slightly beveled to keep the scribe line visible during positioning.

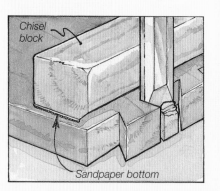

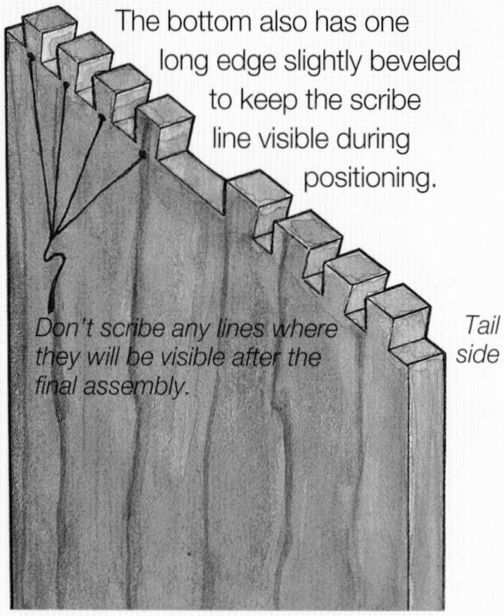

Chisel block

Sandpaper bottom

Don't scribe any lines where they will be visible after the final assembly.

Tail side

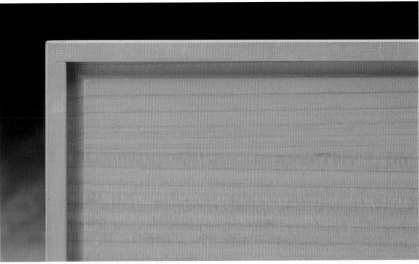

The tray bottom's edge is first shaped with a gentle cove and then captured by stopped grooves routed into the sides.

won't come flying out when pulled open. To achieve this, make the sides a hair closer together at the front of the box than at the back. This way the drawer will move well, but it will slow down as it is pulled further out. Then attach the drawer pocket sides to the box's bottom. (Do a dry run to fine-tune the fit before final glue-up.) When you are satisfied, secure this subassembly into the rabbet on the bottom of the box, applying glue to the rabbet, the top of the pocket sides and the front edge of the divider. This completes the drawer pocket and closes up the bottom of the box.

Forming the Lid, Adding Hinges

As was mentioned earlier, I made the top panel with handmade plywood and trimmed it with edge banding. Form this banding by hand and miter it at the corners. At first I designed the lid with a handle carved out of the front piece of edge banding, but as soon as I made and attached the drawer pull (piece 23), I decided the handle had to go. I simply took the lid to the band saw and removed what looked to me like a second nose on the face of the box. I admit to having felt a little nervous about

Don't scribe a line where it will be visible in the final assembly.

Cut the same side of all the pins and tails at the same time to avoid screwing up.

Pin side

Support

Flattened pencil lead

Scrap Block

4. To transfer the pin pattern to the tail stock, clamp a tall narrow scrap (shown at left) in the end vise and lay your tail stock inside-up, butted against the scrap. Place the pin stock on-end against the scrap. Sand a flat side on your pencil lead and hold the pin piece against the scrap. Mark along the pin sides, being sure to get them all.

5. Slowly work the joint together, paring the tails as you go, to make a snug fit. Where there is too much pressure, the pencil markings will drag and burnish the insides, indicating where to pare. Seat the joint together, about ¾ of the way with hand pressure, the rest with light mallet blows. Never wiggle your joints apart when test-fitting. It will crush fibers and cause a bad fit. Lightly tap the pieces apart, as shown above.

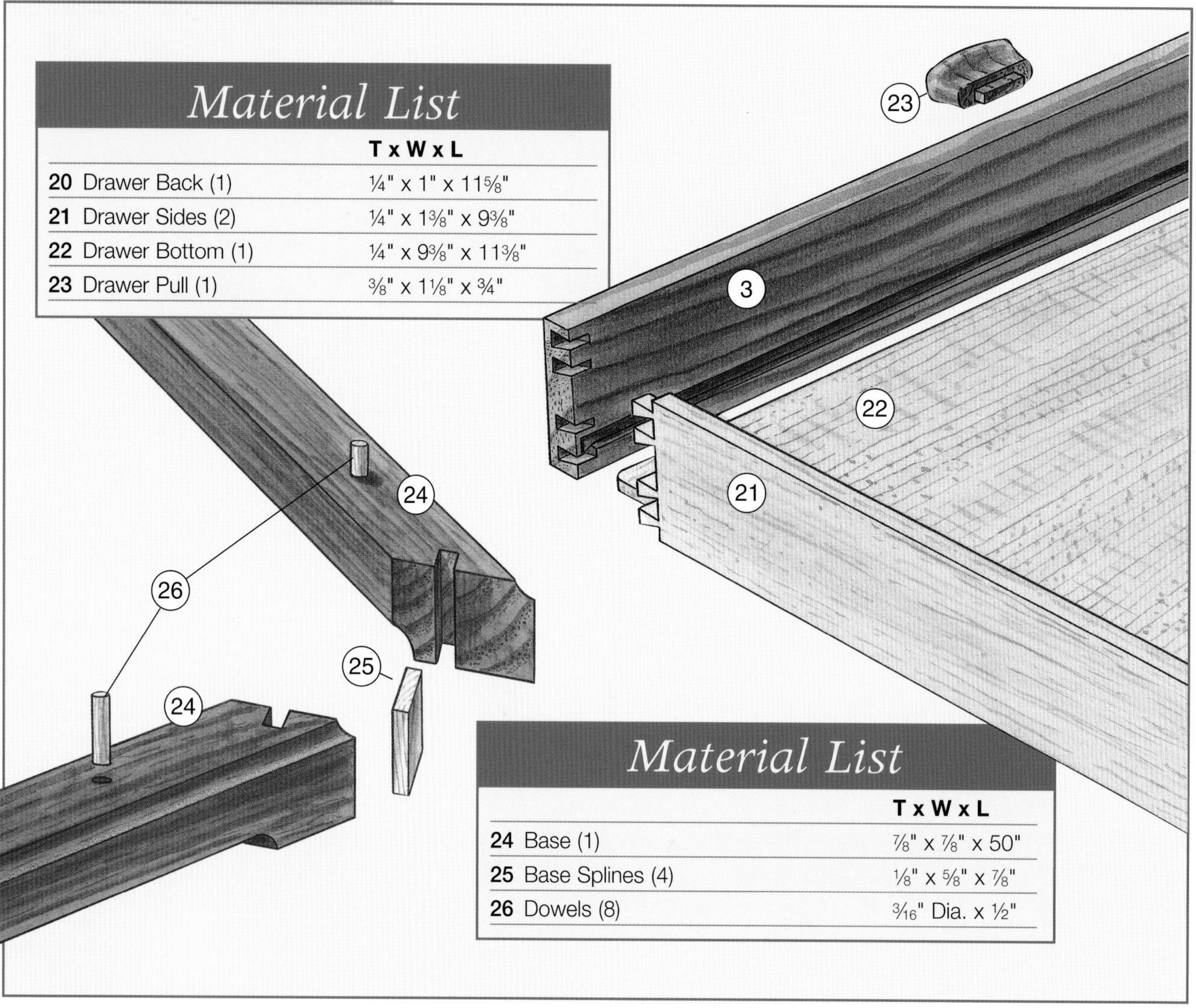

Material List

	T x W x L
20 Drawer Back (1)	¼" x 1" x 11⅝"
21 Drawer Sides (2)	¼" x 1⅜" x 9⅜"
22 Drawer Bottom (1)	¼" x 9⅜" x 11⅜"
23 Drawer Pull (1)	⅜" x 1⅛" x ¾"

Material List

	T x W x L
24 Base (1)	⅞" x ⅞" x 50"
25 Base Splines (4)	⅛" x ⅝" x ⅞"
26 Dowels (8)	3⁄16" Dia. x ½"

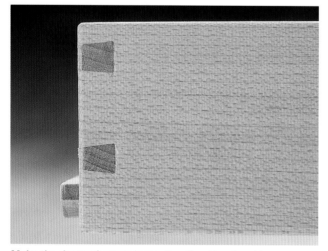

Make the drawer bottom longer than the sides, then trim it to perfectly register the drawer in its opening later in the construction process.

amputating something that had been part of the design from the start, but again, it's important to realize that change is good and woodworking requires flexibility.

Once your lid is finished, attach it to the rest of the box. I used brass quadrant hinges for strength and simplicity. At least the appearance is simple; the actual installation is not so easy. The support arm of the hinge keeps the lid from falling backwards, but it requires a deep channel to rest in. After locating and setting the hinge into the edge of the box, drill a long, deep mortise into the side. Then cut a similar channel into the lid, but more shallow. You may end up filing a little off the top of the support arm so it will fit within the thickness of the lid. The hinges come with screws, but due to the thickness of the top, you'll have to cut half of them quite short to keep from poking through.

The mitered corners on the machiche base were reinforced with splines. The base is attached simply with dowels and glue.

Adding the Base

The last, but definitely not least, aspect of this piece to make is the base. The base (piece 24) visually lifts the box off the surface it rests on and provides a more finished look. I used a species called machiche, which is close in color to the reddish aspect of the narra I used for the other box components. Rip the base pieces to size and then crosscut them roughly to length. Work on the miters until you get a good square fit. It's critical here that the joints meet with the tightest possible seams.

To strengthen the joint, add splines (pieces 25) to the mitered corners. Before gluing, shape the bottom edges to create the feet. Do this final shaping after glue-up, using files and sandpaper. Attach the base to the box with one or two small dowels (pieces 26) per side. A drop of glue ensures that the dowels will make a strong connection.

Always Expect Changes

I took nearly a year to complete this project, with progress broken up by a cancelled wedding, a broken leg, cross-country move and a lost commission in between. The whole process became a lesson for me about the uncertainty of life. Changes can be scary and frustrating but they're almost always for the better. Wood will warp and move, screws will be too long, and things you thought were crucial to the piece will need to be cut off. Such is the beauty of woodworking.

QuickTip

Forget Measuring Twice— Use a Storyboard Instead

Large assemblies with numerous parts can quickly get out of hand, so the pros know the value of a storyboard to keep everything organized. This can be as simple as a large sheet of paper or hardboard laid on the workbench, with a full-size template drawn on it. The template shows how the parts will be oriented to each other after assembly, and a good template can even be used to take measurements while you cut parts to size. Hot-glue small guide blocks to the template, to help line up the larger parts.

Sustainable Exotics

The author purchased the lumber used in this box from EcoTimber®, a company specializing in sustainably harvested wood. You can find them on the web at www.ecotimber.com or call them at 888-801-0855. The narra was salvaged from the bottom of the Mekong river and the machiche was grown in Central America.

Machiche

Narra

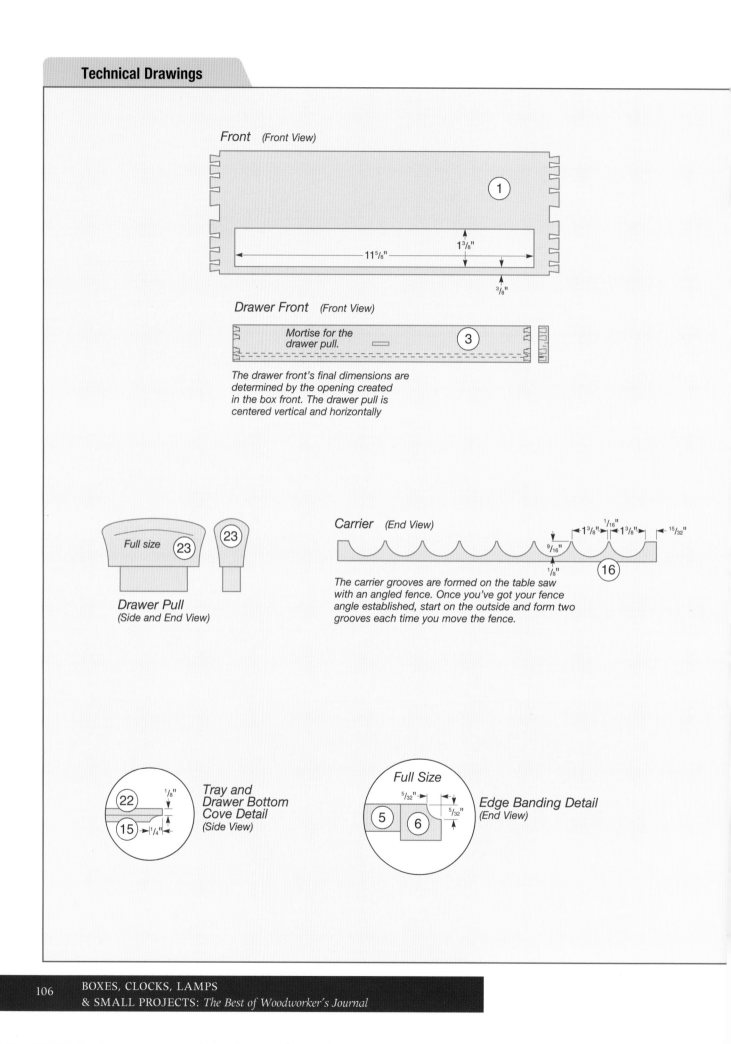

Front (Front View)

①

11⁵/₈" 1³/₈"

³/₈"

Drawer Front (Front View)

Mortise for the
drawer pull.

③

The drawer front's final dimensions are
determined by the opening created
in the box front. The drawer pull is
centered vertical and horizontally

Full size ㉓ ㉓

Drawer Pull
(Side and End View)

Carrier (End View)

1³/₈" 1/16" 1³/₈" 15/32"

9/16"

1/8"

⑯

The carrier grooves are formed on the table saw
with an angled fence. Once you've got your fence
angle established, start on the outside and form two
grooves each time you move the fence.

㉒ 1/8"

⑮ 1/4"

Tray and
Drawer Bottom
Cove Detail
(Side View)

Full Size

5/32"

5/32"

⑤ ⑥

Edge Banding Detail
(End View)

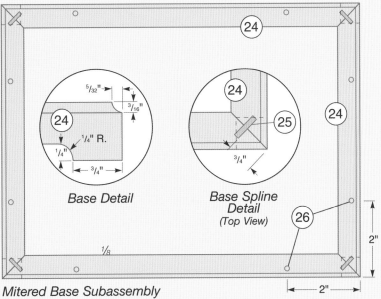

Base Detail

⁵/₃₂" ³/₁₆"

¼" R.

¼" ³/₄"

Base Spline Detail
(Top View)

2"

2"

Mitered Base Subassembly
(Top View)

¹/₈

Tray End (Inside View)

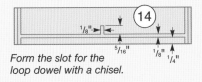

¹/₈" ⑭

⁵/₁₆" ¹/₈" ¹/₄"

Form the slot for the
loop dowel with a chisel.

Tray Corner Detail

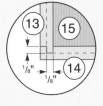

⑬ ⑮

¹/₈" ¹/₈" ⑭

Use a ¹/₈"-kerf saw blade in
your table saw to create the
corner joinery for the tray. Set
the fence 1¹/₈" from the blade
and set the blade ¹/₈" high.
This way, each corner can be
completed with two cuts.

Back (Inside View)

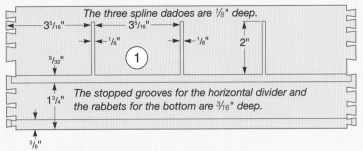

The three spline dadoes are ¹/₈" deep.

3⁵/₁₆" 3⁵/₁₆"

¹/₈" ¹/₈" 2"

⑨/₃₂" ①

1³/₄"

The stopped grooves for the horizontal divider and
the rabbets for the bottom are ³/₁₆" deep.

³/₈"

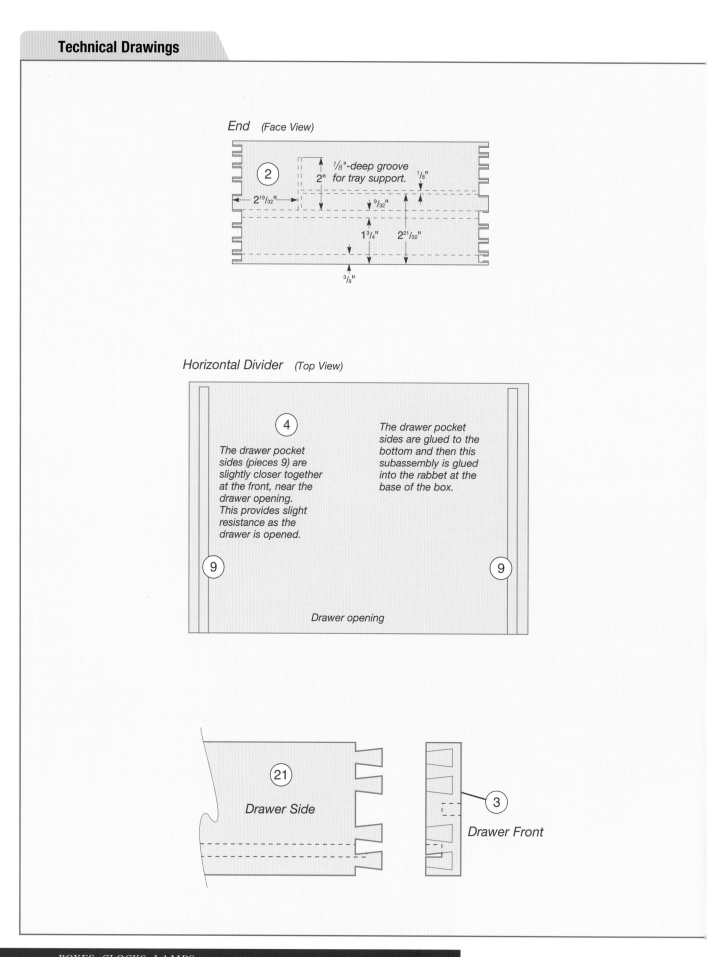

End   (Face View)

②

↕ 2"

⅛"-deep groove
for tray support.

⅛"

2¹⁹/₃₂"

↓ ⁹/₃₂"

1³/₄"   2²¹/₃₂"

³/₈"

Horizontal Divider   (Top View)

④

The drawer pocket
sides (pieces 9) are
slightly closer together
at the front, near the
drawer opening.
This provides slight
resistance as the
drawer is opened.

The drawer pocket
sides are glued to the
bottom and then this
subassembly is glued
into the rabbet at the
base of the box.

⑨   ⑨

Drawer opening

㉑

Drawer Side

③

Drawer Front

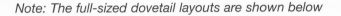

Note: The full-sized dovetail layouts are shown below

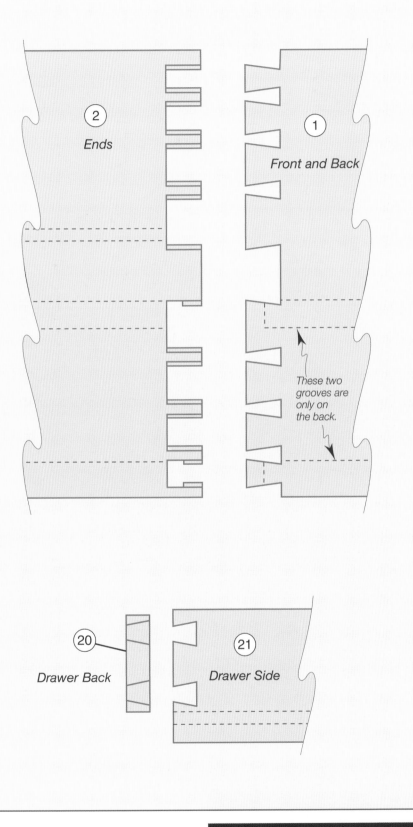

② **Ends**

① **Front and Back**

These two grooves are only on the back.

⑳ **Drawer Back**

㉑ **Drawer Side**

QuickTip

Routers versus Shapers

If, like most of us, your budget will only allow you to buy either a shaper or a large router, the experts all say to go the latter route. Routers are more versatile and less expensive, plus they can do a lot of things a shaper can't, like mortising and using a dovetail jig. A shaper is definitely the right tool in large production jobs, but a big router can do pretty much everything a shaper can, only slower. While an industrial shaper with a 1¼" spindle can easily handle 4" stock in one pass, even a 3HP router will need to make several passes to do the same job. Buy a router that allows for micro-adjustment with provisions for above-the-table bit height adjustment.

After investing in the router, the next logical purchase is a router table. A router table provides the second component to making a surrogate shaper. Choose a router table that has a sturdy base and thick worktop to support a heavy router. Router tables with storage drawers or cabinet compartments are handy, but what's even more important is that the table has a flat, rigid fence that's easy to clamp in place.

by Jim Carroll

May the wonderful
spirit of Christmas
bring joy to You and Yo

The Carroll

TURNING THE "WRITE STUFF"

Even if it's not exactly the night before Christmas, any time of the year is a good time for turners to start turning holiday gifts. Pens are an excellent gift-giving option: they're quick to turn, look great when you're through, and don't cost an arm and a leg. Another pleasant aspect of turning pens is that you get a chance to work with small amounts of exotic stock. It's a cheap route to learn plenty about a variety of different wood species, and every pen you make looks uniquely different.

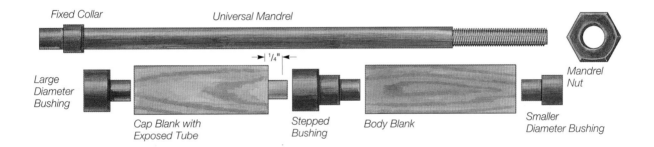

The pen design featured in this article is called Montblanc. It's a common style, and the pen parts retail for about $6 from most turning supply sources. The wood, depending on your approach, will cost from nothing (scrap bin) to a couple of dollars. Not bad, considering you can easily spend over $100 for one of the real things at an office supply store. Pens may just be the ultimate scrap wood projects. With such small blanks, you can really be selective in the material you choose.

The hardware kit you buy should include two brass tubes (a longer one for the body and a shorter one for the cap) and the other various pen parts.

If you're not set up to turn pens, the *illustration* above overviews the other lathe accessories you'll need. These are sold in an inexpensive kit. Also, the pen tubes must fit very tightly into the blank. I recommend that you buy an "O"-diameter bit for making the Montblanc style set.

As far as a lathe goes, all you really need is a mini-lathe.

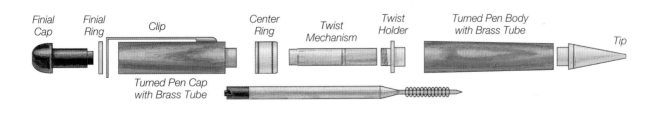

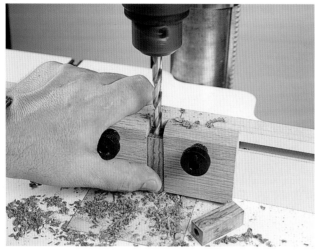

Figure 1: *Equip your drill press with a good fence and stop system for this production project. Remember to continually back out the waste as you drill through the blank to prevent splitting.*

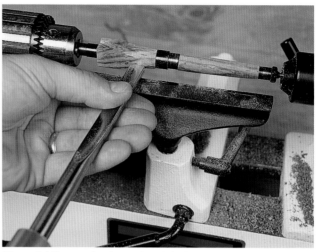

Figure 2: *When turning the pen's elliptical shape, don't get aggressive and trim your bushings. It dulls turning tools and makes for very small pens toward the end of a run. Get close and switch to sandpaper.*

Inserting Brass Tubes into Turning Blanks

To get started, select your pen blank material and machine it into ⅝"-square strips if it doesn't come this way already. Crosscut a group of body blanks to 2⅜" (the exact length of the longer brass tube) and a second group of cap blanks to 1²⁵⁄₃₂", (about ¼" short of the shorter brass tube). Keep the sets together (use a matching number on each set) and be sure your blanks are crosscut perfectly square. This results in a pen with tight joints between the turned material and the fittings.

Make a stop jig for your drill press (see *Figure 1*) and, using an "O" drill bit, drill a hole through all your precut stock. Keep lifting the bit out of the stock to remove waste and be careful—the blank gets warm while drilling.

Before gluing the brass tubes from the pen kit into your freshly drilled blanks, rough up their surfaces with a little steel wool. A great little tip is to jam one end of each brass tube into a raw potato. The resulting plug keeps glue out of the tube. Apply cyanoacrylate glue to the inside of one end of the blank and quickly push the brass tube into this end, until it is flush with the opposite end. The shorter blank will leave about ¼" of the brass exposed. This glue dries very quickly, so only apply glue to one blank at a time during the process. Once all the body and cap blanks have brass tubes inserted, remove any excess glue and use a skinny dowel to pop out your potato plugs.

Turning, Sanding and Finishing

Now you're just about ready to move onto the lathe. You'll need a lathe chuck with a Morse taper and a universal mandrel. Mount your bushing parts and first set of blanks on the mandrel (see the *Elevation Drawing* on page 111), finger-tighten the nut and snug up the tail stock.

Get those safety glasses on, lose the long sleeve shirt and choose your weapons. I use a set of Sorby micro tools that work great for small turnings like this. Start with an 8 mm roughing gouge and wrap up with a 6 mm spindle gouge. The Montblanc style features an elliptical taper on both the cap and the body. Keep this taper in mind as you turn the blanks down almost even with the diameter of the bushings (see *Figure 2*), and then sand through the grits until you're flush with the bushings (see *Figure 3*). Apply finish when the blanks are polished smooth; padding lacquer is an easy-to-use option that produces great results. Once you get the hang of the process, you'll be able to mount, turn, sand, finish and assemble a pen in about half an hour.

QuickTip

Color Your Edges to Sharpen Turning Tools

One way to develop a razor edge on turning tools is to first use a permanent felt-tipped pen to coat the entire cutting edge. This way, you can see how you are progressing while you grind and hone the edge. It's an old machinst's trick that really works.

Final Assembly—Parting Thoughts

Before you start fitting the two halves of your pens together, take time to align the grain. Pens look most attractive if the grain lines up when the pen is capped.

Moderate force is required to press-fit the pen parts and blanks together; once you do, it's just about impossible to separate them. Be sure to develop a system to keep your parts in order. Start with the pen body and press-fit the tip into position, as shown in the *photo* below. Loosen up the clamp and do the same with the unthreaded stem of the twist holder at the other end. Slide the spring onto the ink refill and insert both through the twist holder. Complete the body by screwing the twist mechanism onto the twist holder.

Now switch to the cap assembly and insert the stem of the finial cap through the finial ring and then through the clip's ring. Follow the same clamping procedure to press these pieces onto the cap. Slide the center ring over the exposed brass tube, flush to the shoulder of the pen cap. If the center ring is a little loose, you can carefully glue it into place with a drop or two of cyanoacrylate glue.

Finally, slide the cap over the twist mechanism and sign some lucky relative's card—you're done, at least for the moment. How many more pens you've got to go depends on how many happy relatives you're aiming for this coming holiday season. Have fun!

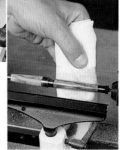

Figure 3: *Sand and apply finish working from the back of the turning. If you're careful, you can accomplish this without removing the tool rest, which speeds things up.*

Once you complete a production run, *a simple padded clamp brings the pens together in short order. Just stay organized during this process.*

by J. Petrovich

BOMBÉ BOX

Carving shapes with your table saw, building a low-tech slot mortiser and cutting finger joints…from a techniques standpoint, this project will give you a woodworking workout. When you're finished, you'll end up with a shapely accent piece with three inner trays for storing jewelry. It's a great project for building skills without breaking the project budget.

The idea for this little chest grew out of my personal fondness for the bombé shape and a pedagogical crisis. About a dozen years ago, I was teaching an advanced cabinetmaking class at a community college. Traditionally, my third-year students were required to produce a final project during the last month of class. On the first day of their last month, the shop lost all of its three-phase power, save to three table saws. The maintenance crew at the college was less than hopeful for a speedy repair.

In a moment born of desperation and inspiration, and tempered with a large dose of blindingly good luck, I was able to lay out the requirements for a new final project that the class dubbed "table saw composition." This small jewelry box was the result.

Reviewing the Key Points for Some "Gee-Whiz" Machining

While cutting the curve of the box at the table saw is the "gee-whiz" part of this project, the corner joinery must come first. The choice of finger joints for this box was part aesthetic and part engineering. Aesthetically, the visibility of the

joints helps to emphasize the "S" curve of the chest. From an engineering standpoint, the box is stronger than it really needs to be. Because the sides of the box rise above the front and back, the top of the sides need to end in a finger. I used 5/4 stock with a dado blade stacked to cut ½" joints. Starting with a space at the bottom of the sides on the 5"-wide stock produces a joint

layout that ends with a finger on top. See the Elevation Drawings, next page, for more details.

Begin by selecting your stock for the front, back and sides (pieces 1 and 2) and cutting them to the dimensions found in the *Material List* on page 116. Then grab your dado set and make those finger joints. If you are new to making them, the *sidebar* on page 118

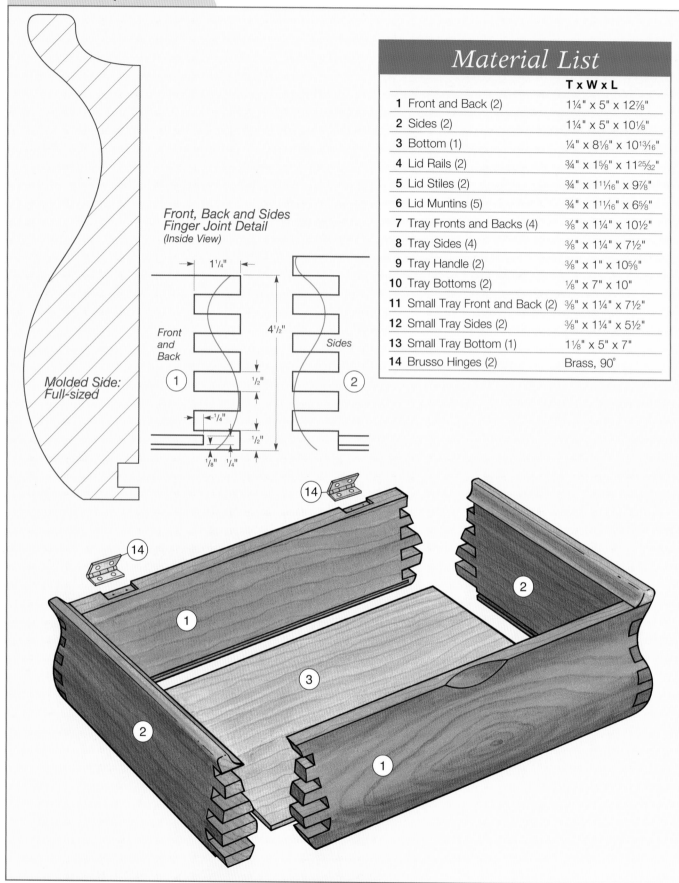

Front, Back and Sides
Finger Joint Detail
(Inside View)

Molded Side:
Full-sized

1¼"

4½"

½"

¼"

½"

⅛" ¼"

Front
and
Back

Sides

Material List

	T x W x L
1 Front and Back (2)	1¼" x 5" x 12⅞"
2 Sides (2)	1¼" x 5" x 10⅛"
3 Bottom (1)	¼" x 8⅛" x 10¹³⁄₁₆"
4 Lid Rails (2)	¾" x 1⅝" x 11²⁵⁄₃₂"
5 Lid Stiles (2)	¾" x 1¹¹⁄₁₆" x 9⅞"
6 Lid Muntins (5)	¾" x 1¹¹⁄₁₆" x 6⅝"
7 Tray Fronts and Backs (4)	⅜" x 1¼" x 10½"
8 Tray Sides (4)	⅜" x 1¼" x 7½"
9 Tray Handle (2)	⅜" x 1" x 10⅝"
10 Tray Bottoms (2)	⅛" x 7" x 10"
11 Small Tray Front and Back (2)	⅜" x 1¼" x 7½"
12 Small Tray Sides (2)	⅜" x 1¼" x 5½"
13 Small Tray Bottom (1)	1⅛" x 5" x 7"
14 Brusso Hinges (2)	Brass, 90°

Lid Stile and Muntin Tenon Detail
(Top and Edge View)

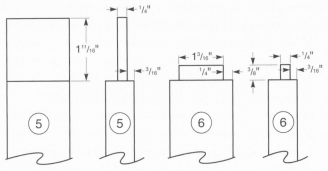

Lid Rail

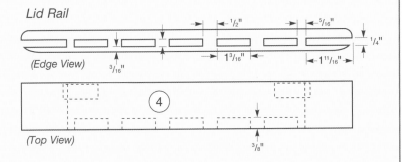

(Edge View)

④

(Top View)

Bombé Jewelry Box Machining Details
(Front View)

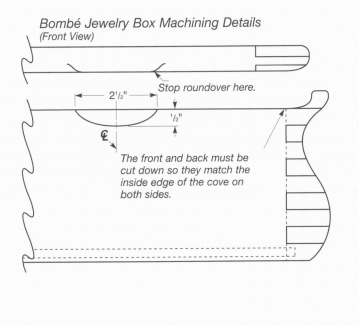

Stop roundover here.

2½"

½"

℄

The front and back must be cut down so they match the inside edge of the cove on both sides.

will get you going in the right direction. Whether novice or pro, testing your setup with scrap wood is more than just being prudent. Once the sides, front and back are correctly machined and fitting well, you can move on to the fun stuff. That said, cut the corner joints.

Shaping the Sides

Shaping wood on the table saw requires a bit of patience and a little imagination. Patience, to make the repeated cuts required to safely mold wood in this fashion…and imagination to forecast the shape of the arc that the blade will cut. With this modified ripping process, instead of feeding the wood directly into the blade, the wood is fed in at an angle controlled by auxiliary fences.

To start, sketch the desired profile onto an end of one of the boards. Use this profile to help align the auxiliary fences to the blade. From the outfeed side of the saw and with the blade raised, sight along the table at the arc of the blade and think of it as a cutting profile (see the *tint box* on page 121 for photos that will help). You are after the angle that best matches the profile sketched on the end of the board.

Once the angle is "sighted-in," securely clamp the two auxiliary fences to the saw table. The resulting "chute" should fit snugly against the box sides, but it should not restrict their movement across the saw table.

Because the ends of the box sides need to be shaped to the same profile, shape the box as a unit. If the box's joinery is tight, you can shape the box without clamping up the parts. If the fingers and slots are a bit loose; however, a clamp or two will secure the joints.

Now set the height of the blade at a little over ¹⁄₃₂" above the table. If you feel uncertain about your angle and how it will look as you mold the sides, use a test piece. When you're satisfied with the test piece, shape the box. Make each pass or cut about ¹⁄₁₆" deep and use a slow feed rate. Don't be too concerned about burning the wood with this slow rate of feed. Continue making passes on all four sides of the box until you have formed the desired profile. To remove the material at the bottom of the profile,

Table-Sawn Finger Joints:
A Quick Refresher Course

Finger joints (also called box joints) are simple to make, nice to look at and very durable. Use a jig (shop-made or manufactured) to form the fingers and slots. The author chose to make a one-time jig using a backer board mounted to his miter gauge. To make your own, cut an opening (using the dado setup prepared for the finger joints) to accept a registration pin in the backer board. In this case, the pin should be ½" X ½" X 1¾". Glue the pin into the opening and reposition the backer board so the pin is moved to the right of the dado head, twice the width of your dado cut (in this case 1"). Now secure the jig to your miter gauge. This may take some tweaking to get exactly right. You are now ready to make your finger joints. Using scrap lumber to make test cuts is the next step in successfully completing the task. A handy trick for making the sides of this box is to clamp one of the completed front or back pieces onto the registration pin and then use it to help register the first cut on the end pieces.

Using a registration pin mounted in a backer board, the author made a "one-time" finger joint jig for his table saw.

use the table saw with the blade tilted. Finish shaping and smoothing the sides with a hand plane and scraper for the convex portions and coarse sandpaper with a shaped sanding block for the convex areas. Final sanding includes more of the same…a lot more!

Next, let in the bottom (piece 3) of the box. I used a ³⁄₁₆" straight bit in a router table and made two cuts per groove just to be sure the groove could properly accommodate undersized plywood. On the box back and front, this is a blind operation (you can't observe the bit cutting the wood directly). Start and stop the cut in exactly the same place by marking the router table or fence with start and stop marks to correspond with marks on the front and back. On the sides, it is a simple through-groove.

Making the Lid

To complement the bombé sides of the box, the lid is a lightly arched frame-and-panel construction. The shape helps to embellish the curve of the sides. Make the lid rails, stiles and muntins (pieces 4, 5 and 6), ripping

them from ⁶⁄₄ plain-sawn stock. If your stock shows quartersawn grain, orient the wood so the lid parts show this figure on the top and bottom surfaces.

The lid's open mortise and tenon joints are easily made at the table saw with a shop-made tenoning jig. The approach is decidedly "low-tech." First attach a tall, hardwood board to the table saw's rip fence (see left *photo*, next page). It should be carefully dressed, flat and true, because this auxiliary rip fence facing will define the path of your stock through the blade. Take another scrap of wood and rest it on top of the auxiliary fence; this piece forms a sliding runner. Set the height of the blade to the width of the frame member, allowing ¹⁄₃₂" extra.

Next, lay out the mortises and tenons as shown in the *Elevation Drawings* on page 117. After adjusting the fence to cut the first pass on the stiles' open mortises, take a piece of scrap wood of the same dimension and rest it on its end against the auxiliary fence and clamp it to the runner. By pushing down on the runner with your right hand and pushing the test piece

See *Elevation Drawings* on page 117.

QuickTip

Foam Board Sanding Block

You'll definitely appreciate having a curve-bottomed sanding block to refine the outer faces of this project. A quick and cheap solution is to use a scrap of rigid foam insulation, and mold it to the correct profile with a rasp. First cut the project parts to shape on the table saw, then make the sanding block based on your final part shapes. It takes just a few minutes of filing to create a mirror opposite of the project's curve, and the foam board will stand up well to hand-sanding. Just wrap it with a piece of sandpaper and you're ready to go to work.

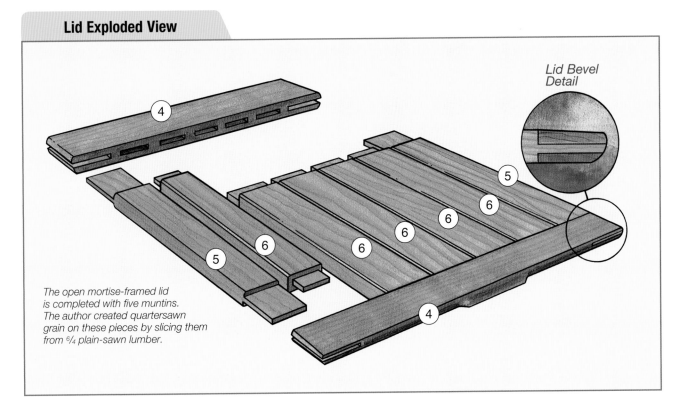

*Lid Bevel
Detail*

*The open mortise-framed lid
is completed with five muntins.
The author created quartersawn
grain on these pieces by slicing them
from 6/4 plain-sawn lumber.*

against the fence with your left, you are ready to guide the test piece through the saw blade. Practice the movement a few times to become comfortable with it. Once the movement is smooth and steady, go ahead and make the other cuts. When you work with the actual pieces, remember to flip the ends

for the cut on the opposite end so the same face is riding against the auxiliary fence. After all four cuts have been made, adjust the fence to make the remaining cuts.

With the open mortises cut to size, you're ready to cut the rails' tenons. Again, a test cut or two saves time and

wood. Line up the blade with the edge of one of the mortise pieces—as though you wanted to enlarge the mortise by the width of the saw blade. Using the clamp and runner, make a test cut on scrap lumber. If the cut is satisfactory, make the four cuts necessary to establish the first side of all four tenons.

Here's a low-tech jig *for making the open mortises on your box lid.
It employs a runner board that slides on top of the rip fence facing.*

Using a stand-off block *to register the cut and a miter gauge
for safety, machine tenons onto the ends of the muntins.*

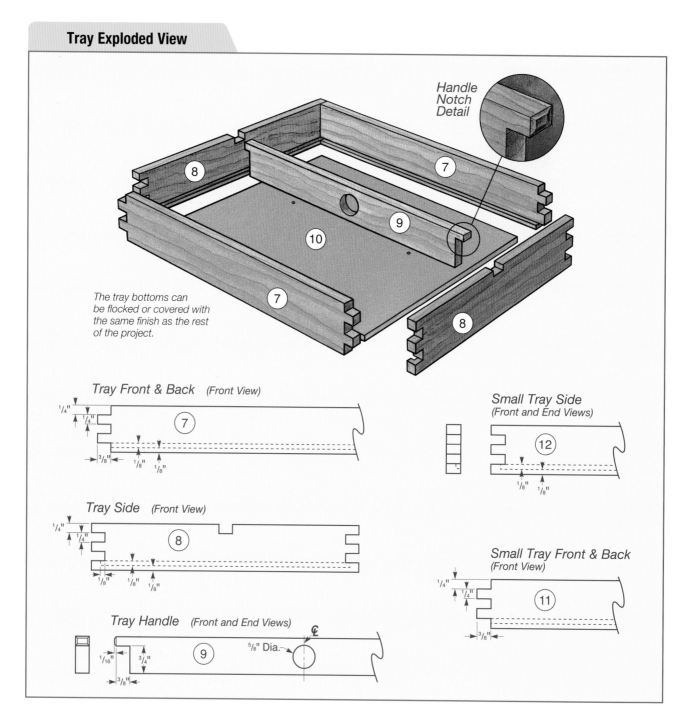

Handle
Notch
Detail

The tray bottoms can
be flocked or covered with
the same finish as the rest
of the project.

Tray Front & Back *(Front View)*

1/4" 1/4" (7) 3/8" 1/8" 1/8"

Tray Side *(Front View)*

1/4" 1/4" (8) 1/8" 1/8" 1/8"

Tray Handle *(Front and End Views)*

1/16" 3/4" (9) 5/8" Dia. ₵ 3/8"

Small Tray Side
(Front and End Views)

(12) 1/8" 1/8"

Small Tray Front & Back
(Front View)

1/4" 1/4" (11) 3/8"

Repeat the procedure for the second cut on the opposite side of the tenon. To establish the clean straight line at the tenon shoulder, use your miter gauge and a standoff block clamped to the rip fence to register the shoulder location. Remember that the depth of cut necessary to remove a tab from one side is less than the other.

Cutting the tenons on the individual muntins requires the same process. The mortises for the muntins are cut at the drill press with a Forstner bit and cleaned up with a mortising chisel. Dry-fit the pieces, and use your table saw to establish the slope on the front and back of the lid. This means running the lid on edge through the blade.

Routing for the Lid

Since the lid of the box is oversized, both the lid and the box will require routing. For the lid, which should be routed as a unit, use a roundover bit. The top of the box sides require a cove, which is done with the box disassembled. Next, cut down the front and back so they meet the cove cut

Creating the classic bombé curve on this box begins on the table saw. The author used auxiliary fences placed at an angle to the saw blade to guide this process. The box is machined while dry-fitted together so the corners of the box are shaped along with the faces of the sides, front and back. The key to this process is to remove only a small amount of material with each pass over the blade.

Two views of the same cut, *from overhead and "looking down the chute" (inset). Determine the fence angle using the "line of sight" method.*

Once you've established your blade angle *relative to the clamped fences, raise the blade ¹⁄₁₆" with each pass. Continue until you have the desired curve on all faces.*

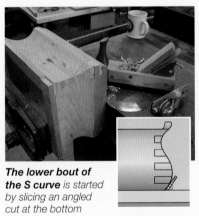

The lower bout of the S curve *is started by slicing an angled cut at the bottom edge of the box, as shown in the inset.*

Finish the box's elegant shape *by planing, scraping and sanding.*

The author used a wide collection of hand tools *and sanding blocks to bring the bombé box to its final shape.*

perfectly (see the *Elevation Drawings*). This creates a recessed area that the lid will fit into, adding subtly to the box's overall curvy shape.

Letting in the small access cove, shaping the front edge of the box and easing the edges comes next. The access cove is done with a cove bit and the lid with a roundover. Note that the bottom edge radius stops at the edge of the access cove, starts again at the other edge and continues. It's a small feature, but it lends a sense of organization.

Now you can assemble the box with glue and clamps, taking plenty of care to be sure it's square.

Building Three Trays

If your project will be used as a jewelry box, there are three trays to construct to organize various jewels, gems and trinkets. Since you're now a pro at making box joints, use them to connect the tray frames. The trays are mostly made out of ¼"-thick hardwood and can be produced in short order. Cut the parts (pieces 7 through 13) to size. Set up another finger joint jig and test-fit the corners on some scrap. Use this setup to form the handle notches, too. See the *drawings* on the preceding page for all your machining details. Rout in the groove for the bottoms and you are almost done. Drill a hole in the handles of the large trays to make them easier to grip.

Mounting the lid requires some sturdy hardware. Brusso makes a sturdy but discreet 90° stop hinge (pieces 14) that is easy to install and perfect for this project.

Finishing Up

With all the construction behind you, it's time for finishing. Sand everything to 220 or finer grit. Use a quality oil or sprayed-lacquer finish, carefully rubbing it down with steel wool between coats. We were more interested in producing a grain-enhancing sheen than a shine. Then top off the finish with a coat of paste wax and a good buffing.

There are a couple options for finishing the trays. You can apply the same finish here as you're using for the rest of the project. Or, skip the finish on the tray compartments and spray them with colored flocking instead for a classic jewelry box detail.

by Rick White

CLASSIC CHESSBOARD

This heirloom chessboard was inspired by a James Krenov design that ingeniously tackles the wood movement problems inherent in using two wood species. If you're a chess junkie as well as a woodworker, you'll be smiling from the first cut through the last check mate with this clever project.

In 1972, the world was transfixed by two men playing a board game for the unprecedented prize of $250,000. Bobby Fischer, who at the tender age of 14 had won the U.S. Chess Open, was locked in combat with the venerable Soviet, Boris Spassky. That event brought chess to main street America, accounting for a massive surge in this ancient game's popularity. Fischer was the last American to become international grand master, and even though he forfeited his title a couple of years later, enthusiasm for the game has remained high.

If you're a fan of combining two great hobbies—woodworking and chess—here's a perfect project to satiate your leisure pursuits. Although the design looks complicated, it's primarily made up of simple moldings. And the clean lines, reminiscent of Art Deco pieces, actually hold two delightful secrets: For one, a pair of almost invisible drawers stow the chesspieces. The other surprise is a more subtle design theme that we'll reveal at the end of this article (if you haven't already guessed by then).

Making the Squares

Chess players are known for their patience, an attribute that will come in handy when making the squares of the chessboard grid (pieces 1 and 2). Begin this task by ripping two 60"-long pieces of stock, one in a dark species—I opted for wenge—and the other light colored, such as the maple used here for contrast. A simple table saw jig equipped with a toggle clamp makes

Figure 1: *This crosscutting jig rides in the miter gauge slots of your table saw and is equipped with a toggle clamp to keep your fingers out of harm's way.*

crosscutting 64 identical 1⅝" squares safe and easy *(see Figure 1)*.

To accentuate the space between the assembled squares, their edges are slightly chamfered on the top and bottom. The only safe way to do this on such small pieces is on a router table with a 45° chamfering bit. You may have to clamp a thin auxiliary fence to your router table's fence if the opening in the machine's fence is large enough to engulf one of these small pieces. Chamfer each square on the top and bottom faces so that, when you assemble the grid, you can choose the best face for the top.

Addressing Wood Movement

We all know how wood expands and contracts with the seasons, so you can imagine my concern when I started discussing the chessboard for this project, which features two distinct species. To avert a potential disaster, I employed a technique I came across in a book written by renowned woodworker James Krenov: A series of dowel pins (pieces 3) are used to assemble the grid.

Figure 2: *A simple jig facilitates drilling a series of accurate holes for the dowels that hold the chessboard grid together.*

A drill press is essential when drilling for these pins, because if the holes (see the *Technical Drawings* for locations and depths) are the slightest bit off, the assembled grid will not be flat. A simple jig (see *Figure 2*) clamped to the drill press table lines up each square with the bit. As you drill, make sure there is no chip build-up in the jig, or the holes will be off center. The squares along the outside edges are drilled three times, while those on the corners are only drilled twice (on adjacent edges). The squares in the field, however, receive four holes each.

Making the Grid Assembly

Dry-fit the grid of squares, picking the best faces for the top. Put a light (maple) square in the right-hand corner closest to each player. Run the grain of both species in the same direction to help with wood movement problems. You'll notice that the 1"-long grid pins are too short to bottom-out in the holes. This is intentional—it allows the wood to move and the spacers to set the correct gap.

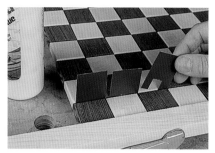

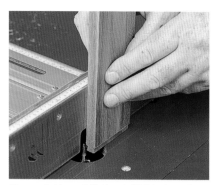

Figure 3: *Use several plastic-laminate spacers to assure proper alignment when gluing up the squares of the chessboard. Cut a recess in each spacer to fit around the grid pin dowels.*

Figure 4: *Use a 14° dovetail bit to form the joints on the drawer sides, fronts and backs.*

Figure 5: *The drawer dividers are ripped and jointed to the correct width and thickness, then held together by half-lap joints.*

Make any corrections during your dry fit because, with the chamfer on the squares, you won't be able to sand the grid flat later. Use a straightedge and several plastic laminate spacers (see *Figure 3*) to keep everything in line and spaced perfectly, then glue up eight strips of alternating dark and light squares. When they're dry, glue the strips together to form the complete chessboard grid.

Milling the Corners

The corners (pieces 4) of the chessboard case are milled from one 12"-long piece of 1¾" square stock that receives decorative fluting and chamfering on two adjacent faces (see *Technical Drawings* for dimensions and locations). These chamfers are the same as those you already milled on the grid squares, so return to the router table to create them. The flutes are also cut on the router table, using a ⅛" core box or round nose bit. Mark the centerline of each cut (see *Technical Drawings*) on the end of a piece of 1¾" square scrap, then set your fence and make practice passes on the scrap for each flute before milling the workpiece.

The inside is formed on the table saw, using a ¼"-wide dado set. To reveal the stepped profile of this piece, make several passes for both safety and quality reasons. Wrap up by cutting the corners to length.

Building the Case Sides and Drawer Fronts

The case sides (pieces 5) and drawer fronts (pieces 11) are made from the same molding. To make this molding, rip your stock to 2⅞", then head for the router table. Use your core box bit to cut the two flutes in the molding, then crosscut the molding to the correct lengths and rip the drawer fronts to 2¾". Finally, go back to the table saw dado set to cut the rabbets on the ends of the sides (see the *Technical Drawings*).

On to Drawer Slides and Supports

The outside edges of the two drawers are quite a distance from the case sides. This presents a problem in that there is nowhere to attach the drawer slides (pieces 6). The solution is to attach supports (pieces 7) to the insides of the corner moldings. Each of these boards features a groove into which the drawer slide is inserted, and both boards can be made at the same time as a single piece of molding.

Making this molding is relatively uncomplicated. Simply cut the stock to the dimensions given in the *Material List*, then create the grooves and rabbets (see *Technical Drawings* for dimensions and locations) on the table saw using the dado set. Mill the drawer slides, then dry-fit the corners, sides, drawer slide supports and drawer slides together.

If everything fits properly, glue and screw the case together (see *Technical Drawings* for screw locations). You probably won't need clamps to hold this small assembly together when assembling the parts.

Building the Grid Frame

The frame that surrounds the chessboard grid is not only decorative, but also functional. This frame is used to attach the grid to the case.

Start making the frames (pieces 8) by ripping stock to size, then set your table saw blade to 45° to create the chamfer on the outside edge (see *Technical Drawings*). Switch to the dado set to cut the two rabbets on the inside edge, then return to your router table to mill the slight chamfer above the top rabbets (also shown on the *Technical Drawings*). Cut the frames to length at a 45° angle using your table saw's miter gauge, then glue up the frame (make sure it is square by measuring both diagonals and adjusting clamps until the measurements are equal).

The two frame braces (pieces 9) and the drawer catch support (piece 10) are ripped to size, then small rabbets are cut on their ends with the dado set (see *Technical Drawings*). Drill pilot holes and countersink for ½" screws, then glue and screw the braces and catch support in place. When the glue is dry, drill four ⅜"-diameter counterbores for 2½" screws in

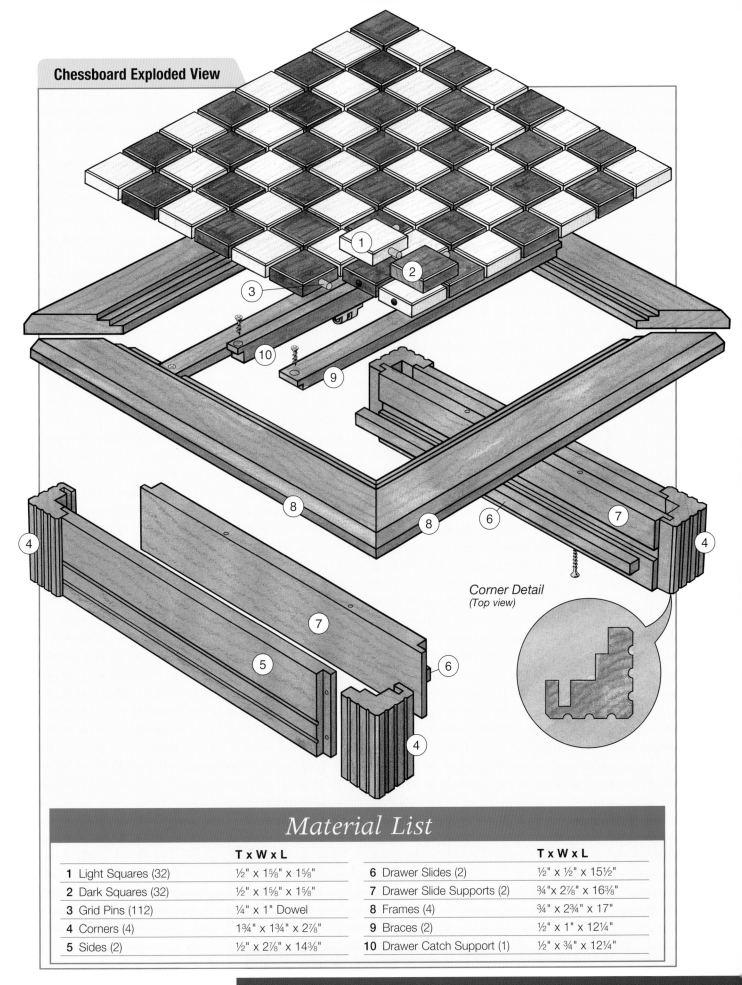

Chessboard Exploded View

Corner Detail
(Top view)

Material List

	T x W x L			T x W x L
1 Light Squares (32)	½" x 1⅝" x 1⅝"		**6** Drawer Slides (2)	½" x ½" x 15½"
2 Dark Squares (32)	½" x 1⅝" x 1⅝"		**7** Drawer Slide Supports (2)	¾" x 2⅞" x 16⅜"
3 Grid Pins (112)	¼" x 1" Dowel		**8** Frames (4)	¾" x 2¾" x 17"
4 Corners (4)	1¾" x 1¾" x 2⅞"		**9** Braces (2)	½" x 1" x 12¼"
5 Sides (2)	½" x 2⅞" x 14⅜"		**10** Drawer Catch Support (1)	½" x ¾" x 12¼"

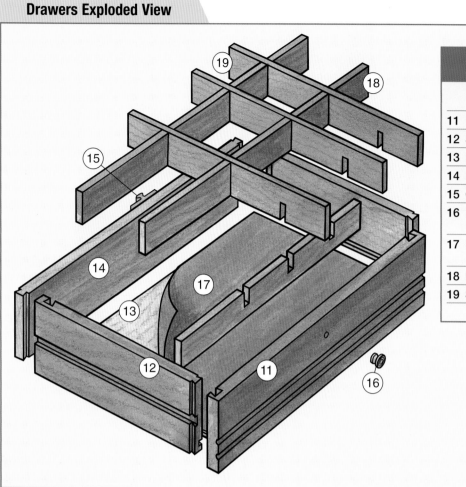

Material List

		T x W x L
11	Fronts (2)	½" x 2¾" x 13¼"
12	Sides (4)	½" x 2¾" x 7⅞"
13	Bottoms (2)	¼" x 12³⁄₁₆" x 7⅝"
14	Backs (2)	½" x 2¼" x 12¼"
15	Catches (2)	¼" x 1¾" Brass
16	Pulls (2)	⅜" Dia. Antique Brass
17	Liner (1)	12" x 24" Green Felt
18	Long Dividers (6)	¼" x 1" x 11⅝"
19	Short Dividers (6)	¼" x 1" x 6¾"

the bottom of the drawer slide supports (see *Technical Drawings*), then screw the side assemblies to the frame.

Constructing the Drawers

You've already created the drawer fronts, so now you can cut the rest of the drawer parts to size. Install the dado set on your table saw to make the drawer slide grooves (see *Technical Drawings*) in the outside faces of the drawer sides (pieces 12). Now cut a ¼"-wide groove on each inside face of the sides and on the drawer fronts for the drawer bottoms (pieces 13). The backs (pieces 14), receive no grooves for the bottoms. Switch to your router table to make the dovetail joints that hold the fronts and backs to the sides, using a 14° bit *(see Figure 4)*. Before using the dovetail bit, however, use a straight bit to remove most of the

waste—it prevents overstressing the dovetail cutter. And test your setups on scrap before milling the workpieces.

You can now glue and clamp the drawers together. The drawer bottoms just slide into their grooves and are then tacked to the drawer back with a couple of ¾" brads, making them replaceable if necessary.

Finishing Up

After sanding the entire project thoroughly, apply three coats of Danish oil. When your finish is dry, install the drawer catches (pieces 15) and pulls (pieces 16). The catches are simply screwed in place (see the *Technical Drawings* for locations), though you will need to drill holes for the pulls (these are also shown on the *Technical Drawings*). To make the drawers glide smoothly, apply friction-fighting Nylo-Tape in the

four drawer slide grooves. Or, apply some paste wax to the bottom edges of the drawer sides.

The inside of each drawer is lined with self-adhesive felt (piece 17), that comes in a sheet. This is simply cut to size and stuck in place. Apply the felt just to the bottom of each drawer. To divide the drawers into individual storage compartments, you can make simple dividers (pieces 18 and 19) spaced out to fit your particular chess pieces. Use your dado set to create half-lap joints where the pieces cross, as shown in *Figure 5*.

Finally, I promised earlier to reveal a second secret: If you look at the completed project, the overall impression is of a boxing ring, complete with ropes and padded corners. So find a worthy opponent and get ready for round one.

Technical Drawings

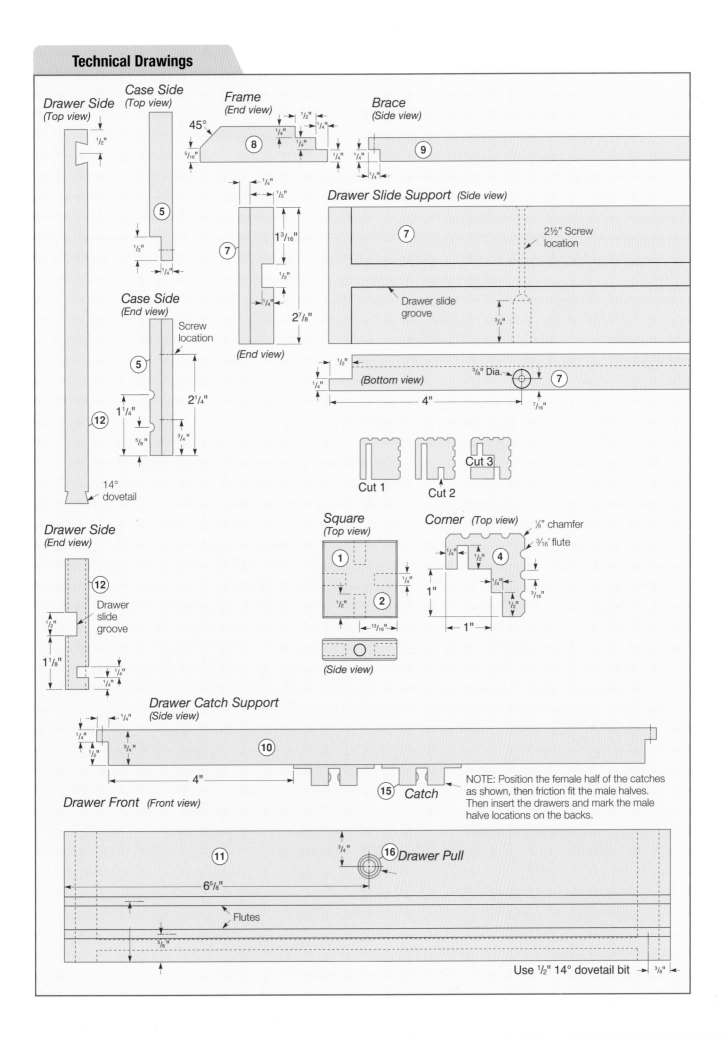

Drawer Side (Top view)
½"

Case Side (Top view)
5
45°
½"
¼"
¼"
5/16"

Frame (End view)
8
¼"
½"
¼"
¼"

Brace (Side view)
9
¼"

¼"
½"
7
1 3/16"
½"
¼"
2 7/8"
(End view)

Drawer Slide Support (Side view)
7
2½" Screw location
Drawer slide groove
¾"

½"
¼"
(Bottom view)
3/8" Dia.
7
4"
7/16"

Case Side (End view)
5
12
Screw location
2¼"
1¼"
5/8"
¾"
14° dovetail

Cut 1
Cut 2
Cut 3

Drawer Side (End view)
12
Drawer slide groove
½"
¼"
¼"
1 1/8"

Square (Top view)
1
2
¼"
13/16"
½"
(Side view)

Corner (Top view)
⅛" chamfer
3/16" flute
4
¼"
½"
1"
¼"
3/16"
1"
½"

Drawer Catch Support (Side view)
10
¼"
¼"
¾"
½"
4"
15 Catch

NOTE: Position the female half of the catches as shown, then friction fit the male halves. Then insert the drawers and mark the male halve locations on the backs.

Drawer Front (Front view)
11
¾"
16 Drawer Pull
6 5/8"
Flutes
5/8"

Use ½" 14° dovetail bit
3/8"

by Marty Lubbers

WALNUT BURL HUMIDOR

A basic exercise in veneering, this attractive 20-cigar humidor with Spanish cedar lining can easily be converted to a stationery holder or jewelry box by simply omitting the lining. We used walnut burl to give the outer panels a rich, warm appearance as well as to provide a continuous grain pattern all around the box.

Fine cigars are built up in layers, each one formed by tightly hand-wrapping leaves one upon the next until perfection is achieved. This humidor is also defined by layers. On the outside is a skin of fine veneers, while the core is a box of ½"-thick solid mahogany. The inside layer of Spanish cedar may be omitted if the box is to serve as a home for stationery, photographs, jewelry or other treasures. But whatever its ultimate role, the best part of building it is the wonderful veneering workout it offers, on a scale that even beginning woodworkers will find welcoming.

Making the Mitered Sides
I chose Honduras mahogany for the sides of this humidor: it's readily available, comes in wide boards, and is both flat and stable enough to form a perfect base for veneer. Begin construction on the sides by ripping a 36"-long board to 5⅛" wide, then set it face-up on your workbench.

The easiest way to ensure a continuous pattern in the veneer on the outside of the humidor is to apply a single piece to the board you just cut, then crosscut it to length after the glue dries: this process will yield the front, back and both sides (pieces 1, 2 and 3). Working with burl veneer (piece 4) can be tricky, especially if it's your first time around. To ensure success, follow the step-by-step instructions (see page 135) for treating and clamping veneer.

When the glue is dry, crosscut the four pieces to length on your table saw according to the dimensions given in the *Material List* on the next page (after first verifying that your miter gauge is indeed set at exactly 90°). Then set the blade to 45° and carefully miter the ends (see *drawings* on pages 136 and 137), without shortening the pieces.

Reset the saw to create the groove for the bottom (also shown on the *Technical Drawings*), cutting it in two passes. Then stay at the table saw to cut the bottom (piece 5) to size. This is also a good time to cut the top (piece 6) to size.

Use clear plastic strapping tape (the 2" wide variety from 3M works best) to attach the ends to the front, as shown in *Figure 1*. Then tape one end to the back, preserving the grain pattern across all three joints as you work. Apply glue to the miters, insert the bottom (don't glue it in), assemble the box and tape up the last joint. Stretch more tape, as tight as you can, across the joints to draw them snug, then make sure the assembly is square before setting it aside to dry.

Veneering the Top

The best way to successfully veneer a pattern is to cut all the parts to size, then tape them together before gluing them onto a substrate (in this case, the mahogany core of the top). Begin by trimming the center (piece 7) to size, then add the mitered ebonized band (piece 8) and the ash matting (piece 9). See the *Top, Veneer Pattern Drawing* on page 136 for layout details.

Center the taped-up assembly on the mahogany top and glue it in place. At the same time, apply veneer (piece 10) to the bottom face of the top, to create a balanced panel that will better resist warping. A lower grade veneer is fine here—it will be ebonized anyway.

Material List

		T x W x L
1	Front (1)	½" x 5⅛" x 11"
2	Back (1)	½" x 5⅛" x 11"
3	Sides (2)	½" x 5⅛" x 5⅞"
4	Case Veneer (1)	5½" x 36"*
5	Bottom (1)	¼" x 5⁵⁄₁₆" x 10⁷⁄₁₆"
6	Top (1)	½" x 6⅞" x 12"
7	Top's Center Veneer (1)	3⅞" x 9⅛"
8	Top's Ebonized Banding (1)	¹⁄₃₂" x ⅛" x 27"
9	Top's Ash Matting (1)	1⅜" x 37¾"
10	Top's Underside Veneer (1)	6⅞" x 12"
11	Bottom Bullnose Molding (1)	¼" x ½" x 37"
12	Feet (4)	⅝" x 2" x 2"
13	Feet Nails (8)	1" Brads
14	Hinges (2)	Brass, Quadrant Style
15	Cedar Liner - Top (1)	¼" x 4⅞" x 10"
16	Cedar Liner - Bottom (1)	¼" x 4⅞" x 10"
17	Cedar Liner - Front & Back (2)	¼" x 4⅜" x 10"
18	Cedar Liner - Sides (2)	¼" x 4⅜" x 4⅞"
19	Hygrometer (1)	50mm Solid Brass
20	Hygrometer Ring (1)	Brass Mounting Ring
21	Humidifier (1)	The Tube™

* Note: This veneer is listed slightly oversize to allow for trimming.

Figure 1: *Clear strapping tape is the perfect clamping solution when it comes to applying equal pressure to mitered box sides.*

QuickTip

Smoother Shifting on Your Table Saw

Table saw blade height and tilt adjustments will be easier to make if you apply the correct lubricant to the gears. What's the best lubricant to use? If the gears on your saw are already stiff, chances are what's currently there is petroleum-based grease. Use a spray-on automotive grease remover and bristle brush to remove it (and the accumulated sawdust crud that it collects), and replace it with silicone-based spray or a dab of paste furniture wax. Either of these options will repel sawdust and wood pitch, which will keep those gears meshing smoothly.

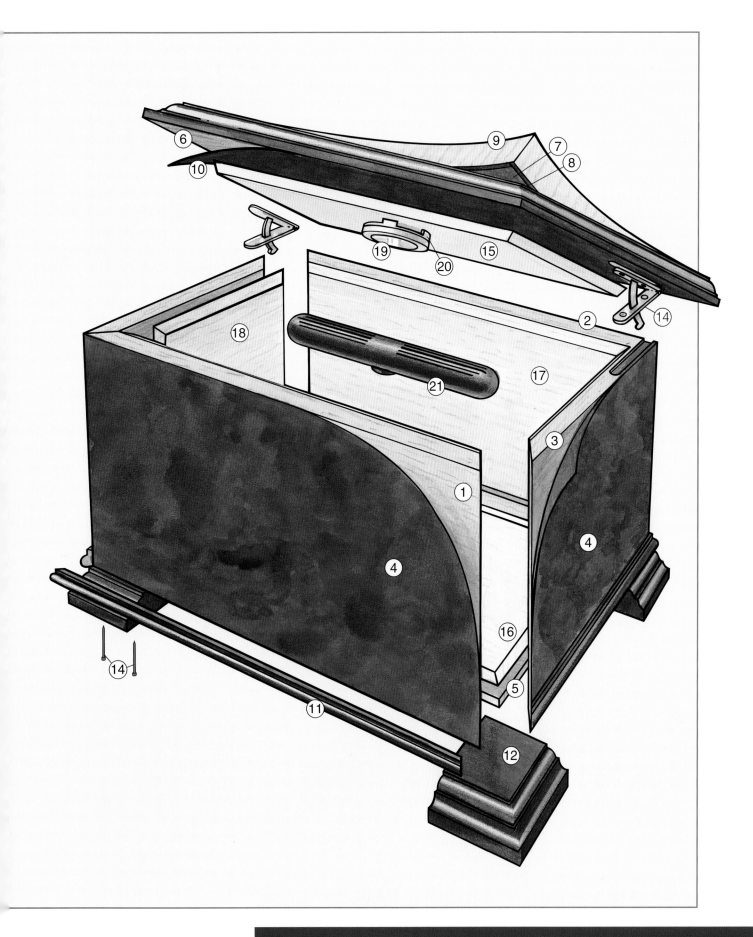

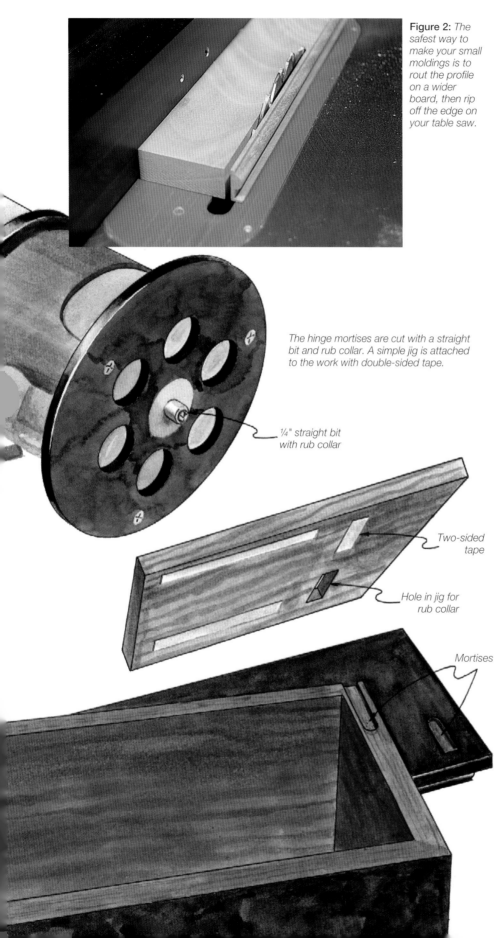

Figure 2: *The safest way to make your small moldings is to rout the profile on a wider board, then rip off the edge on your table saw.*

The hinge mortises are cut with a straight bit and rub collar. A simple jig is attached to the work with double-sided tape.

¼" straight bit with rub collar

Two-sided tape

Hole in jig for rub collar

Mortises

Making the Moldings on a Router Table

At this point, turn your attention to the router table to create some interesting details for this piece. You'll start with a bullnose molding (piece 11) for the bottom edges of the sides and then change bits to cut the edges of the top and feet (pieces 12).

The bottom bullnose is cut with a ³⁄₁₆"-radius half-round bit. If you already own a ¼" radius bit that creates a ½"-wide bullnose, this will also work but it might not look as elegant. For safety reasons, form the profile on the edge of a wider board, then rip off the molding on the table saw, as shown in *Figure 2*.

The edge profiles on the top and feet are cut in a two-step process. Begin by milling a cove with the workpiece standing on edge and using a ½"-diameter cove bit chucked in the router (see *Figure 3, inset*). Now move the fence, install a roundover bit with the guide bearing removed, and run the piece through again to make the second cut (see *Full-Size Section View* on page 137 for dimensions). As with the bullnose molding earlier, it's safer if you machine the feet on a larger piece of stock and cut them to size later.

Ebonizing...A Little Black Magic

Before installing the feet, bottom trim and box top, all three are ebonized. To do this, sand the top thoroughly, then apply masking tape to your glued-up veneer pattern. Apply a primer and two coats of matte black paint using an over-the-counter aerosol can. Sand between coats with 400-grit paper to remove any dust nibs.

Glue and clamp the bottom trim in place, then install the feet with glue and two small brads (pieces 13) in each. Rout mortises for the hinges (pieces 14) in both the bottom face of the top and the top edge of the box, according to the dimensions given in the *Technical Drawings* (you should double-check these locations as your stock may not match ours exactly in all dimensions). The easiest way to create the mortises is with the simple jig (see *Hinge Mortising Jig* on page 136). This is just a template for a standard guide bushing (also called a rub collar) that guides a ¼" straight bit. Since this is a rather tricky cut, I recommend that you practice with scrap stock before milling the actual workpiece.

After installing the hinges, remove them and sand the project one last time before applying a semi-gloss finish: sprayed lacquer or brushed polyurethane are both good options. When the finish dries, reinstall the hinges and turn your attention to the Spanish cedar inserts.

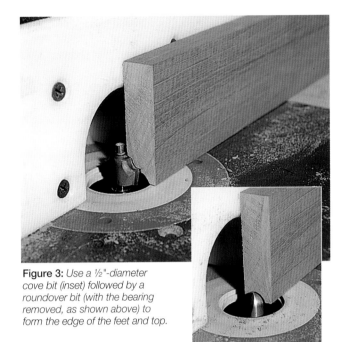

Figure 3: *Use a ½"-diameter cove bit (inset) followed by a roundover bit (with the bearing removed, as shown above) to form the edge of the feet and top.*

---

*Quick*Tip

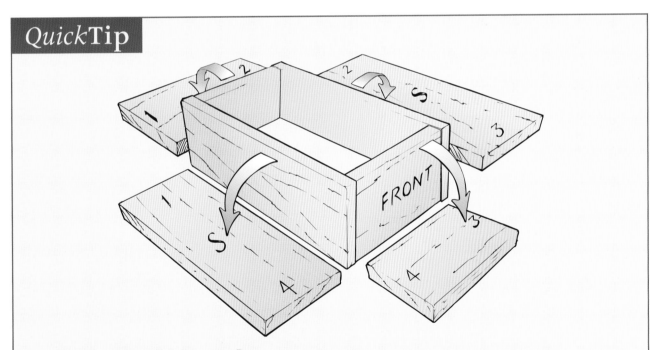

Ordering Dovetail Joints on a Box

Adding dovetail joints to the corners of a box can get you into trouble if you don't keep the parts oriented carefully. The above illustration shows a good method for ordering each corner joint. Make a small sample box to keep on hand in the shop every time you need to lay out a box worth of dovetails, to remind you of just how to arrange the parts and organize your joint-cutting procedure.

Figure 4: *Drop the Spanish cedar bottom and sidewall liners in place, but don't glue them in so you can replace them in a decade or two.*

Installing Humidity Controls

Regulating the humidity level in your humidor is important: you don't want your cigars to dry out. To monitor the humidity level, purchase a small surface-mounted hygrometer (piece 19) and secure it with a brass ring (piece 20) and screws to the cedar on the humidor lid. Humidity is added to the cigars' environment by means of a self-contained torpedo shaped humidifier (piece 21), similar to the one in the opening photo on page 128.

Now all that's left to do is select twenty or so fine cigars, open a dignified old bottle of brandy and sit back to admire your magnificent new walnut burl humidor.

*Quick*Tip

Trimming Laminate without Burning

Trimming plastic laminate can lead to burned pilot bearings on your router bits. This typically happens if the bit encounters excess contact cement along the edges of the laminate. One way to reduce the burning and keep your bits cleaner is to apply a thin coating of petroleum jelly to the bearing before you begin trimming the laminate. It will help prevent melted glue from sticking to the bit.

Adding a Cedar Lining

The cigars in this humidor will be enclosed in an air-tight, six-sided Spanish cedar compartment. This species is rich in aromatic oils that enhance the flavor of the smoke, which explains its popularity among humidor builders. You probably won't be able to find Spanish cedar at your local woodworking store, but it's easy to find from specialty internet lumber suppliers as well as from Rockler. Don't use aromatic red cedar—it won't impart the same pleasant taste.

Make the compartment by cutting liners for the top, bottom, front, back, and ends (pieces 15, 16, 17 and 18) to the dimensions given in the *Material List*, then trim their edges at 45°.

Drop the bottom and side liners in place without any glue *(see Figure 4)*, then dry-fit the top gently in place. Put a dab of hot-melt glue on each corner of the top, and add a couple more dabs down the middle. Then, working quickly before the glue sets, gently close the lid tight. Wait a couple of minutes before opening, to allow the glue to fully harden.

Veneering Basics

As burl and highly figured veneer dries after slicing, it tends to become wavy and brittle. Over-the-counter glycerine treatment will solve this problem. Just soak your veneer in the water-soluble treatment (see the package for diluting instructions), then place it in a shop-made drying press, as shown below.

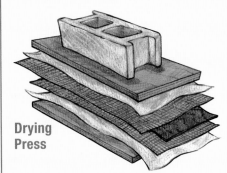

Drying Press

Crossbearer

Caul

Veneer

Clamping Press
After clamping the crossbearers in place to apply pressure to the center, install more clamps to increase pressure to the perimeter.

The press is basically a sandwich with the veneer at its center. On either side are layers of window screen, kraft paper and ¾" plywood. Place a heavy weight on top and then leave the entire assembly to dry for a couple of days.

Once the veneer is removed from the press, it's important to use it within a few hours: figured veneer tends to have memory, and it will quickly return to the wrinkled, wavy stage if allowed.

Gluing Up Veneer
To glue veneer to a substrate, you need to build a simple veneer press. The most convenient and versatile version is made with a couple pieces of plywood (known as cauls) and

several bow-shaped clamping beams (crossbearers). Apply a thin even coat of regular white or yellow woodworking glue to both sides of your substrate (white glue is preferable because it's more elastic). After cutting the veneer slightly larger than the substrate to allow for trimming, set the pieces in place. Lay kraft paper between the veneer and cauls and use the crossbearers to apply pressure to the center of the press as you clamp. Once everything is locked in place, add additional clamps around the perimeter. The goal is to provide even pressure across the entire piece.

Creating Patterns
To make the top of the humidor, join several pieces of veneer to create a pattern. This is simply a matter of

cutting the elements to size and taping them together from the top before using your veneer press.

A veneer saw or sharp knife works well to make these cuts; just be sure to score the veneer before you trim across the grain to avoid tear-out. After the glue dries, peel or sand off the tape.

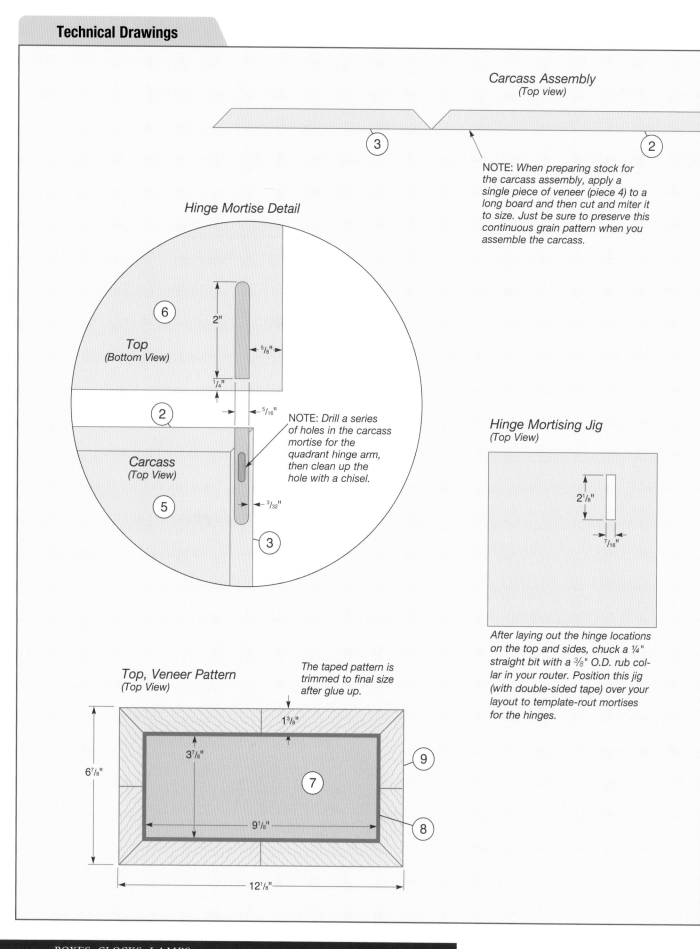

Carcass Assembly
(Top view)

③   ②

NOTE: *When preparing stock for the carcass assembly, apply a single piece of veneer (piece 4) to a long board and then cut and miter it to size. Just be sure to preserve this continuous grain pattern when you assemble the carcass.*

Hinge Mortise Detail

⑥

Top
(Bottom View)

2"

5/8"

1/4"

②

5/16"

Carcass
(Top View)

⑤

3/32"

③

NOTE: *Drill a series of holes in the carcass mortise for the quadrant hinge arm, then clean up the hole with a chisel.*

Hinge Mortising Jig
(Top View)

2 1/8"

7/16"

After laying out the hinge locations on the top and sides, chuck a ¼" straight bit with a ⅜" O.D. rub collar in your router. Position this jig (with double-sided tape) over your layout to template-rout mortises for the hinges.

Top, Veneer Pattern
(Top View)

The taped pattern is trimmed to final size after glue up.

1 3/8"

3 7/8"

⑨

6 7/8"

⑦

9 1/8"

⑧

12 1/8"

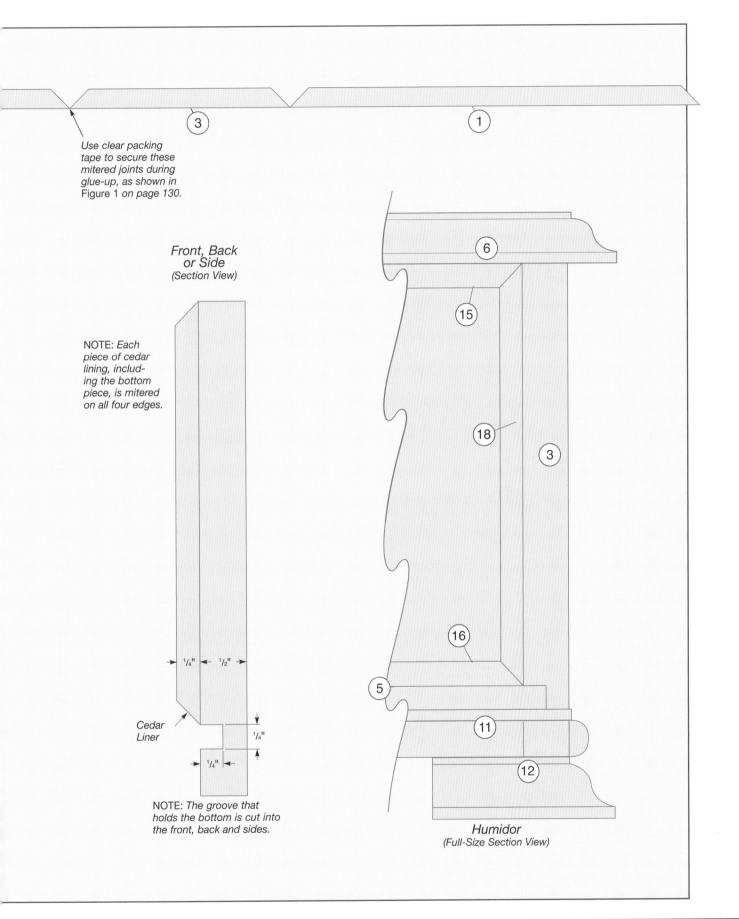

Use clear packing
tape to secure these
mitered joints during
glue-up, as shown in
Figure 1 *on page 130.*

③

①

Front, Back
or Side
(Section View)

NOTE: *Each
piece of cedar
lining, includ-
ing the bottom
piece, is mitered
on all four edges.*

Cedar
Liner

$^1/_4$" $^1/_2$"

$^1/_4$"

$^1/_4$"

NOTE: *The groove that
holds the bottom is cut into
the front, back and sides.*

⑥

⑮

⑱

③

⑯

⑤

⑪

⑫

Humidor
(Full-Size Section View)

by Craig Lossing

ZESTFUL TURNINGS

Start with several pieces of scrap cherry and maple, stir well and add a few hours on the lathe. Now you're ready for the salt and pepper. A small turning project like this is a perfect candidate for a "production run" to suit holiday gift-giving, not to mention a nice way to bring a bit of the shop into the kitchen.

Like recipes, turning projects have an organic quality to them. Most are best presented as ideas so each turner can make changes to suit a project to his or her own tastes. This salt and pepper set is a good example. If you enjoy contemporary tableware, these shapes will blend right in with that look. You can follow the full-size drawings on page 141 to make exact duplicates, or take off with your own ideas to create your own style.

The construction of the salt shaker includes a useful ring joint that you may want to try out on other sectional designs like candlestick holders, vases or vessels that are made with separate pieces of wood.

Making the Pepper Mill

The first thing you should take care of before starting this project is purchasing the salt and pepper mechanisms, available from Rockler and other turning supply sources. Having the hardware in hand when you begin cutting will save you from possible mistakes.

Cut your pepper mill wood blanks slightly oversize, and begin working on the cherry top first. Drill a ¾"-diameter by ¼"-deep hole in one end of the cherry block, then mount it on the lathe with the hole facing the tail stock. Turn the block into a cylinder with a ½" gouge, then use a parting tool to form the neck. Continue with the gouge to round over the top, and smooth the surface with a skew. Increase your lathe speed to sand the cherry to 220 grit, then dismount the top and drill a ¼"-diameter hole through the wood.

Now put the maple between centers on the lathe and turn it to shape with the ½" gouge. Again, use a skew and

Figure 1: *When you're ready to drill the cores, a wooden handscrew clamp will help keep the mill from spinning during drilling as well as align the workpiece for an accurate through hole.*

sandpaper to refine the surface. Part off the maple piece from the lathe and drill three holes into the mill: First, a 1½"-diameter by ½"-deep hole in the bottom of the piece, then a 1¼"-diameter by ⅜"-deep hole in the top end. Use the indents from the lathe drives to find the drilling centers for these two holes. The third hole is 1" in diameter and passes from the top end all the way to the bottom. To get greater control and accuracy while drilling this hole, clamp a wooden handscrew to the mill (see *Figure 1*).

Once these holes are drilled, insert the grinding mechanism in the mill and secure the retaining plates after drilling pilot holes for the screws. The top should turn freely when you loosen the nut, which, by the way, also allows the peppercorns to slip into the teeth of the gears so they can be ground.

Turning the Salt Shaker

Mount your curly maple salt shaker blank into the lathe and rough it with a gouge into a 2" cylinder. Next, make the ring joint by turning one end of the cylinder down to a 1½" diameter with a parting tool. Take your cherry block over to the drill press and drill a 1½" hole through it. Remove the maple from the lathe and use yellow glue to secure its ringed end inside the cherry block.

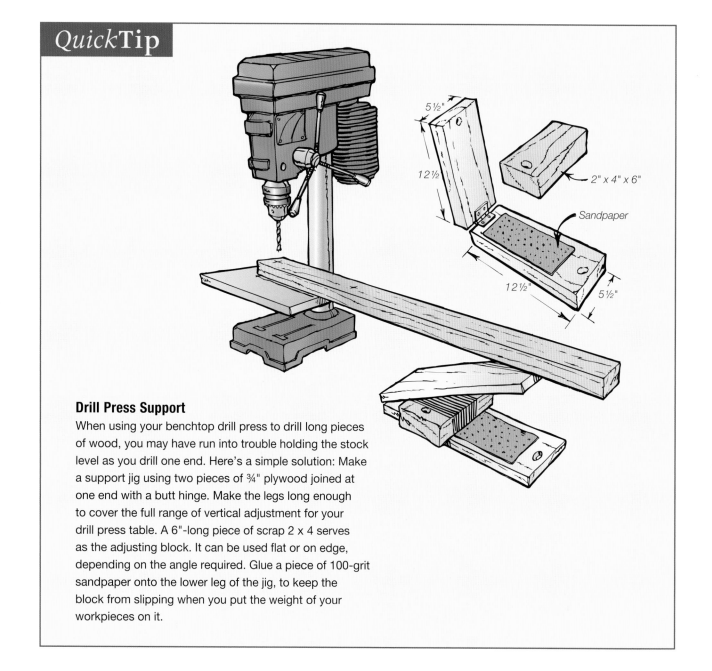

QuickTip

5½"

12½

2" x 4" x 6"

Sandpaper

12½"

5½"

Drill Press Support

When using your benchtop drill press to drill long pieces of wood, you may have run into trouble holding the stock level as you drill one end. Here's a simple solution: Make a support jig using two pieces of ¾" plywood joined at one end with a butt hinge. Make the legs long enough to cover the full range of vertical adjustment for your drill press table. A 6"-long piece of scrap 2 x 4 serves as the adjusting block. It can be used flat or on edge, depending on the angle required. Glue a piece of 100-grit sandpaper onto the lower leg of the jig, to keep the block from slipping when you put the weight of your workpieces on it.

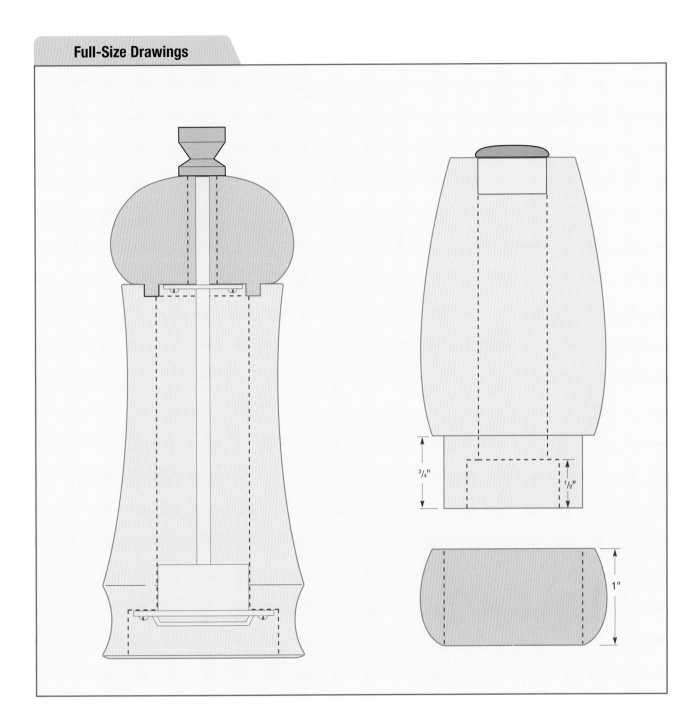

Once the glue dries, remount the shaker on the lathe and turn it to final shape. Sand the piece to 220 grit, then part off the top end. Take the shaker back to the drill press to bore the holes, making sure to use the handscrew clamp again to control the turning. Drill a 1"-diameter hole ½" deep in the bottom of the shaker, then turn the piece over and drill a ¾"-diameter hole through the full length of the body.

Finishing Up

Dismantle the pepper mill to give it and the salt shaker a final burnishing with fine steel wool. Apply three coats of tung oil to the outside of the set to really bring out the curly pattern in the maple.

Let the finish dry for two days before reassembling the mechanism in the pepper mill and adding the top to the salt shaker. Once this is done, pour in your salt and your peppercorns, and cap off the openings. Your salt and pepper set is now ready for work. Bon appetit!

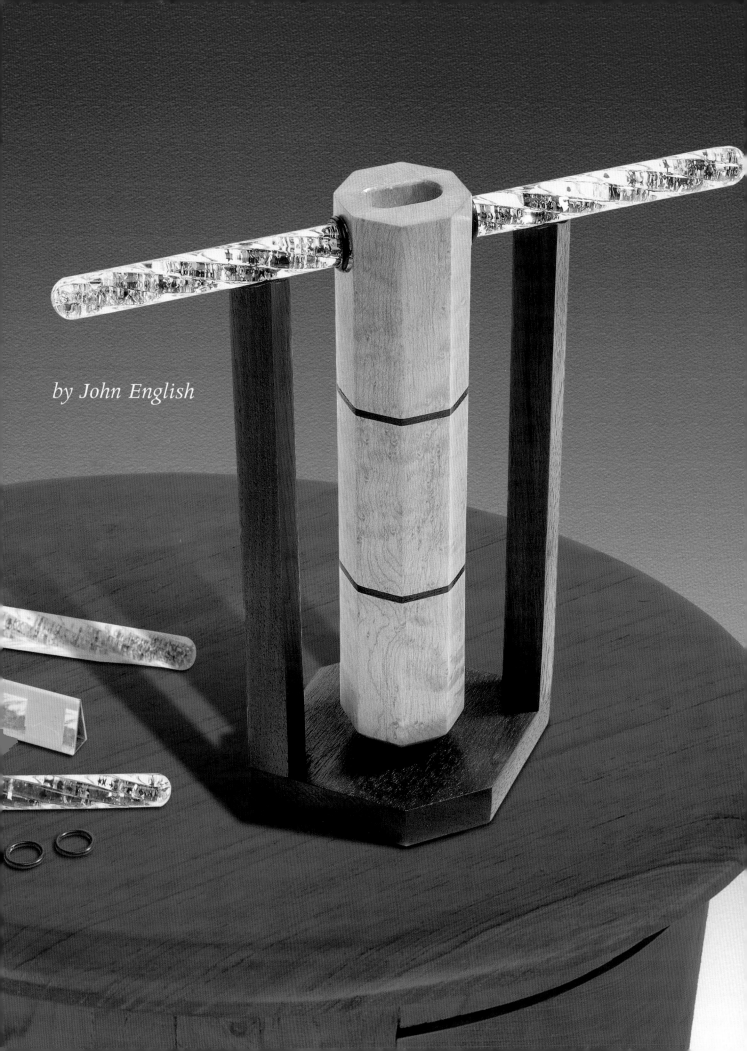

by John English

KALEIDOSCOPE

Look no further: here's the perfect production project for the next holiday season. A kaleidoscope will bring you right back to your childhood, and it's just as amusing to today's internet-generation kids. Building a toy is also a delightful change of pace from larger, more formal or labor-intensive projects.

One of Scotland's most distinguished sons, physicist Sir David Brewster (1781-1868), is credited with inventing the kaleidoscope. Brewster discovered numerous physical laws that govern the behavior of light, including Brewster's Law, which helps define such things as polarized sunglasses. But you don't need to study optics to build this kaleidoscope: Just head for the shop and dig out some 10"-long pieces of 2" x 2" hardwood from the scrap bin. This is a great production project, so look for several pieces of stock. If you can't find 2"-square blanks in your favorite species, just face-glue three pieces of ¾" stock, then trim the two outside faces evenly so the middle piece is centered.

Finding Necessary Hardware

You'll need some inexpensive hardware to complete this project. Here's what to buy: 1) A set of three 1" x 7¾"-long mirror strips; 2) A ½"-diameter plastic lens; 4) A 6" oil-filled wand to generate the colored light effects; and 5) A pair of ⅝"-diameter O-rings. These supplies can be purchased from Southern Front Inc. (www.southernfront.com; phone 281/890-5860). Find the O-rings in the plumbing section of a home center.

Milling the Segments

Once you have your hardware and wood blanks, the first step in construction is to mark one surface of each blank with random pencil lines. That way you'll always be able to orient the pieces correctly. Next, use a try square to mark off the three sections of each blank and the ⅛" spaces between them (see the *Technical Drawings* on page 146). Crosscut the blanks through the spaces on your table saw, then move to the drill press to start milling.

Forstner bits are ideal for making projects like this: They provide clean walls and flat-bottomed bores.

The lens segment (piece 1) is bored three times, each with a different diameter bit. Set up your drill press so that a 1¼" bit is centered on the end of the segment: This is the end that will be glued to the middle segment (piece 2) upon reassembly. Set the depth gauge on your drill press to stop the bit ½" from the other end of the segment, then clamp the workpiece firmly in place as shown in *Figure 1* on page 145, and bore the hole. Now switch to a ½" bit and drill ¼" deeper into the wood, then turn the segment end-for-end and bore a ¼"-diameter hole all the way through it.

Milling the middle segment is a lot simpler: Just bore it all the way through with the 1¼" bit, then use the same bit to drill a 2¼"-deep hole in the wand segment (piece 3). Drill this hole into the end that will be glued to the middle segment.

There are two more milling operations that should be completed before the segments are reglued. Begin with the 1¹⁄₁₆"-diameter hole for the wand (see the *Technical Drawings* on page 146 for its location). An 1¹⁄₁₆" Forstner bit may be hard to find, so this can be made with a sharp spade bit—if you place a piece of scrap under the exit point to prevent tearout.

Finally, bore a series of ⅝"-diameter holes through the undrilled end of the

Kaleidoscope Exploded View

Material List		
		T x W x L
1	Lens Segment (1)	2" x 2" x 3 1/8"
2	Middle Segment (1)	2" x 2" x 3 1/8"
3	Wand Segment (1)	2" x 2" x 3 1/8"
4	Lens (1)	1/32" x 1/2" Glass
5	Vertical Mirrors (2)	1/16" x 1" x 7 3/4"
6	Horizontal Mirror (1)	1/16" x 7/16" x 7 3/4"
7	Inlay Banding	1/8" x 3/16" x 16"

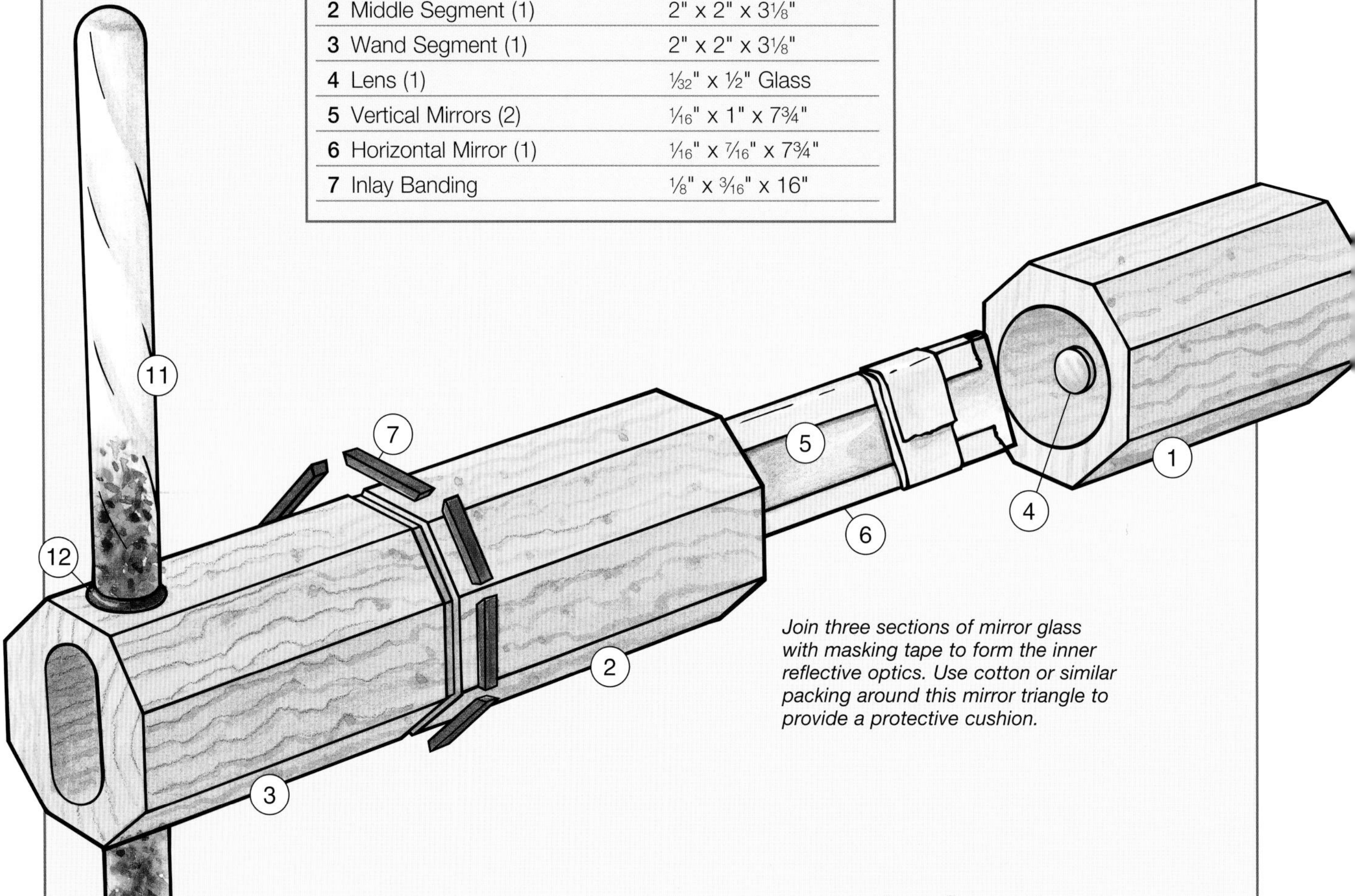

Join three sections of mirror glass with masking tape to form the inner reflective optics. Use cotton or similar packing around this mirror triangle to provide a protective cushion.

Lens Segment
(Side view)

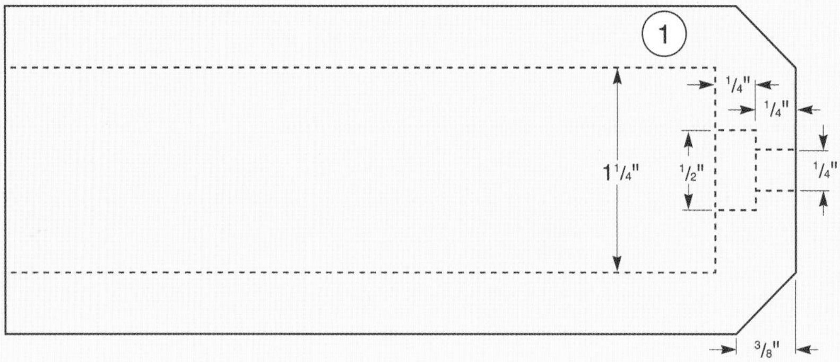

wand segment, creating the hole that allows light into the kaleidoscope (see *drawings* for locations), and straighten the two long sides of this opening with a rasp.

Adding the Lens and Mirrors

The lens (piece 4) is just a ½" disk of plastic inserted into the lens segment. It's then glued in place in the ½"-diameter bore you created earlier. The easiest way to seat the lens is to secure a ⅜" dowel vertically in your bench vise, then place the disk on its end. Spread some slow-drying (at least 30 second) super glue on the ledge inside the segment, and just lower the segment onto the dowel *(see Figure 2)*.

Next, use masking tape to join the three mirror strips to create an equilateral triangle (as shown in *Figure 3*), and insert it into the lens segment after blowing the dust out. Use cotton or a similar material to pack the mirror so it is centered on the lens. Now apply a liberal amount of glue between the lens segment and the middle segment. Working quickly before the glue sets, pack cotton wool into the middle segment, then apply glue to the joint between it and the wand segment. Make sure the mirror triangle lines up properly with the elongated hole in the end of the wand segment (see *drawings*), then apply clamps and let this assembly dry.

When it's dry, set your table saw blade to 45°, remove any excess glue from the glued-up body—a scraper or sandpaper block works well for this—and cut all four chamfers. With the blade still set at 45°, this is a good time to chamfer the lens end of the kaleidoscope using your saw's miter gauge. You can find these dimensions on the *Technical Drawings* on page 146, as well.

Installing the Inlaid Band

Inlaying the band is a lot simpler than it looks. Set your table saw blade back to 90° and adjust the height for a ⅛"-deep cut. Clamp a stop to the miter gauge fence so the blade is centered on one of the joints in the kaleidoscope body, and make a series of cuts all the way around.

Repeat this process on the other end, then raise the blade and rip some ⅛"-wide strips of a contrasting species for the inlay banding (pieces 7). Cut sections of these strips slightly longer than you need. Sand each end to 22½° with a fine belt on your stationary belt sander. Use super glue to secure the banding in the saw kerfs, and sand off the excess when the glue is dry. A sanding block works better than a power pad sander here: The latter tends to round over the chamfers.

Assembling the Stand

The stand is just two pieces of ¾"-square stock (pieces 8), screwed and glued to a base (piece 9). Cut the base to shape according to the *drawings*. The curved tops of the uprights

Figure 1: *Set up your drill press to bore each of the three segments. Safety is paramount here: Make sure the workpiece is firmly clamped to prevent it from spinning during drilling.*

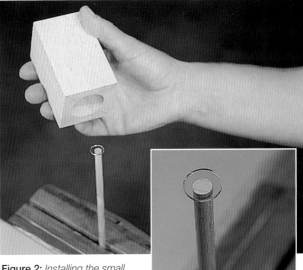

Figure 2: *Installing the small lens can be tricky. One good technique is to place it on the end of a dowel that is locked in a vise. Apply glue inside the lens segment, then gently lower the segment onto the lens. You can watch through the lens hole as you align the two parts.*

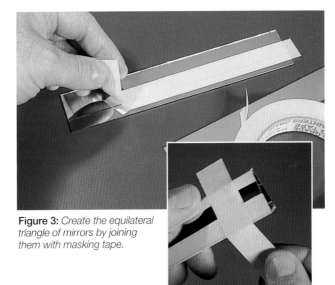

Figure 3: *Create the equilateral triangle of mirrors by joining them with masking tape.*

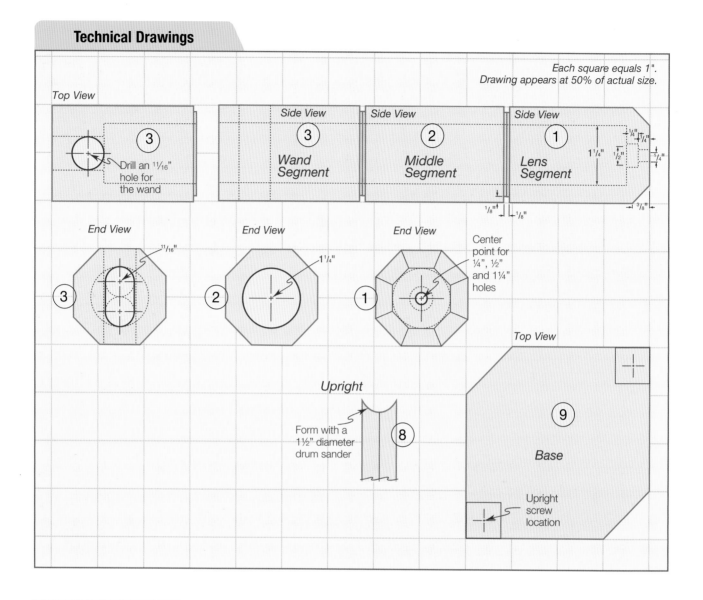

Each square equals 1".
Drawing appears at 50% of actual size.

Top View

③

Drill an ¹¹/₁₆" hole for the wand

Side View ③ **Wand Segment**

Side View ② **Middle Segment**

Side View ① **Lens Segment**

1¼" ¹/₄" ¹/₄" ¹/₂" ³/₄"

¹/₈" ¹/₈" ³/₈"

End View ③ ¹¹/₁₆"

End View ② 1¼"

End View ① Center point for ¼", ½" and 1¼" holes

Upright

Form with a 1½" diameter drum sander

⑧

Top View

⑨ *Base*

Upright screw location

QuickTip

Inexpensive Dust Collection

Keep sanding tasks cleaner at the bench by building a simple dust catcher from a plastic register air diverter. These diverters come with magnets, so they can be mounted and removed in seconds. Attach the hood to a small box with a couple of 20d nails driven in the sides for the magnets to grab. Cut a hole in the box and install a collar around it for attaching your shop vac hose nozzle. Mount the box to your bench so it's ready when you need it.

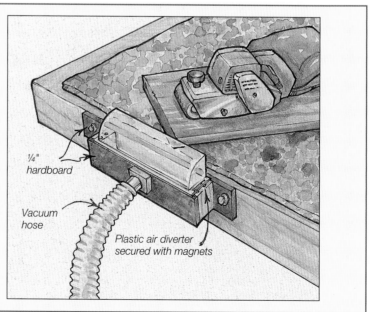

¼" hardboard

Vacuum hose

Plastic air diverter secured with magnets

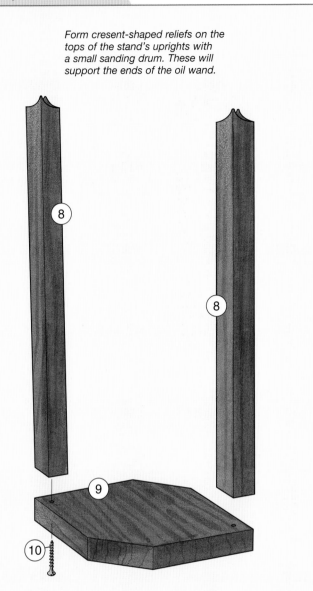

Form cresent-shaped reliefs on the tops of the stand's uprights with a small sanding drum. These will support the ends of the oil wand.

Material List

		T x W x L
8	Uprights (2)	¾" x ¾" x 9"
9	Base (1)	¾" x 4" x 4"
10	Screws (2)	1⅝" Wallboard Screws
11	Wand (1)	¹¹⁄₁₆" x 11½", Glass
12	Rubber O-Ring (2)	⅝" I.D.

are shaped on a 2" drum sander in the drill press, then the uprights are glued and screwed (pieces 10) in place. Finally, break any sharp edges with sandpaper.

Finishing Up

At this stage, you can insert the wand (piece 11) in its hole, turn the kaleidoscope toward daylight, and test your handiwork. Assuming that everything looks right, remove the wand and mask off all the holes in the body to prevent dust from getting into the mirror. Then sand all visible surfaces down through the grits to 180. Remove the masking tape and apply three or four coats of oil finish, sanding between coats with 400-grit wet/dry paper. Make sure no oil gets into the mirror.

When the last coat of oil dries, slip a rubber O-ring (piece 12) onto the wand, insert the wand into the kaleidoscope and install the second O-ring to secure the wand. Now rotate the kaleidoscope so the material inside the wand begins to fall, and watch through the lens. For a more interesting effect, twirl the wand as you watch those magical patterns develop inside your kaleidoscope.

*Quick*Tip

Solid Surface Worktops

For worktops on outdoor projects like grills, tables and barbecue carts, some solid surface materials like Corian® work extremely well. You can pick up a sink cutout at a cabinet shop for a minor charge, or even for free. Although some products aren't certified for outdoor use, they seem to hold up well to the elements.

CLASSIC CANISTER SET

Here's a bygone kitchen accent whose time has come again. Regardless of what you store in yours, these octagonal beauties are fun to make, and you can crank out multiples at a time if you follow the production methods we describe here.

In the new culinary world order, flour, sugar and salt are "so twentieth century," but coffee and tea are definitely "in." And so a familiar kitchen staple—the canister set—is destined for a comeback, only it's holding trendy new ingredients for a new millennium.

This project has been designed for customization. You can make one or six canisters, and you can make each as tall or short as your kitchen setup requires. You just can't make them fatter (at least not without major modifications to these plans). Our

production-style approach, as you can see in the left *photo* on the next page, is to create one long glued-up octagon cylinder and then cut each canister to length.

Getting the Bevel Right Before Moving On

When you're making a segmented project like this, setup is all-important. If you set your bevels at 22¼° instead of 22½°, for instance, you'll get a quick lesson in the power of multiplication. A ¼° times eight equals...well, it equals a

very leaky canister. So get some scrap wood out and set your fence and blade. (Use the Material List and the Elevation Drawings on page 150 for all your construction details.) When you're sure you've got your setup right, cut eight test pieces to width and wrap them up with tape. Even a ¹⁄₃₂° alignment error will multiply up to a poor fit. So accuracy is the watchword here.

Once you've tested your setup, go ahead and choose your stock. Remember, you're making a number of canisters from the same glue-up, so

by Brad Becker

Absolute accuracy is never in doubt if
you make your canisters from one glued-up
octagon. A flip-stop miter attachment makes
it easy to crosscut the canisters accurately.
(If you don't have a flip stop, attach a scrap
stop to your miter gauge instead.)

A "Green" Hardwood

Lyptus®, a natural hybrid of
Eucalyptus grandis and
E. urophylla, is a new,
plantation-grown
hardwood
from Brazil.
"Manufactured" by
Aracruz Wood Products,
it is distributed in North
America through an exclusive agreement
with Weyerhaeuser.

Lyptus is being used for diverse applications where
the beauty and appearance of mahogany or cherry
is desired. In its natural state, the wood has a pleasant cherry
color and variation between hardwood and sapwood boards. Left unstained,
the natural figuration in Lyptus is similar to quartersawn oak. It oxidizes similarly
to cherry and will turn a beautiful patina in a very short time.

Lyptus compares favorably to the density, strength and technical properties of
oak and beech. It machines well (little tearout along or across the grain as it is sawn
or shaped) and has the surfacing qualities of genuine mahogany. It requires
only minimal after-shaping touchup sanding.

Weyerhaeuser predicts that Lyptus will become the
most important hardwood species of our generation for
two very important reasons:

1. Rapidly renewable—the growth rate is unprecedented.
   Four-year-old trees are already 45 feet tall. Lyptus is
   harvested in 15 years (as opposed to 50 to 120 years
   associated with other hardwoods). After Lyptus is
   harvested, it regrows from the stump without the need to
   replant or disturb the forest floor.
2. Lyptus is reversing the loss of native forest lands—100%
   of Lyptus productivity comes from previously barren land
   that has been reconstituted through the reintroduction
   of native species indigenous to the region. Plantations
   of Lyptus are grown in a mosaic pattern interspersed
   with indigenous trees to preserve native ecosystems and
   create biodiversity.

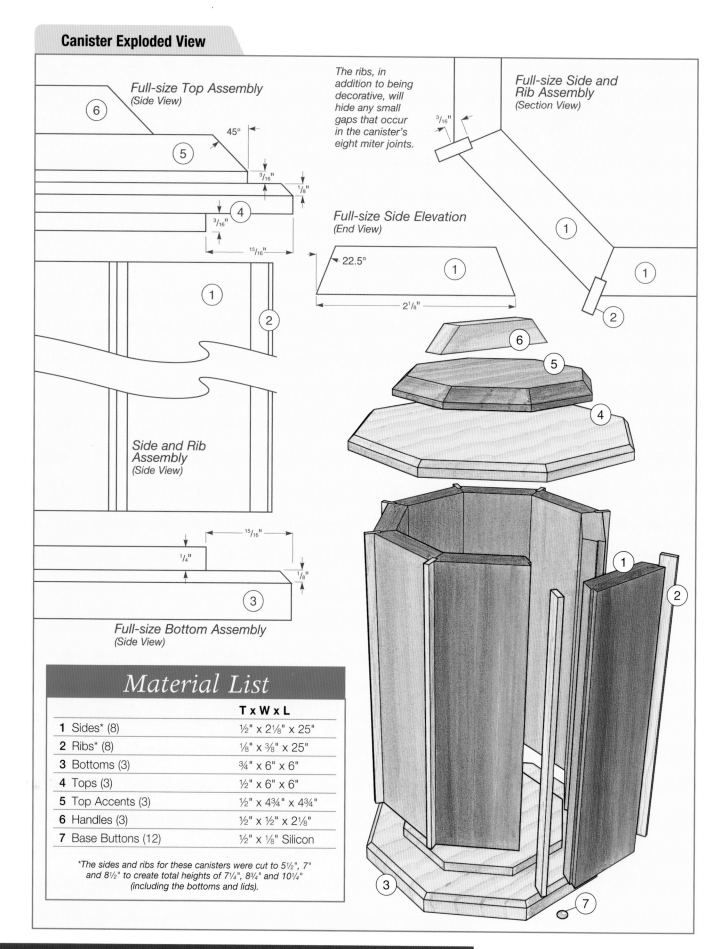

Full-size Top Assembly
(Side View)

45°

3/16"

1/8"

3/16"

15/16"

The ribs, in addition to being decorative, will hide any small gaps that occur in the canister's eight miter joints.

Full-size Side and Rib Assembly
(Section View)

3/16"

Full-size Side Elevation
(End View)

22.5°

2 1/8"

Side and Rib Assembly
(Side View)

15/16"

1/4"

1/8"

Full-size Bottom Assembly
(Side View)

Material List

		T x W x L
1	Sides* (8)	½" x 2⅛" x 25"
2	Ribs* (8)	⅛" x ⅜" x 25"
3	Bottoms (3)	¾" x 6" x 6"
4	Tops (3)	½" x 6" x 6"
5	Top Accents (3)	½" x 4¾" x 4¾"
6	Handles (3)	½" x ½" x 2⅛"
7	Base Buttons (12)	½" x ⅛" Silicon

The sides and ribs for these canisters were cut to 5½", 7" and 8½" to create total heights of 7¼", 8¾" and 10¼" (including the bottoms and lids).

make sure you have nice uniformity in grain and color. Lyptus®, the wood I selected for my project, comes in a range of colors, as you can see from the three pieces shown on page 149. I picked a ½"-thick board and jointed one edge dead straight before moving to the table saw. Decide the heights of your three canisters, throw in a few inches of waste for good measure, and crosscut your board to length. Draw some diagonal lines on each side with different colored chalk to keep things lined up and then proceed to cut the sides (pieces 1).

Keep milling until you have enough sides to create a complete octagon. I recommend that you cut a few extra pieces, just for good measure. Now you're ready to create the "master cylinder." Get out the glue, some packing tape and a set of web clamps.

The next step is going to be a real breeze, since you've used up lots of cheap scrap wood testing your bevel setup before moving into the expensive hardwood (right?!). For that reason, everything is going to fit together perfectly and you're going to end up with a perfect "master cylinder." Remember, the origin of the famous woodworker's anthem "measure twice, cut once," can be traced to segmented projects.

As you can see from the *photo* sequence at right, the first step is to lay a few strips of packing tape out on your work surface. Secure each end of this tape to the bench to ensure that things don't bunch up or move around you as you lay your pieces down, each touching the one next to it. Your chalk lines will help you with the sequencing. Just be sure to have a good look at the outside of each piece as you work through your layout process. If you spot a ding or a piece that has warped or twisted, now is the time to grab one of those extras and replace the defective piece.

Once all the pieces are lined up, (and your web clamps are close at hand), use a foam brush to apply glue to the matching bevels (including the first and last ones). Because these canisters are going to end up in the kitchen, use a waterproof glue with adequate open time. The new Titebond® III is a good choice here. It's waterproof, gives you plenty of open time (eight minutes) and cleans up easily with water. Move quickly to apply the glue and then, using the tape, slowly roll up your master cylinder. Cinch up the web clamps until the joints close, and you're ready to move on.

Once the glue dries on your master cylinder, crosscut them to their various lengths. The first *photo* on page 149 shows how this works. Use your miter fence and a good stop and move slowly…this is no time to mess up all the work you've done already. I found that Lyptus® mills pretty nicely, but I still sanded both ends smooth (using a block to prevent

Packing tape provides a convenient way to align and hold the cylinder side pieces together for gluing. Remember, when you're doing a multiple-step glue-up like this, always pay close attention to your glue's open time.

The first step *is to carefully lay all your mitered pieces on top of the packing tape with their ends squared up. Make sure the miters butt from one end to the other, and then quickly spread your glue in all the miters.*

As soon as you've applied the glue, *pick up the two ends of the packing tape and start rolling. The miters will come together easily, and the tape will temporarily "clamp" your cylinder together.*

Bring on the muscle with a few web clamps, *one at each end and one in the middle. Tighten the clamps securely, and then use a damp rag to wipe off as much excess glue from the inside of the cylinder as possible.*

The simple jig shown at right will ensure that all your rib cuts will be perfectly located on the miter joints of each cylinder. As with many of the steps in this project, test your saw setup with a waste section from the cylinder glue-up.

rounding), through 120 grit. I added maple "ribs" that run the length of the eight miter joints. They not only create a design element that visually connects the maple top and bottom pieces, but if your miter joint has a small gap, no one will ever see it. You've got to like that!

To help accurately locate the rib veins, your next step is to make yourself a sled like the one shown above. Use a square scrap of plywood to create the base. Then attach two beveled pieces and two cross ties. The bevels (22½°) can be formed on the table saw. After cutting them to size, place the two pieces right up against each other on the base, screw them in position and then screw the two cross ties to them. Set your fence so the blade is directly in line with the point where the bevels meet and raise your blade high enough to cut through the base and the joined edges of the bevels, but be sure and stay below the cross ties: they'll be the only thing holding the jig together after the first cut is made. Adjust your blade height using a leftover segment of the master cylinder in the jig; you want the ⅛" blade to penetrate the canister miters to a depth of exactly ³⁄₁₆". With all that in mind, go ahead and cut all the rib veins.

Creating the Ribs

After jointing one edge smooth, rip your ribs (pieces 2) to width on the table saw, as shown in the *photo* at right. Be sure to use a push stick with this ⅛"-thick stock and make sure there are no knots or cracks in sight. Test the fit in the scrap you used to set your blade depth: you want a nice, tight fit: half in, half out. Once your ribs fit the miters, rip enough

material for all three canisters and, after a light sanding, crosscut them to their three lengths. Place packing tape to work during the glue-up phase; it brings just enough pressure to bear to hold the ribs steady and tight while the glue dries. When all the ribs are in place and the glue dries, remove the tape and sand through 180 grit, softening the edges and making the tops and bottoms perfectly flush.

Forming the Octagonal Tops, Bases and Accents

With your three cylinders ready to go, it's time to move on to the bottoms and tops (pieces 3 and 4) and top accents (pieces 5). These pieces start out as squares and are cut into octagons on the miter saw. It's a simple process—just set your miter saw to 45° and either use tape as a marker or clamp a stop to your fence. Measure in from the corner of the square piece, as shown in the top left *photo* on the next page. Once again, I strongly recommend testing your setup with scrap. Work your way around each of the three tops and do the same thing with the three accent pieces. Then, move over to the table saw and, using a ¾" dado head, form the rabbets on the bottom of the lid and the top of the base piece (see the *Elevation Drawings*). Keep rotating the pieces while you nibble away the waste. Sand the saw marks off of the rabbets.

The final step with these pieces is to form the chamfers along their top edges. Carry out this machining step on a router table with a chamfering bit. Work your way around each piece and take a sanding pass to smooth everything out.

Making the Handles and Gluing Everything Together

The final pieces to mill are the handles (pieces 6), which are also machined on the miter saw. Mill your stock to overall size and start with the blade set at 45°. Cut off one end, flip

Select clear ⅛" maple for the ribs and joint one edge before firing up the table saw. With thin stock like this, a push stick is especially important. Also, be sure your stock is completely free of defects.

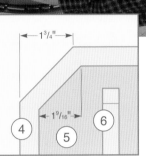

Line up some tape on your miter saw's fence as a "stop" when you're ready to create the top, base and accent pieces. Use the illustration at right to lay out your cuts. Again, you can't go wrong using scrap to make a couple of test cuts.

The handles are also formed on the miter saw, once again using tape on the fence to create a stop. After each cut, flip the stock over to form opposing miters.

your piece over and slide it forward to your tape "stop" on the fence. The second cut creates the first handle. Keep cutting and flipping until you have all three handles. Sand these through the grits, softening their edges as you go.

Now you're ready to bring everything together. Glue the bases to the cylinders first (using epoxy) and then glue the handles to the top accents, pointing the handles in the direction of the grain. Once that subassembly dries, glue it to

the lid, keeping everything centered and making sure the grain on both pieces runs in the same direction. Test your fit and do any necessary final sanding at this time. Glue the silicon bumpers (pieces 7) to the bottoms of each canister and use a tack cloth to get ready for finishing. See the *sidebar* below for finishing recommendations. Then your canisters will be ready for those exotic teas and coffees you've been itching to try.

Food-Safe Finish Options

Whether you find some liners for your canisters or store your coffee beans right in the "wooden boxes" as they did in the good old days is up to you. If you're going au naturel, be sure and use a food-safe finish on the inside, like General Finishes' Salad Bowl Finish shown here.

For the outside, we were more concerned with moisture hitting the surface on a regular basis, so we added silicon buttons around the bottoms and applied three coats of a wipe-on polyurethane gel finish on all the exposed surfaces.

DOVETAIL PUZZLE MALLET

Even though this intriguing mallet design has been around for centuries, the method for building it had nearly been lost. Thanks to the counsel of an experienced hand tool woodworker, we've revived all the methodology here. And, making this mallet provides a double bonus—you'll have a beautiful tool to display and a worthy workhorse around the shop.

by Stephen Sheperd

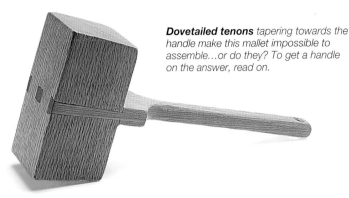

Dovetailed tenons *tapering towards the handle make this mallet impossible to assemble...or do they? To get a handle on the answer, read on.*

There will always be a place in woodworkers' hearts for trick joinery, if only for the sheer delight of stumping their friends with the finished product. But seemingly impossible joints can also be useful and fun to make.

This mallet is a classic example of a puzzle joint that is both useful and a great exercise in hand tool joinery. It is mystifying because the dovetails appear to taper in two conflicting directions that would make it impossible to assemble.

The secret is that the dovetails are "ramped," or double-tapered, as shown in the *Elevation Drawings* on page 156. A small shoulder where the pins meet the handle covers up the fact that the dovetail is deeper at the bottom of the head. The joint is tricky to assemble because the two dovetail pins on the handle have to be bent in order to get them started into the ramped dovetail slots on the sides of the head.

Though this puzzle mallet design has been around for centuries, the method for making it had nearly been lost. In this article, we'll explain how to make this useful shop tool that doubles as a great shop conversation piece.

Making the Head First

When making a puzzle mallet, it's a good idea to start with the head and then fit the handle to it. This is roughly the same as cutting the tails of a conventional dovetail joint first and then making the pins to fit.

You can use any type of wood for the head, as long as it is hard enough to stand up to the abuse you plan for it. Red oak, rosewood, lignum vitae, ebony, maple and walnut are all good options that take a real pounding (no pun intended).

Cut the head from a single block of wood, with the grain parallel to the direction of swing, as shown in the *drawings*. Slope the faces of the head 5° from top to bottom to provide a natural striking angle.

It is not critical to create a center tenon in the mallet's head, but it will add strength, even on mallets with narrow heads. You might even consider switching to a round tenon in the center rather than a square one. This way, you can drill a hole through the center of the head—much easier than chopping a long, narrow mortise.

Lay out the dovetail slots on the sides and the ends of the head exactly as they will appear in the completed mallet (see the *drawings* on page 156 and *photos* on the next few pages). At the handle end, the dovetail is twice as deep as at the top of the mallet head. This creates the secret taper that makes the joint possible. It is important that the widest part of the ramped dovetail is the same width at both ends, as you'll see in the *drawings*.

The best and safest way to create the dovetail slots in the head is with

Step 1: *Gauge the depths of the dovetails on the top and bottom of the head, then mark the width of the tails on the centerline.*

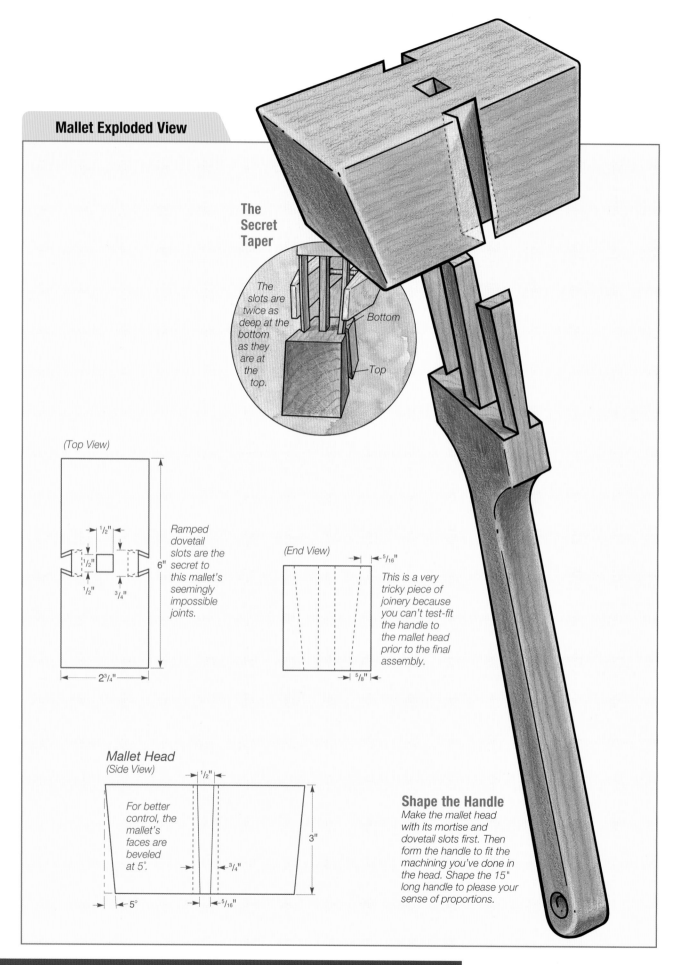

The Secret Taper

The slots are twice as deep at the bottom as they are at the top.

Bottom

Top

(Top View)

¹/₂" ¹/₂" ³/₄" ¹/₂"

6"

2³/₄"

Ramped dovetail slots are the secret to this mallet's seemingly impossible joints.

(End View)

⁵/₁₆"

⁵/₈"

This is a very tricky piece of joinery because you can't test-fit the handle to the mallet head prior to the final assembly.

Mallet Head
(Side View)

¹/₂"

For better control, the mallet's faces are beveled at 5°.

³/₄"

3"

5°   ⁵/₁₆"

Shape the Handle

Make the mallet head with its mortise and dovetail slots first. Then form the handle to fit the machining you've done in the head. Shape the 15" long handle to please your sense of proportions.

Step 2: *The dovetails are half as deep at the top of the mallet head as they are at the bottom (where the handle enters). Scribe the depths with a marking gauge.*

Step 3: *Connect the scribe marks with a reliable straightedge and a sharp marking knife to ensure precise layout lines.*

a dovetail saw, followed by a sharp chisel to remove the waste material. Saw the angled sides of the dovetail slots first, then cut a couple more kerfs between them, stopping at your layout lines on the top and bottom ends of the head, as shown in the *photo* sequence on the page 158. These kerfs provide a depth reference when you're removing the waste wood with a chisel. Once the slots are cut, drill or chisel out the mortise for the center tenon.

Making the Handle

The wood you pick for the handle must be strong enough to stand up to the abuse a handle on a mallet gets, yet it should be flexible enough that the pins may be bent. We've found that ash and hickory both work well and that quartersawn stock in either species is best for both strength and bending qualities.

Lay out the tapered dovetail pins and the center tenon to match the slots in the head. Make the handle slightly wider than the head so the pins will stand proud when assembled. Also, allow about ⅛" of extra length on the pins and ½" on the tenon for ease of assembly, as we'll explain later.

Band-saw the waste between the pins and the tenon, then cut the bottom shoulders and sloped sides of the pins with a handsaw. A backsaw works well for this purpose. If the wood is straight-grained enough, you can carefully split it away with a chisel. Pare the pins until they align with your layout lines using a sharp chisel.

This is a difficult joint because you can't dry-fit the handle to the head to check the fit. You have to carefully check all of the measurements and angles on your pins and tails to make sure they match their corresponding surfaces perfectly. It's

*Quick*Tip

Quick-Release Clamp Pads Save Effort

Wood blocks make good clamp pads to protect workpieces from getting crushed by the clamp jaws. Trouble is, it feels like you need six arms to hold your workpiece, clamp and blocks in place to clamp everything up. One way to eliminate a few arms is to first use spots of hot-melt glue to fix the blocks to the clamp jaws. When you're finished clamping, it's easy to break the glue bonds with a paint scraper and pop the blocks off.

Step 4: *Saw the sides of the dovetail slots with a backsaw. Slice kerfs in the slot's middle to help you gauge the depth when paring.*

Step 5: *Chop out the waste with a chisel, working your way up from the bottom end.*

exacting work, but the end result is quite satisfying if you work carefully and keep your patience in check.

Once you've cut the pins and tenon, band saw the rest of the handle to its approximate shape, but leave the final smoothing until later.

Assembling the Mallet

In order to assemble the mallet, you will need to bend the pins inward to meet the grooves in the head. The pins are likely to be too stiff to bend easily, so soak the pin end

Step 6: *Clean up the slots with a sharp paring chisel. Note the gradual slope of the opening, top to bottom.*

of the handle for a few minutes in boiling water to make it more pliable. Use filtered or distilled water to reduce mineral staining. Cold water will also work, but it will take longer to soften the wood, and you risk staining the wood if you soak it for a long time.

Check the softening process periodically by squeezing the pins together. As soon as they bend easily, you're ready to assemble the mallet. Start by tightening one clamp across the flat of the handle (below the pins) to prevent the wood from splitting as the pins are bent inward. Then, place another clamp near the ends of the pins and tighten it until the pins are close enough together to fit into the dovetail ramps in the head, as shown in the *photo* on the next page.

Line up the center tenon with its mortise and tap the end of the handle with another mallet to force the joint together. Since the center tenon is longer than the pins, it goes into the mortise first and helps align the pins when you engage them in the head.

Once the pins are partway into the slots, you can remove the end clamp; the sides of the slots will guide the pins the rest of the way. To protect all the work you've done on the handle, leave the other clamp in place until it is completely seated in the head.

Even with a tight friction fit, it's still a good idea to secure the joints with glue. I use hot hide glue. It has a suitable working time and is compatible with the moisture saturating the boiled tenon and pins. With the tenon engaged and the hide glue brushed into the openings, firmly drive the handle home with a mallet. Wipe off any excess glue that has been squeezed out, then clamp the handle tightly into the head until the glue and wood dries thoroughly.

Finishing Up

When the wood and the glue have dried, trim the ends of the pins and tenons flush with the head and scrape or sand them smooth. Then you can softly bevel the edges of the head and chamfer or round the handle to final shape.

To fill any slight gaps in the joints, after they shrink, use an authentic 19th-century mixture of linseed oil, whiting and a little dry powdered pigment. This mixture takes a few days to dry, so you might prefer a faster drying mix such as wood flour (fine sawdust) and hide glue.

When the filler is dry, sand or scrape the joints flush. The scraper imparts a smooth hand finish on the tool that feels wonderful to the touch. As a final finish, soak the mallet in a 50/50 mixture of turpentine and linseed oil. It's an appropriate finish for wooden tools and easy to reapply as necessary.

Once the finish dries, it's time to put your new handmade mallet to work. Reach for it the next time you have some serious mortises to square up. There's nothing quite like swinging a mallet you've made yourself.

After soaking the pins in boiling water to make them pliable, clamp the ends together until they line up with the oversized dovetail slots. The second clamp keeps the handle from splitting at the base.

*Quick*Tip

Custom Wax Dispenser

Carnauba wax is easier to apply to small turnings if melted into small sticks using standard ¼" OD plastic drinking straws for forms. The resulting 7⁄32" stick fits handily into eraser holders sold at office supply stores. The wax, when set, will slide right out of the straws.

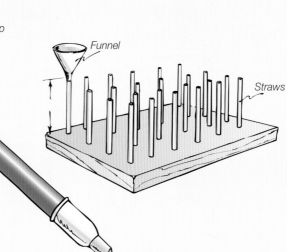

After the wax cools, slip it out of the straw and into an eraser holder

Funnel

Straws

More Great Books from Fox Chapel Publishing

Jigs and Fixtures for the Table Saw & Router
By Editors of Woodworker's Journal
Learn the tricks of the trade with over 25 jig and fixture projects from the experts at Woodworker's Journal.
$17.95
ISBN 978-1-56523-325-6

Craftsman Furniture Projects
By Editors of Woodworker's Journal
17 Craftsman-style projects from the experts at Woodworker's Journal.
$17.95
ISBN 978-1-56523-324-9

The New Complete Guide to the Bandsaw
By Mark Duginske
Learn to master the workshop's most important saw. Contains over 500 photographs and illustrations.
$19.95
ISBN 978-1-56523-318-8

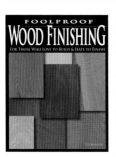

Foolproof Wood Finishing
By Teri Masaschi
Take the mystery out of finishing with easy-to-follow exercises designed by one of the nation's premier finishing instructors.
$19.95
ISBN 978-1-56523-303-4

Woodworker's Pocket Reference
By Charlie Self
Everything a woodworker needs to know in an easy-to-read, quick-to-find format.
$14.95
ISBN 978-1-56523-239-6

New Woodworker Handbook
By Tom Hintz
Includes tips, techniques, tool overviews, shop setup, and detailed woodworking plans.
$19.95
ISBN 978-1-56523-297-6

LOOK FOR THESE BOOKS AT YOUR LOCAL BOOKSTORE OR WOODWORKING RETAILER

Or call 800-457-9112 • Visit www.FoxChapelPublishing.com

Learn from the Experts

You already know that Fox Chapel Publishing is a leading source for woodworking books, videos, and DVDs, but did you know that we also publish two leading magazines in the woodworking category? *Wood Carving Illustrated and Scroll Saw Woodworking & Crafts* are the magazines that carving and scroll saw enthusiasts turn to for premium information by today's leading artisans.
Contact us today for your free trial issue!

WOODCARVING
I L L U S T R A T E D

- Written BY carvers FOR carvers
- Improve your skills with premium carving patterns and step-by-step instruction for all skill levels
- Learn from today's top artists with helpful hints and new techniques for every style of carving
- New product and tool reviews
- Stay in touch with the carving community with biographies, show coverage, a calendar of events, and galleries of completed work

SCROLLSAW
Woodworking & Crafts

- Written by today's leading scroll saw artists
- Dozens of attractive, shop-tested patterns and project ideas for scrollers of all skill levels
- Great full-color photos of step-by-step projects and completed work presented in a clear, easy-to-follow format
- Keep up with what's new in the scrolling community with tool reviews, artist profiles, and event coverage

To Get Your Free Trial Issue or Subscribe:
Call 800-457-9112 or Visit www.FoxChapelPublishing.com